iMovie™ 2 Solutions™

Tips, Tricks, and Special Effects

Erica Sadun

SYBEX® San Francisco • London

Associate Publisher: Dan Brodnitz

Acquisitions and Developmental Editor: Bonnie Bills

Editor: Pete Gaughan

Production Editor: Molly Glover

Technical Editor: Clark Kyle McCabe

Production Manager: Amy Changar

Book Design and Composition: Owen Wolfson

Proofreader: Dave Nash

Indexer: Ann Rogers

CD Coordinator: Dan Mummert

CD Technician: Kevin Ly

Cover Designer: Lori Barra, Tonbo Designs

Front Cover, Kayak Photo: Michael DeYoung, Alaska Stock

iMovie 2 Solutions

Tips, Tricks, and Special Effects

Acknowledgments

Writing a book is truly a team effort. An author's name, alone on a cover, does not reflect those many people who brought this book to life. Let me take a moment to acknowledge this effort and say thank you. I could not have written this book without your help, advice, effort, information, and time.

Let me start by thanking the fantastic Sybex team who transformed this book from a vague idea into a concrete reality. Bonnie Bills, Molly Glover, Pete Gaughan, Owen Wolfson, Dan Mummert, Kevin Ly, Amy Changar, Dave Nash, Ann Rogers, and Dan Brodnitz all put in a huge effort during this exciting project. Thank you all.

Next, let me thank Neil Salkind, my agent, and the wonderful team at Studio B, including Sherry, David, Jessica, Craig, Kevin, Kristen, Stacey, Tom, and the rest. You've all been troopers, and I very much appreciate your help.

I want to thank all of the companies that have graciously offered review hardware and software. This book could not have been written without these items. I very much appreciate your generosity and timeliness.

I offer my gratitude to all those people whose outstanding knowledge, insight, and courtesy helped this process enormously. These include Pam Swartwood and Travis White of Ulead; Alan Williams of Adobe; Bruce Gee of GeeThree.com; Eric Bin and Natalie Jacques of Totally Hip; Alex Ljung of alc sounddesign; Darrin Cardani of Buena Software; Daniel Azuma, creator of FileTyper; Jim Rathburn of FreePlay Music; Jaime Nichols of Triangle Images; Bernhard Jenny, author of SoundRecorder; Alberto Ricci, who built SoundEffects; Sarah Davis of Bender/Helper Impact; and Kari Bulkley and Bruce Herbert of Sorenson Media.

Thank you to everyone who volunteered and participated in the beta test program for this book. In particular, let me single out Dana McCown, who went far above and beyond the call of duty. You were amazing! Your diligence and attention to detail was truly remarkable, and I cannot begin to express my gratitude for your help. Special thanks as well to Miraz Jordan, Bill Quattlebaum, Fabian Ius, Franklin E. Miller, Larry Richardson, Sabrina Silvernale, Gary Bertoia, John Mitchener, Joseph Keenan, and Sam Kimery—your feedback was invaluable. Let me also thank those who volunteered but for whatever reason could not eventually participate in the program: Guy Bowring, Marty Levenson, Richard Martino, Daniel Beck, Brad Veneracion, Adrienne Allen, Bakari Chavanu, Chuck Van Pelt, Jason W. Denzel, Michael Smith, and Dave Rodenborn. Thank you all.

On a personal note, I thank Alberto Sadun for his continued, inexplicable, but well-appreciated patience, and Emma and Sofia Sadun for their general wonderfulness. Particular thank-yous to Ben Sadun, Hayden Starr, Pat Bates, Norma Lajoie, 'chelle Parmele, Nicole Campos, Annie Toran, Heidi Foster, Paula Vitaris, Olympia Fafoutis, Yuko Caruso, the entire June 1997 Mommies List, everyone at the BMH-BJ Preschool—particularly Ellen, Jo, Nurit, Olga, and Cindy—and everyone else who got me through this.

Finally, to anyone I've overlooked in these acknowledgments, please accept my apologies and my thanks.

For all the wonderful librarians at the Virginia Village and Schlessman Family Libraries, who, for years now, have kept me in books, words, and happiness.

Foreword

In the near future, video production will move from being an arcane art to become simply another basic skill, like reading or writing, that plays a daily part in our professional and personal lives. Not many people yet think of this once-exclusive occupation as an everyday task, but the transition is inevitable. This is not to say that everyone will need to be an expert video editor. Video production will be used by a range of people in a variety of ways. Just as there are a few people who write for a living and many others who use writing as a tool, so video production will be a primary profession for some and just part of the job for many others.

There is no doubt that Apple's iMovie is the video-editing tool for the "non-expert" editors of the future. The fact that everyone from adolescents to grandparents is already using iMovie testifies to its simplicity—not to mention that they're generating video of broadcast quality. This is video that just ten years ago would have taken hundreds of thousands of dollars to produce.

But iMovie's strength as an easy-to-learn and easy-to-use editing application is also its greatest limitation. In order to keep the interface simple and uncluttered, the program's power is limited: many common special effects are beyond the capability of iMovie—and moviemakers like to use effects! While there's always the alternative of moving up to iMovie's big brother, Final Cut Pro, that would be massive overkill for most people. Final Cut Pro is a tool for professional producers; it has a steep learning curve, it's fairly pricey, and thus it isn't a realistic alternative for most iMovie users.

Author Erica Sadun helps you surpass this limitation with *iMovie 2 Solutions: Tips, Tricks, and Special Effects*. She plumbs the depths of iMovie to create effects you wouldn't think possible with this "simple" program. She also takes advantage of the most underrated piece of software in the Apple stable, QuickTime Pro, to make edits and effects that you couldn't achieve in iMovie alone. QuickTime Pro is a powerhouse little editor. In my professional life, I use it almost every day to trim a soundtrack (often completely rebuilding a script), or to paste in a still image to fix a small defect in a movie or audio file. QuickTime Pro is an obvious answer to taking iMovie to the "next level."

In teaching Final Cut Pro and QuickTime classes, I've surprised many people with the power that exists in QuickTime Player and they always ask where they can get more information. Imagine my surprise when I discovered that *iMovie 2 Solutions* contains many tips and techniques for QuickTime Pro! From *iMovie2 Solutions* I not only learned a whole set of new tips and tricks for using iMovie 2 and QuickTime Pro, I also now have a resource to recommend when I'm asked where the tricks from my classes can be found.

Erica Sadun has done a wonderful job of keeping it all easy to understand with plenty of practical examples and techniques. *iMovie 2 Solutions* will definitely fill the void for iMovie-makers who want to get the most out of their movies, without breaking the bank.

PHILIP HODGETTS
President and CEO, Intelligent Assistance, Inc.
"The Software Guy," DVGuys.com

Contents

Introduction

iMovie can do a lot more than you might ever expect from a free product. It is one of the best-designed products to ever hit the desktop. It combines real movie-making power with amazing ease of use. And, as digital camcorders gain popularity, more and more people are turning to the Macintosh to provide a complete video-editing solution.

In mid-2001, I approached my editor with the idea to write an iMovie book. "Some people think iMovie's nothing but a pretty toy," I told her. I knew that iMovie was getting a bad rap. "You can create thousand-dollar effects," I said, "with a hundred-dollar budget. And you don't have to move up to Final Cut Pro and Premiere to do this."

"Okay," she replied. "Show me."

The result is the book you're holding in your hands.

The first iMovie release was a nice little package, but with iMovie 2, Apple set the standard for consumer-grade excellence. They introduced a huge number of new features and a far better design. Sitting down with iMovie 2 for the first time is an eye-opening experience. It's fun—really fun—and amazingly simple to use. Users can create movies literally in minutes.

But the fun doesn't stop with simple movies. iMovie hosts many wonderful, innovative, but not especially obvious features. These features can take users out of the "title-footage-credits" mindset into a fun and exciting world of special effects. You can create diverse and intriguing videos. You'll find many of these techniques detailed in the pages of this book.

Add QuickTime Pro to the equation, and things really start to take off. This often overlooked utility ($29.99, www.apple.com/quicktime) brings iMovie the technological power usually associated with much more expensive packages. With iMovie and QuickTime Pro, you really can make thousand-dollar effects. You can, for example, add logo and watermarks to your movies, create picture-in-picture effects, introduce streaming subtitles, or add custom "skins" around your movies. All of these are things most people wouldn't associate with iMovie, but they're there and available to anyone with another thirty bucks to spend.

QuickTime Pro and iMovie form the perfect pair. iMovie provides a great interface and terrific movie-editing capabilities. QuickTime Pro adds the razzle-dazzle. It produces fantastic special effects and adds the multiple-video-track editing missing from iMovie. To anyone who dismisses iMovie as a toy, I reply "nonsense!" iMovie and QuickTime Pro offer a powerful one-two punch that can produce movie effects as sophisticated as those from high-end software.

How to Use This Book

iMovie 2 Solutions: Tips, Tricks, and Special Effects offers a complete hands-on introduction to building a wide variety of movie effects with iMovie and QuickTime Pro. You'll learn each technique by working through a step-by-step project. Each project focuses on a different topic and allows you to gain expertise while creating your movies. Here are some tips for making the best use of this book.

Note: Our book development team spent a lot of time to make sure that a typical reader could follow each project. A panel of beta testers worked through every project. These testers helped point out where the original material was vague, confusing, or just wrong so that the instructions could be fixed before publication. When you try out these projects, you'll be the beneficiary of the panel's hard work.

Sit at your computer. You'll gain the most from this book when you work through each project as you read. This book offers a hands-on method of experiential learning. The philosophy behind this is that actual experience provides the best way to absorb the techniques presented here. So sit down, launch your computer, open the book, and get ready to learn.

Watch the sample movie. Most projects in this book offer a sample movie that showcases the effect you're trying to build. You'll find the name of the associated movie next to the CD icon on the bottom of the second page of each project. By watching the movie first, you'll discover the technique you're about to master.

Find the supporting files and programs. The CD icon points you to supporting files as well as sample movies. Your CD provides a wealth of material, including source images, text files, programs, and any other resources you'll need to complete each project. For the more advanced projects, you may find a self-extracting archive containing the materials relevant to that project, including some resources that allow you to go beyond the steps in the book to experiment on your own. Supporting files include versions for both NTSC readers (U.S., Canada, Japan, etc.) as well as PAL readers (England, Europe, Australia, etc.) where applicable.

Read and work through the steps. Each project in this book is formed of a series of easy-to-follow steps accompanied by full-color images. Read through each step, and examine the image. Each picture showcases how your project will look as you work through the step, offering visual as well as textual reinforcement.

Read the sidebars. Alongside each project you'll find one or more sidebars covering related or helpful topics. The sidebars point out shortcuts and advanced tricks, warn you about common mistakes and bugs, detail differences for OS 9 and OS X users, and point you to more great resources for your movie-editing work.

The Companion CD-ROM

The CD that accompanies this book provides a major component of these projects. You'll find many videos, images, and software tools, all of which will help you better work your way through these projects.

Most projects are accompanied by a sample video. This video allows you to see the final result that you're building and offers a sanity check to ensure that you're moving in the right direction.

The CD also contains image and text files. These are the same ones I used to create the projects. Wherever possible, I have included materials in both NTSC (U.S., Canada, Japan) and PAL (U.K., Australia, France, Italy, etc.) format. In addition, I've collected some useful image files into a set of general resources that are not project-specific.

I built some special-purpose utilities (file typing programs) to help the readers of this book. Look for these utility programs on the CD when you reach a project that calls for them: DVmaker, MakeiMovieProject, MakeSimpleText

Tools

Meet the tools you'll use throughout this book. These software packages provide everything you need to create thousand-dollar effects on a bargain-basement budget. Each of these items offers amazing functionality with a very low price tag; many are completely free.

You'll find several of these software titles on the accompanying CD in a variety of forms. Photoshop Elements comes as a thirty-day demo. It's a time-limited program with full-functionality, but it only works for the specified period of time unless you buy a license. FileTyper and SoundEffects are both shareware. These allow you to try the product before you buy. If you like the software, please send the requested fee to the developer.

iMovie www.apple.com/imovie; free on new Macs.

iMovie offers a terrific, easy-to-use application that allows you to import, edit, and produce digital movies. Don't be fooled by the low price tag. You can do far more with iMovie than you might think.

QuickTime Pro www.apple.com/quicktime; $29.99 from Apple.

QuickTime Pro is an amazingly powerful package that complements and expands iMovie's functionality, bringing pro effects to a consumer software product. For only thirty dollars, you can unlock your QuickTime player and bring out all the built-in Pro features. Go online to Apple's website and enter a credit card number. You'll receive a license and an unlock code, ready for immediate use. If you buy just one software package to complement iMovie, buy this one. Between iMovie and QuickTime Pro, you have a powerful movie-editing suite.

Adobe Photoshop Elements www.adobe.com/products/ photoshopel/main.html; $99 new, $69 upgrade (from PhotoDeluxe, Photoshop LE, and earlier versions of Photoshop Elements; other products may qualify for competitive upgrades). *You'll find a thirty-day trial version of this software on the companion CD.*

Photoshop Elements combines the power of Photoshop with consumer-friendly interface features. At a fraction of the price, most users won't miss (or even know about) the few highly specialized production features excluded from this package but present in the larger Photoshop application. I cannot think of a better bang-for-the-buck for consumer-grade image editing.

iMovie Plug-In Packs www.apple.com/imovie/ (OS X users) and www.apple.com/imovie/macos9/ (OS 9.x users); free.

Apple offers Plug-In Packs for both OS 9.x and OS X iMovie versions. These free add-ins provide essential functionality for your iMovie work. Download the appropriate version and add it to your iMovie Plugin folder for a quick and easy functionality upgrade.

MakeEffectMovie and MakeEffectSlideShow

ftp://ftp.apple.com/developer/Sample_Code/QuickTime/
QuickTimeIntro/MakeEffectMovie.sit; free.
http://developer.apple.com/samplecode/Sample_Code/QuickTime/
Effects/MakeEffectSlideShow.htm; free.

These two utilities allow you to merge visual resources (both videos and still images) and add special effects that bridge between them. These utilities offer enormous convenience in a completely free package.

GeeThree Slick Transitions and Effects (Volumes 1 and 2)

www.geethree.com; $29.95 each downloaded volume or $49.95 for both. CD orders cost slightly more. *You'll find a free GeeThree sampler on the accompanying CD.*

Want to accessorize iMovie? The GeeThree packages provide fantastic iMovie add-ons. They completely expand the visual vocabulary of your iMovies, adding a huge variety of transitions and effects. You'll find quite a lot of plug-ins in these volumes. I only regularly use a subset of about a dozen or so of them, but I use that subset a lot. Those few alone are well worth the price! Treat the rest as a bonus.

FileTyper   www.ugcs.caltech.edu/~dazuma/filetyper/;

$10 shareware, single license. *A copy of this fantastic app is on the accompanying CD.*

FileTyper isn't just a great iMovie utility, it's a great Mac utility. FileTyper allows you to associate your files with applications and data types. The included MakeAutoTyper program is a particular gem. I used this to create DVmaker and the other type utilities for this book found on the accompanying CD.

SoundEffects   www.riccisoft.com/soundeffects/; $15 shareware.

I've included SoundEffects on the companion CD.

Although no longer in development, the 0.9.2 release of Sound Effects provides an excellent sound-editing utility that I use on a regular basis.

Conventions Used in This Book

You'll see a few small, helpful icons throughout the book:

"Twirl" key: ⌘ Of course, this is how most of us see the Command key on our Mac keyboards.

Cross-references: ⌒ The "see" eyeglasses let you know that you can find more information on a related topic elsewhere in the book.

Other Outstanding Resources

These resource packages provide the reason that many of the sample videos look and sound so great.

FreePlay Music (www.freeplaymusic.com) FreePlay Music offers amazing royalty-free sound tracks that you can use directly in your personal, private use iMovies without paying a penny. (FreePlay receives revenue from electronic hardware manufacturers and broadcast royalties.) You will find certain exclusive tracks, as well as access to the complete FreePlay Music suite, on your personal iDisk on Apple's website (www.apple.com/idisk).

Ulead Royalty Free Media (http://rfm.ulead.com) Ulead offers a wide range of royalty free media including stock video clips, computer-animated video clips, image stills, and so forth. Most of the stills and video clips used in this book derive from Ulead's extensive collection. Their media is priced well and aimed at the hobbyist and business user rather than the high-end video production world. Each media set comes in a nicely designed package with a visual quick-reference that allows you to browse quickly through the image and video contents.

Triangle Images (www.eyewire.com/products/motion/triangle/) Triangle Images offers many collections of high-end professional video clips. Subjects range from individuals to business environments and beyond. Triangle Images provided the beautiful clips of people used in this book—if you see a face in these pages, it's likely to be a Triangle Images clip.

The iMovie Interface

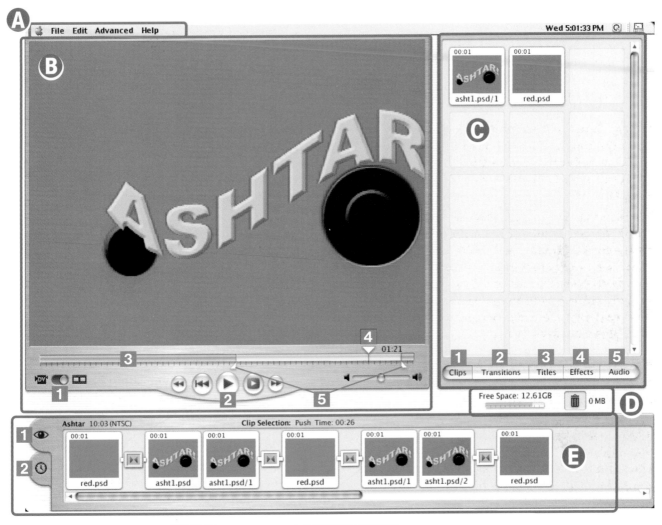

A **MENU BAR**

B **MONITOR**
1 Import/Edit toggle
2 Playback controls
3 Scrubber bar
4 Playhead
5 Crop markers

C **THE SHELF**
1 Clips Shelf button
2 Transitions Palette button
3 Titles Palette button
4 Effects Palette button
5 Audio Palette button

D **FREE SPACE INDICATOR AND GARBAGE PAIL**

E **CLIP VIEWER**
1 Clip Viewer tab
2 Timeline tab

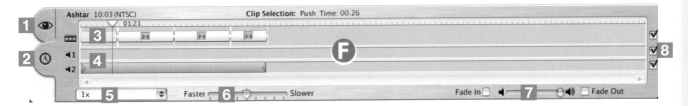

F **TIMELINE**
1 Clip Viewer tab
2 Timeline tab
3 Video track
4 Audio tracks
5 Timeline Zoom pop-up
6 Clip Speed slider
7 Volume and Fade controls
8 Track Mute buttons

iMovie Shortcuts

iMovie Clip Selection Shortcuts

⌘-**A** Select everything in the current context, whether it be the clips shelf, Clip Viewer, Timeline, scrubber bar, track, etc.

⌘-**D** Unselect everything in the current context, whether it be the clips shelf, Clip Viewer, Timeline, scrubber bar, track, etc. (This is the Select None command.)

Shift-drag just under the scrubber bar Make a selection based on the start and end of the drag.

Left arrow and Right arrow (playhead on either crop marker) Extend or contract the selection by one frame in the direction indicated.

Shift-Left arrow or Shift-Right arrow (playhead on either crop marker) Extend or contract the selection by ten frames in the direction indicated.

iMovie Timeline Shortcuts

Left arrow or Right arrow (audio clip selected); Control-Left arrow or Control-Right arrow (video clip selected) Move the start of the clip by one frame in the direction selected.

Shift-Left arrow or Shift-Right arrow keys (audio clip selected); Control-Shift-Left arrow or Control-Shift-Right arrow (video clip selected) Move the start of the clip by ten frames in the direction selected.

⌘-**L (audio clip selected)** Lock the audio clip at the current playhead location.

⌘-**R (video clip selected)** Reverse the selected clip or clips.

Shift-⌘-**V** Paste video from the Clipboard over the video at the playhead, entirely replacing that video for the duration of the pasted clip. The original audio remains unaffected and, if not already split out, is extracted from the original and placed on the voice track in the Timeline. No audio from the pasted clip is used.

⌘-**J (video clip selected)** Extract the audio from selected video clips and place that audio on the voice track in the Timeline. If only part of the clip was selected, the clip splits as needed to accommodate. The audio automatically locks in place.

iMovie Clip Editing Shortcuts

⌘-**X** Remove the selection from your movie, saving it in the Clipboard. If the middle of a clip is removed with this command, the right and left parts of the clip become two new clips.

Delete Remove the selection from your movie, without saving it in the Clipboard. If the middle of a clip is removed with this command, the right and left parts of the clip become two new clips.

⌘-**C** Copy the selection to the Clipboard.

⌘-**V** If no selection exists, paste the data from the Clipboard after the current clip. If a selection has been made, overwrite the selection with the Clipboard data, potentially splitting unaffected areas of the original clip into new clips. No scaling is done by a paste operation, and the pasted data remains otherwise unaltered.

Shift-⌘-**V** Paste video from the Clipboard over the video at the playhead, entirely replacing that video for the duration of the pasted clip. The original audio remains unaffected and, if not already split out, is extracted from the original and placed on the voice track in the Timeline. No audio from the pasted clip is used.

⌘-**J** Extract the audio from selected video clips and place that audio on the voice track in the Timeline. The audio automatically locks to the clip location.

⌘-**L** Lock the audio clip at the current playhead location.

⌘-**K** Remove everything from your clips in the scrubber bar except the selection.

⌘-**T** Split the clip in two, at the current location specified by the playhead.

Shift-⌘-S Create a still clip of the frame specified by the playhead, without otherwise altering the current clip.

⌘-Z Undo the last command, moving back one step in your history. Take care when emptying your trash and when saving your project: Doing so will remove not only the stray clips and other items you've discarded, but will zero-out your history buffer as well.

⌘-Shift-Z Redo the last command, moving one step forward in your history

iMovie Playback Shortcuts

Spacebar Toggle playback on and off.

Up arrow or Down arrow Adjust volume up or down.

Home Reset the movie to the beginning.

End Reset the movie to the very end.

Left arrow or Right arrow (video clip selected) Move playhead by one frame in direction selected.

Shift-Left arrow or Shift-Right arrow (video clip selected) Move playhead by ten frames in the direction selected.

Left arrow or Right arrow, held down (video clip selected) Continuous scroll in the direction selected.

⌘-] (video clip selected) Fast forward.

⌘-[(video clip selected) Fast rewind.

Miscellaneous (but Useful) iMovie Shortcuts

Shift-⌘-I or double-click a clip Reveal clip information, including media file and clip name while allowing you to set fade-in and fade-out for the clip.

⌘-? Go directly to the iMovie help center.

⌘-F Bring up dialog to save an image of the frame at the playhead out to disk.

⌘-I Bring up dialog to import a wide variety of file types that you can add to your iMovie project.

⌘-E Bring up dialog to export the project back to the camera or create a QuickTime file for iDVD or for other purposes.

QuickTime Shortcuts

QuickTime Playback Shortcuts

Spacebar, Return key, or Control-M Toggle playback on and off.

⌘-Left arrow or ⌘-Right arrow Play movie in the direction indicated.

Up arrow or Down arrow Adjust volume up or down.

Option-Down arrow Mute the volume.

Option-Up arrow Adjust volume to the maximum setting.

Control-\ and Control-] These two key shortcuts act, respectively, as the left and right arrows if your keyboard does not have separate arrow keys.

Left arrow or Right arrow Move the playhead one frame in the direction indicated.

⌘-. Stop playback.

Option-Left arrow or Option-Right arrow Move to the next major feature in the direction indicated. Major features include movie start, left crop marker, right crop marker, and movie end.

Control-Play button Play back without audio

⌘-T Toggle playback between play-entire-movie and play-selection-only.

⌘-L Toggle playback between play-once and play-looped.

⌘-M Open movie playback controls.

⌘-0 Playback half size.

⌘-1 Playback normal size.

⌘-2 Playback double size.

⌘-3 Play back large size.

QuickTime Selection Shortcuts

⌘-A Select the entire movie.

⌘-B Select nothing.

Control-Shift-[A less well behaved equivalent of ⌘-B, the Select None command.

Shift-Left arrow or Shift-Right arrow Move the playhead one frame in the direction indicated and expand the selection to that frame.

⌘-Shift-Left arrow or ⌘-Shift-Right arrow Move the playhead one frame in the direction indicated, expanding the selection to that frame, and then start movie playback, moving the crop marker with the play of the movie until the Command and Shift keys are released.

Shift-mouse drag Adjust the selection according to the placement of the mouse along the scrubber bar.

QuickTime Editing Shortcuts

⌘-X Remove the selection from your movie, saving it in the Clipboard.

⌘-C Copy the selection to the Clipboard.

⌘-V If no selection exists, paste the data from the Clipboard at the playhead. If a selection has been made, overwrite the selection with the Clipboard data. No scaling is done by a paste, and the pasted data remains otherwise unaltered.

Option-⌘-V Create a new track, adding the data from the Clipboard to that new track, starting at the playhead location.

Option-Shift-⌘-V Create a new track, adding the data from the Clipboard to that new track, scaled to the start, end, and duration of the current selection.

About the Author

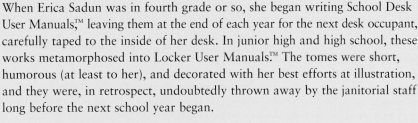

When Erica Sadun was in fourth grade or so, she began writing School Desk User Manuals,™ leaving them at the end of each year for the next desk occupant, carefully taped to the inside of her desk. In junior high and high school, these works metamorphosed into Locker User Manuals.™ The tomes were short, humorous (at least to her), and decorated with her best efforts at illustration, and they were, in retrospect, undoubtedly thrown away by the janitorial staff long before the next school year began.

Nevertheless, a pattern had been set, and Sadun spent many of the years that followed gaining technical knowledge of obscure minutia and translating such knowledge into accessible documentation. While working on her doctorate, she began writing how-to texts professionally, for the first time earning money at what she loved. (Sadun earned her master's degree in digital imaging from the University of Pennsylvania and her doctorate in visual languages and inter-face design at Georgia Tech's renowned Graphics, Visualization & Usability Center.) She continues to write, focusing on bringing technical material to general audiences.

1 Power Tips

Get the Most out of iMovie and QuickTime Pro

There's more to iMovie and QuickTime Pro than meets the eye. Both programs offer unexpected functionality and flexibility. In this chapter, we'll dive behind the scenes and discover a few lurking secrets. You'll discover some of my favorite techniques for making the best use of your movie media—the video and sound clips that make up your movie and the project files that put them together. You'll also learn how to manipulate your clips and transfer them between iMovie and QuickTime Pro.

Reveal iMovie's Secret Files

Get Started with QuickTime Pro

Move between iMovie and QuickTime

iMovie Power Edits

Reveal iMovie's Secret Files

Apple Inc. designed iMovie surprisingly well. It doesn't have many secret files or mysterious data types, although it does have some. Fortunately, you can bypass these barriers in a few steps. iMovie stores your settings and project files as plain text, but it takes a little fiddling to gain access. Once in, you can admire the elegance and power that lies behind the seemingly simple interface. In this section, you'll learn how to sneak past the guard and uncover those gems that iMovie hides away from view. You'll learn how iMovie projects are put together, explore iMovie preferences, and learn how to manipulate transitions and sounds hidden away in your iMovie media folder so you can reuse these elements for other purposes.

Meet the Project

iMovie projects are very straightforward. In these steps, you'll navigate through the various resources that make up your iMovie project.

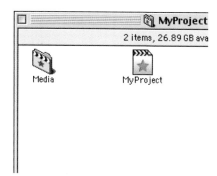 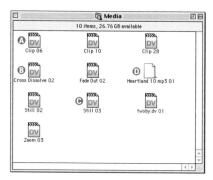

1. Whenever you start a new project, iMovie creates a project folder to hold all the materials associated with that project. Opening the project folder reveals a subfolder called Media and a project file. The project file has a distinct icon with a star and a "clapboard"-style top.

2. Your Media folder holds the multimedia clips associated with your project: all stills, video, audio, and special clips. These clips include the transitions, effects, and titles you have added to your project. Here's a Media folder from a fairly typical project; it includes clips, transitions, stills, and an audio track.

Ⓐ Clip   Ⓔ Still
Ⓑ Transition   Ⓓ Audio Clip

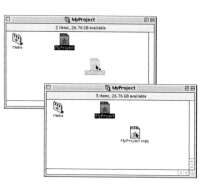 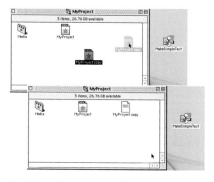

3. Your project file details, in plain text, how each clip is placed and used, the order frames appear in, and whether transitions and effects have been applied. OS X users, open your file with TextEdit. OS 9.*x* users follow these remaining steps. Option-drag your project file out of the Media folder to create a copy.

4. Drag the copy to the MakeSimpleText utility (which can be found on the companion CD). The copy automatically converts after you drop it on MakeSimpleText, becoming a SimpleText document. (The converted file stays in its original folder.)

5. Open the copy by double-clicking its icon. If you do this with any newly created project, you'll find a completely empty document. However, if you choose a project that you've been working on, you'll be rewarded with an interesting and somewhat readable project description.

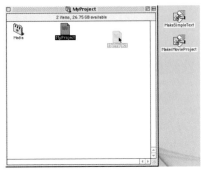

6. If at any time, you accidentally convert an actual project file to SimpleText, fear not. Recover by dragging your converted file to the MakeiMovieProject utility, which is also found on the companion CD.

iMovie Help

Are you new to iMovie? If you are, the built-in tutorial offers the best and easiest way to get up to speed. Select Help ▷ iMovie Tutorial to begin. With this tutorial, you work your way through a hands-on introduction to iMovie. The tutorial takes about one to two hours to complete, but the time is well invested. After finishing, you'll have mastered most of the skills needed to put together your own movies.

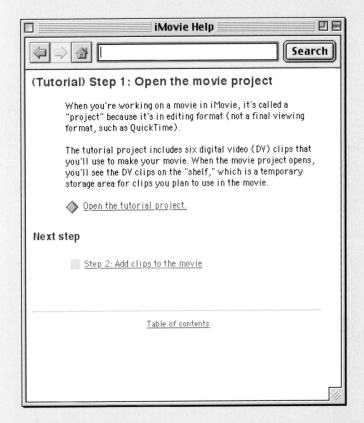

Available help does not end with the tutorial. The iMovie Help Center offers even more documentation and information. Select Help ▷ iMovie Help (or ⌘-?) to open the Help Center window. From here, you can read more about setting up, editing, exporting, and so forth.

Note: Apple offers additional iMovie support at **www.info.apple.com/ usen/imovie/**. Find the QuickTime support page at **www.info.apple.com/usen/ quicktime/**.

MakeSimpleText, MakeiMovieProject

Reset Your iMovie Preferences

At times, you may want to reset your copy of iMovie back to fresh out-of-the box settings. Doing so couldn't be easier. Just drag your current preferences (from the Preferences folder in the System Folder) to the Trash. The next time you launch iMovie, it will automatically create a newly initialized preferences file. Further, iMovie will display the rather spiffy animated introduction dialog that allows you to start a new project, open an existing project, choose the tutorial, or quit.

Resetting preferences also helps when iMovie tries switching country systems on you. For example, sometimes it insists on starting an NTSC project when you have a PAL camera attached. To fix this, trash your preferences, restart your computer, and launch iMovie with your PAL camera attached and powered on.

Note: Before attempting to edit your preferences, make sure you've saved all prior work. You may want to start a new, empty project before beginning, just to be on the safe side.

Edit Your Preferences

iMovie stores your preferences in a clear text-based format. Follow these steps to change preferences using a text editor. You'll set some preferences you cannot change in iMovie itself.

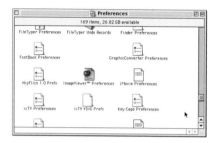

1. Make sure iMovie isn't running, and locate your iMovie preferences file. You'll find it in your System Folder in the Preferences subfolder. Notice that it's just a plain text file.

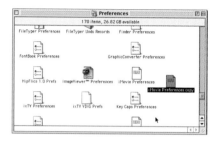

2. Option-drag the preferences file somewhere else, to create a backup copy—just in case. (If you prefer, select the file and choose Edit ▷ Duplicate or type ⌘-D, instead.)

3. Double-click the *original* preferences file to open it in SimpleText (OS 9.*x*) or in TextEdit (OS X). Take particular note of the warning at the top of the file; to quote, "Do not edit this unless you know what you're doing."

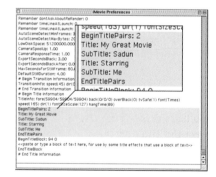

4. To see an example of how preferences can be changed in this file, scroll down to the bottom, to find the section on Title Pairs.

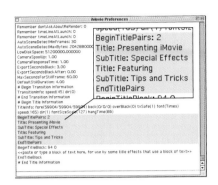

5. You can edit these title pairs to change your default titles. This proves particularly helpful when you use the same titles across several movies. Set these as desired and save your file.

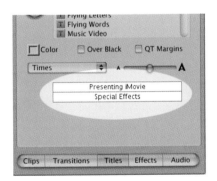

6. When you next launch iMovie, you'll see these changes when you select the Titles palette.

Your iMovie Preferences File: Other Changes

iMovie does not respond the same way to all preferences file changes. For example, iMovie will usually ignore a change to the VideoStandard (PAL, NTSC, or SECAM). Other items respond better to simple edits. You can easily customize some items, like title pairs, in the preferences file—modifications you cannot set in the program itself.

Default Font Size On the TitleInfo line, you'll find an entry similar to fontSizeScale(127). Valid font sizes range between 1 and 255. I like to set this item to fontSizeScale(255) so that my iMovie titles will always default to the maximum font size.

Default Title Block To change the initial settings for Scrolling Block titles (an effect in the menu of the Titles palette), replace the text on the lines between BeginTitleBlock and EndTitleBlock. Then count the number of characters of text, including spaces and punctuation. Update the *first* number after BeginTitleBlock (it's originally 94) to correctly reflect this new size.

Title Pairs By setting the number just to the right of BeginTitlePairs, you can add more (or fewer) default titles pairs. This proves helpful when you wish to use the same set of title pairs in several projects. Make sure to place the correct number of Title and Subtitle lines to match.

OS X Note: Find your iMovie preferences in ~/Library/Preferences. OS X uses an XML version named com.apple.iMovie.plist.

Note: In many ways, TextEdit is like SimpleText on steroids. Offering rich text features, and a wider variety of formatting options, TextEdit allows you to work on any text file from a stylized note to structured programming code.

Searching for Your Transition

iMovie stores your transitions as normal DV files in your Media folder. For reasons I do not begin to understand, it assigns them an odd file type, TRFX. This stops you from importing your transitions back into iMovie, since iMovie only accepts DV files with a dvc! file type. (The transition files do not even appear in the Open File window when you attempt to import them.) Given that you can achieve some of the most interesting special effects by overlaying transitions with other transitions, this can prove limiting. Fortunately, these steps present a way to bypass this limitation, in order to import and reuse your transitions as needed.

Note: Transition files look just like other DV files in your Media folder. You cannot tell the difference by simply looking at them. To determine which files are importable, select File ▷ Import (⌘-I) in iMovie. Only those files with proper types will appear in the Import File dialog box.

Extract Your Transitions

In these steps, you'll recover transitions from your project media folder. This allows you to layer iMovie effects and transitions on top of your recovered clips.

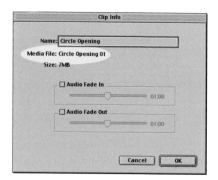

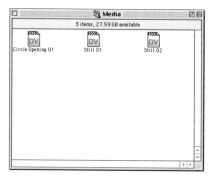

1. In iMovie, open one of your projects that includes transitions on the Timeline. Select any of these transitions. Choose File ▷ Get Clip Info (Shift-⌘-I, or just double-click the transition) to bring up the associated Clip Info window. Make a note of the name of the media file associated with your transition.

2. Return to the Finder and locate your project folder. Open it and then open the Media folder within. Inside you'll find the materials that make up your iMovie project. In this case, we have two stills and our transition.

3. Option-drag this media file (in this case, Circle Opening 01) to the Desktop. Always use a *copy* of your files. Do not attempt to modify the original transitions in your Media folder; doing so may permanently damage your iMovie project.

4. Now transform the transition into a properly identified DV stream: DVmaker, a utility on the included CD, can do this; it updates the file type and creator to bring a clip into compliance with iMovie's requirements. Drag the copy of your media file onto the DVmaker icon. The file type automatically converts to dvc!.

5. Import your newly converted media file into iMovie.

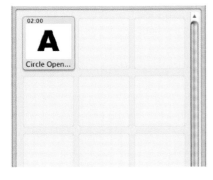

6. The clip will appear in your clips shelf as a fully editable, manipulable normal clip without any of the restrictions associated with normal transitions.

iMovie File Types

Every file, whether in OS 9.*x* or OS X, has a file type and file creator associated with it. This file "metadata" allows your Macintosh to associate your file with an application and open the correct program when you double-click the file icon. And although implementation details vary, the file-conversion utilities included on the companion CD work under both operating systems. Here's a brief list of the major iMovie file types. If you attempt to set these by hand, using a program such as ResEdit, make sure to pay special attention to capitalization, punctuation, and so forth.

ELEMENT	TYPE	CREATOR
Sounds (AIFF, MP3, voice, etc.)	AIFF	Hway
Transitions	TRFX	Hway
Video clips (clips, imported clips, titles, effects)	dvc!	Hway
Stills	StiL	Hway
Project file	TeXT	Hway
iMovie preferences	TEXT	Ttxt
MP3 files (recognized for import only)	MPEG	TVOD

Change Types in FileTyper

FileTyper, which can be found on the accompanying CD, allows you to change file attributes directly within its program. Simply open a file, edit either the type or creator field, and click Change to save your changes.

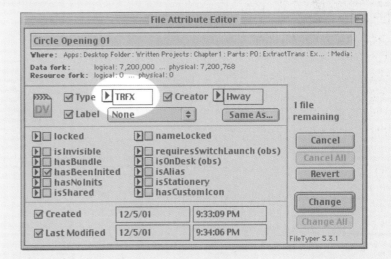

DVmaker, FileTyper

Import and Extract Sounds

iMovie allows you to import sounds in either AIFF or MP3 format—although it converts the latter to AIFF in your Media folder. (Up-conversion to AIFF will not improve any degraded, tinny MP3 quality.) You can also import audio directly from a CD or record sounds from your microphone, using the Audio palette. In addition, you can disassociate the audio from your video clips to gain direct access to the audio track for editing or other purposes. To extract audio, start by selecting all or a portion of a video clip or clips. Then invoke Advanced ▷ Extract Audio (⌘-J). iMovie will separate the audio and place it in the voice track on the Timeline, in orange. If you extract just a portion of a clip's audio, iMovie automatically splits the clip as needed to preserve the unseparated portions.

Normalize Sounds

When sound quality is too low, you can "normalize" your audio—extend its dynamic range—using a sound-editing program. Follow these steps to extract and normalize an iMovie audio track.

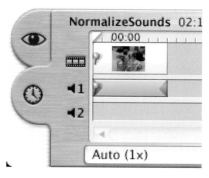

1. For this example, we'll normalize sound from a video clip. Select the clip you wish to work on and press ⌘-J to extract the audio.

2. iMovie automatically switches to the Timeline display, extracts the audio, and displays it in bright orange.

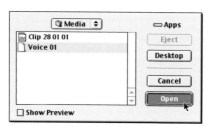

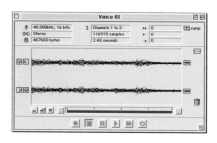

3. Save your project. Make sure you've allocated enough memory for your favorite sound-editing application to open and edit your sound file, then launch the app. (Here, I use SoundEffects, a shareware package on the companion CD.) Select File ▷ Open and open the Voice file from your project's Media folder.

4. Examine your sound's waveform. A poor sound usually has little variation and lies very close to the centerline. When you see a fuzzy waveform, as shown here, do not expect too much in the way of clarity. You'll be able to make things louder, which will help differentiate voices, but the background noise will get louder too.

Use Sound Effects Judiciously and Effectively

Although many sound editors offer spiffy special effects, like robotic-sounding voices, tunnel effects, and echoes, use these with care. Every time you alter your sounds, you're more likely to remove quality than add it. There are times, however, when you're looking for a particular result. For those times, be sure to experiment on a copy of your audio file.

Each of the two audio tracks in the Timeline is inherently stereo. Use either track for audio content. You can even overlap audio clips on the same track, maintaining full stereo in each clip.

Note: Some sounds can be very short and therefore hard to move in iMovie. Instead of changing your sound clip's position, you may end up resizing or just selecting it. When you find a sound that seems too small to move, crank up the zoom: The Timeline zoom pop-up can magnify your small sounds. At 10x or above, most sounds become large enough to grab and manipulate without having to touch the resizing arrows at either end.

5. Select the entire waveform by choosing Edit ▷ Select All (⌘-A).

6. Determine where your editor offers the normalization function. In the case of SoundEffects, you will find this under Effects ▷ Normalize. This feature varies by editor.

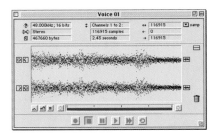

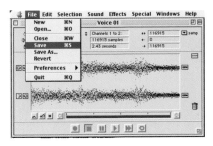

7. After normalizing, your waveform will look different. All the amplitudes will extend, offering a much larger dynamic range. Play the sound clip to hear the difference.

8. If you like the result, select File ▷ Save, which updates your sound file right in place! When you return to iMovie and click Play, the sound plays back as altered. If you feel less brave, use Save As and save to another file. Import that file into iMovie to substitute it without altering the original.

Get Started with QuickTime Pro

QuickTime Pro is a powerful movie-editing tool. It works with multiple video tracks, creates cool special effects, and goes way beyond iMovie in power. iMovie, in contrast, works only with a single video track and does not handle such professional features as masking, transparency, and video resizing. Unfortunately, QuickTime Pro does not provide the friendliness and usability that make iMovie such a pleasure. Don't let this dissuade you from using QuickTime Pro. It is an amazingly flexible and useful program, and you can get up to speed quickly. The overviews and examples presented here will get you running in short order.

Note: You'll find the basic QuickTime 5 player on the companion CD. Visit www.apple.com/quicktime to buy a license to unlock the Pro features ($29.99; the viewer-only version is free). Be sure, either way, that you're using version 5 or later.

Getting Help

QuickTime Pro does not come with a tutorial, but you can access documentation through your computer's Help menu and the online QuickTime help site. In these steps, you'll see how to find these resources.

1. To access the QuickTime Help Center, start by selecting Help ▷ Help Center from the Finder, iMovie, or any application that offers Help Center support.

2. From the Help Center menu, choose QuickTime Help.

3. View individual help topics by clicking any of the categories (Editing Movies, in this example).

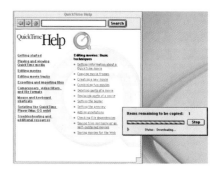

4. Click a help topic to read it. By default, your Macintosh does not store these write-ups. You'll need an active Internet connection to download the information the first time you access it.

QuickTime Pro Playback Shortcuts

Use these shortcuts to help you control the playback of your QuickTime movie.

SHORTCUT	ACTION
Spacebar, Return key, or Control-M	Toggle playback on and off.
⌘-Left arrow or ⌘-Right arrow	Play movie in the direction indicated.
Left arrow or Right arrow	Move the playhead one frame in the direction indicated.
Option-Left arrow or Option-Right arrow	Move to the next major feature in the direction indicated. Major features include movie start, left crop marker, right crop marker, and movie end.
Up arrow or Down arrow	Adjust volume up or down
Option-Up arrow or Option-Down arrow	Adjust volume to the maximum setting or mute.
Control-\ or Control-]	These two key shortcuts act as the left and right arrows, respectively, if your keyboard does not have separate arrow keys.
⌘-. (period)	Stop playback.

OSX Note: The OS X Help Center does not offer exactly the same subjects and looks quite different from the OS 9.*x* Help Center. However, both use the same online help site.

Other Resources

You can find other QuickTime Pro resources on the Internet. Here are just a few.

Usenet The **comp.sys.mac** newsgroups may be able to help with your QuickTime questions.

Apple support Apple offers a comprehensive, searchable knowledge base at **http://kbase.info.apple.com/**. Plug in your QuickTime question and discover what answers Apple has on hand.

QuickTime mailing list Sign up for a QuickTime-specific mailing list at **http://lists.apple.com/mailman/listinfo/quicktime-talk**.

Help
- About Balloon Help...
- Show Balloons
- **On-line QuickTime Player Help**
- Update Existing Software...
- QuickTime Web Site

5. You can access another source of QuickTime help from the player itself. While running QuickTime Pro, select Help ▷ On-line QuickTime Player Help.

6. You'll connect to helpqt.apple.com, Apple's QuickTime help site. The topics and coverage found there vary a little from those found in the Help Center, so it's worth taking the extra time to browse through what you can find here.

Set Your QuickTime Pro Preferences

When you first start to work with QuickTime Pro, you'll want to set your preferences. Establishing these will make your life a lot easier when you actually set down to work. Select Edit ▷ Preferences ▷ Player Preferences.

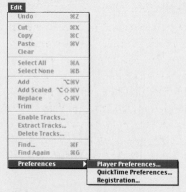

There's one particular preference I find vital. Ensure that Open Movies In New Players has been selected and click OK. This changes the default File ▷ Open Movie option to File ▷ Open Movie In New Player. When you open a movie, QuickTime adds a new window without automatically closing any windows that are already open.

Know Your Tracks

Follow these steps to view and work with the tracks that form your movie.

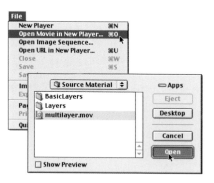

1. To open a movie, select File ▷ Open Movie In New Player. (If you haven't set your preferences, the menu item will read File ▷ Open Movie. Press the Option key before you click File to reveal the alternate menu item.) Navigate to your movie and click Open.

2. With your movie window open, select Movie ▷ Get Movie Properties or ⌘-J. This opens the Movie Properties window, which is the heart and soul of QuickTime and allows you to directly control and manipulate the tracks associated with your movie.

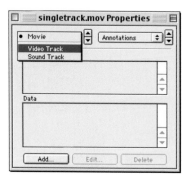

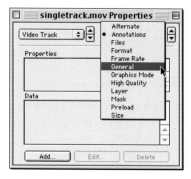

3. The Movie Properties window offers two pull-down menus. The left menu gives you direct access to each track in your movie, including all audio, video, and the main "movie" track. Here's what a standard movie with a single audio and video track looks like.

4. The right pull-down menu offers track-specific options. With this menu, you can alter such features as placement (the Size option), layer ordering, and graphics mode.

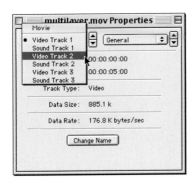

5. When more than one video or audio track are added, they are numbered accordingly. (You can change a track's name from this automatic numbering system with the General palette, if desired.) In this example, I've added three sound and video tracks to this movie.

6. To remove a track, select Edit ▷ Delete Tracks. Choose the track or tracks you wish to remove, and click Delete. If you remove a track or tracks by accident, select Edit ▷ Undo (⌘-Z) to restore them.

7. QuickTime assigns layer numbers to each video track. Layers with smaller (or, typically, "more negative") numbers lie on top of—and may obscure—layers with higher numbers. In this example, Video Track 3 (seen in the window at –6) lies above Video Track 2, which in turn lies above Video Track 1.

8. To change track order, adjust the layer number for any track. Here, we select Video Track 2 and choose Layer palette from the right pull-down menu.

9. By lowering the layer number (clicking the small down-arrow), we place the second track in front. The up and down arrows adjust the layer number, one level at a time. Here, we click the down arrow to adjust the second track. At a layer of –8, it arrives in front.

10. With QuickTime Pro, you can change more than layer ordering. To change image orientation, select Size from the right pull-down menu. Clicking the first arrow button mirrors your image horizontally; the second mirrors vertically. The last two rotate your image clockwise and counterclockwise. Click Normal to revert to your original footage.

multilayer.mov

QuickTime Pro Sizing Shortcuts

QuickTime Pro does not offer many (or very useful) editing shortcuts, but there are some to be had when working with a track after you click Adjust on the Size palette:

- Hold down the Option key while resizing to automatically snap between full-size and ¼-size.
- Hold down the Shift key to limit movement and resizing along one direction.

You can also center a ¼-size image fairly accurately by resizing into one corner and then using the original crossed circles as placement guides, as I do here.

Know Your Tracks *continued*

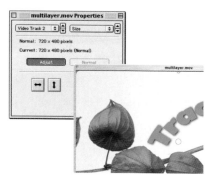

11. To change the image size, click the Adjust button to begin. Small red handles appear in the center, the corners, and the middle of each edge. These handles allow you to size and reorient your image.

12. Drag any corner handle to resize. If you press the Option key while dragging, you'll automatically snap to full-size or, as shown here, ¼-size. Notice how resizing Video Track 2 reveals Video Track 3 underneath.

13. You can reposition the video by dragging in the middle areas (avoiding the circle at the center). Here, we move the image roughly to the center of the window. (Pressing the Shift key constrains you to only horizontal or vertical movement.)

14. The small crossed circles, at the middle of each side, allow you to skew your video.

15. To rotate the image, drag out from the center circle. A handle will appear, following your mouse. Use this handle to control the degree of rotation. You may find a longer handle easier to manage than a short one.

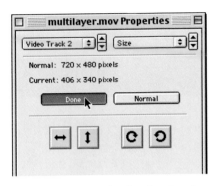

16. Click Done to finish adjusting the video track, or click Normal to revert to the original size and orientation.

17. Now select another track to resize.

18. Click Adjust and the red handles appear for the newly selected track. Notice that the track ordering does not change. In this example, I resize track 3 in place, as it lies behind track 2.

19. Proceed to adjust the current track. Then click Done to finish.

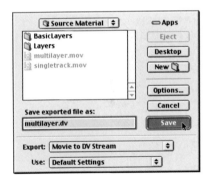

20. To transform your creation into a form you can use in iMovie, select File ▷ Export (or ⌘-E). Navigate to where you wish to save the movie, select a DV Stream export with default settings, and click Save.

Sound Advice

Take care when using Add Scaled to add a movie with a soundtrack. As the video stretches or squashes to fit the selected timeframe, so does the audio. Squeeze it into a shorter space, you'll end up with a high-pitched audio. Similarly, if you stretch your audio track, you'll wind up with a low-toned, slowed-down effect. Any audio overlay without some fade-in and fade-out will produce sharp, noticeable, and uncomfortable transitions between the original and added soundtracks. You can hear an example of audio scaling in scaled_audio.mov on the companion CD.

Note: To save your work after adding tracks, use File ▷ Save (⌘-S). Select Make Movie Self Contained to create a file containing all the tracks—originals and new ones. Selecting Normal takes up much less space, but you have to keep all the source files with the movie. Your movie needs these extra files. If you lose one, your movie won't play back properly.

Add Tracks to Your Video

Follow these steps to add new tracks to your video. You can add tracks in a QuickTime video, much as you add layers in a Photoshop or Photoshop Elements image.

1. Open your base movie in QuickTime Pro.

2. Next, open the movie you intend to add to the first. Select the entire movie track (Edit ▷ Select All, ⌘-A) and copy it (Edit ▷ Copy, ⌘-C). Then close the movie and return to the base movie.

3. Position the playhead where you wish to add the second movie. Use Edit ▷ Add (Option-⌘-V) to add a new track to your movie starting at that position. Don't confuse "Add" with "Paste;" the Paste command doesn't add a new track.

4. After you add the track, QuickTime Pro moves the playhead automatically to the end of the new material. The new footage may appear above the original, replacing it in the view if the movie endings coincide, as shown here.

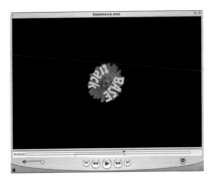

5. At times, you may wish to specify the exact range of frames you wish to overlay with a new track. This will stretch or squeeze your footage to exactly fit the duration of those frames. (This works particularly well when adding still images to moving footage.) Start by selecting the frames you wish to overlay.

6. Copy the footage you wish to add, as per Step 2. Instead of using Edit ▷ Add, choose Edit ▷ Add Scaled (Option-Shift-⌘-V).

7. As with the previous method, the playhead automatically moves to the end of the addition after you add the new track. Once again, if the movie endings coincide, the newer footage will be placed above the original. In this case, the additional material ends well before the original; the original footage remains in the window.

8. Resize the new track. Select Adjust from the Size palette and use the red resizing handles to change the size of your track until you see both tracks at once (☞ "QuickTime Pro Sizing Shortcuts" earlier in this chapter).

9. Move the playhead outside the dark-gray selected area, to either side. The new track disappears—it wasn't added to that part of the movie.

10. Move the playhead into the selected area and the new track reappears.

scaled_audio.mov, track1.mov, track2.mov, track3.mov, multi-track.mov

Royalty-Free Material

Take care when using clips, sounds, and other elements that you did not yourself capture or create. Know whether you comply with fair use guidelines and whether you need to pay royalties. Royalty-free footage, stills, and sound effects are easily purchased from a variety of vendors. You can use these elements in your videos without having to pay any further fees. Ulead (rfm.ulead.com) offers a wide range of royalty-free products in their Royalty-Free Media series. Titles include Pick-A-Video, Pick-A-Sound, and Pick-A-Photo.

Note: Ulead has recently introduced a new line of royalty-free footage: computer-generated animation. These new CG titles include money, finance, festivities, and seasons, among others, and work particularly well as backdrops for your other video material.

Annotate Your Movies

QuickTime Pro offers a handy way to annotate your movies. Annotations (viewable by anyone with a QuickTime player) can take the form of credits, copyright notices, and other labels.

1. Bring up the Movie Properties window (⌘-J) and select Movie from the left pull-down menu and Annotations from the right. Click the Add button.

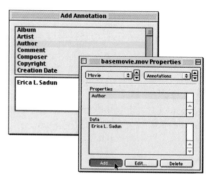

2. Scroll through the available annotations, select one, and enter a value in the text area. Click Add to finish. Here, Author now appears in the Annotations palette as one item of a scrolling list in the Properties panel; when this item is clicked, my name appears in the Data panel.

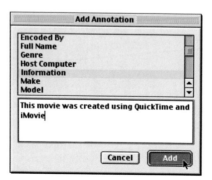

3. In the Movie Properties window, click Add to add another annotation. In the Add Annotation dialog, select an annotation, enter a value, and again click Add to finish.

4. The new one appears with the original in the Properties panel of the Annotations palette. Click any label to view the associated information.

5. Select an annotation and click Edit to update the stored information.

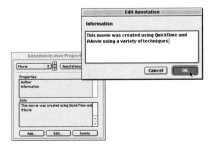

6. Enter a new value into the pop-up Information window and click OK. Select File ▷ Save (⌘-S) to save the annotations with your movie.

Annotations

Don't feel limited to the annotations used in this project. QuickTime Pro offers an extensive collection of predefined annotations. Pick those that best match your documentation needs. The full list includes Album, Artist, Author, Comment, Composer, Copyright, Creation Date, Description, Director, Disclaimer, Encoded By, Full Name, Genre, Host Computer, Information, Make Model, Original Artist, Original Format, Original Source, Performers, Producer, Product, Software, Special Playback Requirements, Track, Warning, Writer, URL Link, and Edit Date 1 through Edit Date 9.

QuickTime Pro Selection Shortcuts

Use these shortcuts to help create selections in a QuickTime Pro editing window.

SHORTCUT	ACTION
⌘-A	Select the entire movie.
⌘-B	Select nothing at all; deselect (this is the Select None command).
Control-Shift-[	A less-well-behaved equivalent of ⌘-B/Select None.
Shift-Left arrow or Shift-Right arrow	Move the playhead one frame in the direction indicated and expand the selection to that frame.
Shift-⌘-Left arrow or Shift-⌘-Right arrow	Move the playhead one frame in the direction indicated, expanding the selection to that frame, and then start movie playback, moving the crop marker with the play of the movie until the ⌘ and Shift keys are released.
Shift-drag	Adjust the selection according to the placement of the mouse along the scrubber bar.

Move between iMovie and QuickTime

While iMovie and QuickTime Pro are both excellent, powerful programs, the problem at times is that they aren't, in any way, the *same* program. So you end up shuttling your data between one and the other a bit more than you might like to. What's worse, these programs use slightly different shaped pixels. This can turn into a major pain, producing stretched or squashed pictures, or pictures lined with black bars.

Moving footage between these programs becomes vital when you need to take advantage of QuickTime Pro's capabilities. It also helps when you want to produce your movies in a form that you can reuse in multiple projects. It pays to spend some time learning how best to transfer your files between these two programs. With a little practice and a bit of foresight, you can save yourself a lot of heartache while producing quality videos.

Export and Import DV Movies

Unfortunately, no single common file type exists to transfer DV movies between iMovie and QuickTime Pro. Instead, follow these steps to move your footage back and forth.

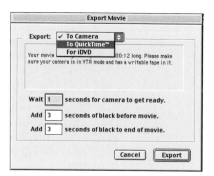

1. From within iMovie, select File ▷ Export Movie (⌘-E). This instructs iMovie to open the Export dialog. Choose To QuickTime from the pull-down menu.

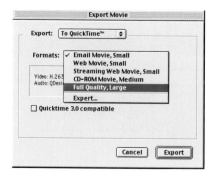

2. Choose Full Quality, Large from the Formats menu to create a QuickTime movie with DV compression. Click Export and wait for the Save As dialog to appear.

3. Navigate as needed to the folder where you wish to save your file. Name the file and click Save. It may take some time to finish exporting.

4. From QuickTime Pro, open the movie you just created (File ▷ Open Movie In New Player, ⌘-O). The movie appears with a proper screen ratio and otherwise looks normal.

5. To export back from QuickTime to a format that you can open in iMovie, select File ▷ Export (⌘-E). Choose the Movie To DV Stream option. I recommend you use the default settings.

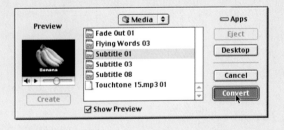

6. When you return to iMovie, select File ▷ Import File (⌘-I). Navigate to where you exported the QuickTime file. You will now see the DV file you created. Select it to open it in iMovie.

Combine and Conquer

Exporting your footage from iMovie offers a great way to combine edited footage together to create a single block of video. I do this often when I want to create a video clip that I'll reuse for several videos. Another reason I do this is to keep my projects simple. Instead of editing a large project in a single file, I'll use several projects to keep each section isolated. Exporting the footage allows me to combine the chunks from each project into a final unified form. This practice offers several advantages:

- A big mess-up in any one subproject will not affect any other part.
- It reduces export times for any block of video.
- It allows me to focus specifically on a single section, without having to worry about tying down sounds and video clips unrelated to that section when I add or remove material.
- It helps avoid any problems associated with file-size limits.

Note: Beware of the iMovie 2 GB file-size limit! Do not attempt to export and then import footage that exceeds about 10 minutes in length. When you keep this limit in mind, you'll avoid some unpleasant surprises—such as programs that mysteriously stop or data that gets lost forever.

Sneak into Your DV Clip Collection

You can open the DV files stored in your project folder directly from within QuickTime Pro. Simply navigate to your project's Media folder, select a file, and click Convert. The QuickTime file dialog even lets you preview your video clips before you select them.

Know Your Still Sizes

QuickTime and iMovie use slightly different pixel shapes. A still that works perfectly in iMovie may appear distorted in QuickTime and vice versa. QuickTime circles may appear as iMovie ovals and iMovie circles as QuickTime ovals. This happens because computers generally use square pixels while television and broadcast video use rectangular pixels. Since iMovie pixels are rectangular, they occupy more "space," allowing the same-size video to appear with fewer pixels. Fortunately, most image editors easily allow you to resize your image—squeezing or stretching to fit. The exact image size varies by broadcast system, as shown here:

	NTSC	PAL
iMovie	640x480	768x576
QuickTime	720x480	720x576

Transfer Stills

If you want to transfer a single still, you'll need to resize it in an image editor. Here, you will see how to export a still from QuickTime, resize it, and then properly import it into iMovie.

1. Standard DV movies occupy 720x480 pixels (720x576 for PAL systems), as you can see here from the QuickTime Pro Movie Info window (Window ▷ Show Movie Info or ⌘+I).

2. Export a still from QuickTime Pro using the bitmap export feature (File ▷ Export or ⌘+E). Choose Movie To BMP and use default settings.

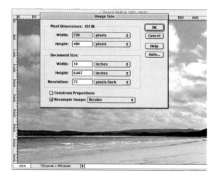

3. When you import this still into iMovie, the odd size forces black bands above and below the image.

4. To correctly import the still, you must first resize it. This example uses Photoshop Elements, a demo of which is available on the companion CD, but the same method should work in any good image-editing program. Open the still in Photoshop Elements and select Image ▷ Resize ▷ Image Size.

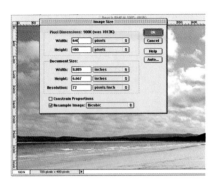

5. First, ensure that Constrain Proportions is unchecked. Enter the correct new pixel dimensions and press OK. In this case, we're converting a 720x480 picture to 640x480. Enter 640 in the width field and click OK.

6. Save the converted file back to disk, in preparation for importing to iMovie.

7. In iMovie, the newly resized image fits perfectly without needing "filler" bands to pad the picture.

8. You can see the size difference clearly in QuickTime. Here's what it looks like when imported into QuickTime and overlaid on top of the original DV footage.

Create a Still in iMovie

Creating stills in iMovie is as easy, or even easier, than in QuickTime Pro. To create one, just press ⌘-F (File ▷ Save Frame As), enter a name, and press Save. Wherever the playhead is located, iMovie will save that frame. You can save in either of two formats: JPEG or PICT; select one from the Save Frame As Image dialog. While JPEG offers smaller files and better transportability between programs and people, PICT offers higher image quality and less compression.

Small Video Direct to DV

As you might expect, you can export your small-sized videos directly to DV format with QuickTime Pro. However, you may or may not like the results. QuickTime must scale your movie to standard DV size (720x480 pixels for NTSC, 720x576 for PAL). Whenever you enlarge a video in this way, you magnify defects and expand the "blockiness" that results from low resolution.

To create a DV file from your smaller-than-normal video in QuickTime Pro, select File ▷ Export (⌘-E) and choose Export: Movie To DV Stream.

Note: QuickTime export allows you to convert a variety of file types that you might not expect to use with iMovie, including MJPEG and AVI. As a rule of thumb, if you can open a file with QuickTime Pro, you can probably export it to a format that iMovie accepts.

Prepare Non-Standard Sized Video

Small-sized video comes from web cams, USB digitizers, TV cards, or other sources. In these steps, you'll create a virtual matte that preserves video size and resolution when exporting to an iMovie-compliant DV stream.

1. Use Photoshop Elements to create a 720x480-pixel blank RGB still (720x576 for PAL) filled with any color. (Screen resolution does not matter. Choose any resolution you like.) Save to disk in a .psd file and open it in QuickTime Pro.

2. In QuickTime Pro, select all of the blank still (⌘-A), copy (⌘-C), and close the matte (⌘-W). Then, open your small-sized video. (In this example, I use a 320x240 clip imported from an old, analog camera.)

3. Select all (⌘-A) and add the matte with Edit ▷ Add Scaled (Option-Shift-⌘-V). The window will resize, and the blank matte will overlay the video. This virtual matte, like the cardboard rectangles used by framing stores, surrounds your picture.

4. Open the Movie Properties window by typing ⌘-J. Select Video Track 1 from the left pull-down menu and Layer from the right menu.

5. Press the down-arrow button to adjust the layer until your video appears in front of the matte. *⊘* You can read more about this in the earlier project "Know Your Tracks."

6. Select Size from the right pull-down menu and click the Adjust button.

7. Manually, move your video track into place as desired (*⊘* "Know Your Tracks"). Finish by clicking Done.

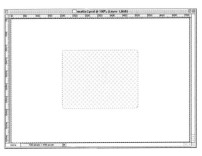

8. When you are satisfied with your video placement, select File ▷ Export (⌘-E) and choose Movie To DV Stream from the Export pull-down menu. Navigate as needed, name your file, and click Save.

9. When dealing with video that has small tracking problems and other flaws around the edges, you may want to use a different matting technique. You'll find this sort of feedback when you import from traditional video sources, such as VHS, Hi-8, and Beta.

10. Create a new RGB, transparent image (720x480 NTSC, 720x576 PAL). Fill it with white. Select a rectangle that's smaller than your video—here, 310x230 pixels. Selection ▷ Feather softens the edges for a seamless overlay. Edit ▷ Cut (⌘-X) removes the selection, adding the hole. Save to a .psd file.

matte.psd, chicken.mov, emchick.mov

Matte over Video

It may seem counterintuitive to add the matte to the video, but there's a good reason. You add it over the video because you want to scale that matte for the entire video duration. If you were to reverse this procedure, adding the video over the matte, you'd end up with either an extremely short video (when using Add Scaled) or the matte would disappear after a single frame (when using Add). It may be a little annoying to have to re-layer, but it is actually vital in creating a proper matte track that extends for the full length of your movie.

Note: Most Macintosh image editors allow you to save to Photoshop (.psd) format. This format allows you to use transparency in QuickTime Pro, as you do in the example shown here.

Prepare Non-Standard Sized Video *continued*

11. Open the matte in QuickTime (File ▷ Open Movie In New Player or ⌘-O), select it (⌘-A), copy it (⌘-C), and close it (⌘-W). If using a white matte, as seen here, you will not see the "hole" because the graphics mode defaults to Dither Copy.

12. Open your movie in QuickTime, select all (⌘-A), and add the scaled matte (Edit ▷ Add Scaled or Option-Shift-⌘-V). Then open the Movie Properties window by pressing ⌘-J.

13. Select Video Track 2 from the left pull-down menu and Graphics Mode from the right. Choose Straight Alpha from the list of choices. The hole you created in your image editor will now appear.

14. Select Video Track 1 from the left pull-down menu and Size from the right, then click the Adjust button.

QuickTime Pro Editing Commands

These QuickTime Pro shortcuts affect your selection in various ways.

15. Drag your video into place behind the opening in the matte. Click the Done button on the Movie Properties window.

SHORTCUT	ACTION
Cut, ⌘-X	Removes the selection from your movie, saving it in the Clipboard.
Clear	Removes the selection from your movie, without saving it in the Clipboard.
Copy, ⌘-C	Copies the selection to the Clipboard.
Paste, ⌘-V	If no selection exists, pastes the data from the Clipboard at the playhead. If a selection has been made, this command overwrites the selection with the Clipboard data. No scaling is done by a paste, and the pasted data remains otherwise unaltered.
Trim	Removes everything from your movie except the selection.
Add, Option-⌘-V	Creates a new track, adding the data from the Clipboard to that new track, starting at the playhead location.
Add Scaled, Option-Shift-⌘-V	Creates a new track, adding the data from the Clipboard to that new track, scaled to the start, end, and duration of the current selection

Add Creative Mattes

There's no reason to limit yourself to plain white when matting your video. Feel free to design clever and interesting elements, so long as they do not overly detract attention from the actual footage.

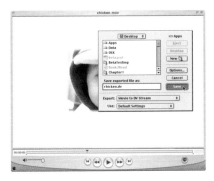

16. Test your movie, make any further adjustments needed, and then export to a DV stream to use your movie in iMovie.

iMovie Power Edits

Sometimes, the non-obvious way to do things provides the best results. When using iMovie to edit your footage, you should be aware of some alternative editing techniques. Here, you'll find some tricks that I use to edit my movies. They may not be the simplest way, and they may not be the most straightforward way, but they are dependable. For example, my cutaway technique separates the audio before performing the cut, avoiding unpleasant sound glitches that crop up as an iMovie bug. This bug and others may get fixed in later versions of iMovie, but all the techniques shown here work correctly now.

Perfect Cutaways

Cutaways are a common technique to jump from one video source to another—continuing the original soundtrack avoids confusing your viewer. You've surely seen this on TV and in movies.

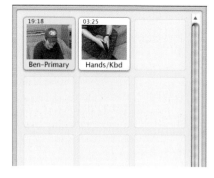

1. Import your primary and cutaway footage into iMovie. Here, we will cut away to footage of hands opening a keyboard as the subject discusses how the keyboard can be expanded.

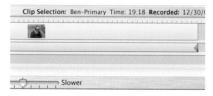

2. Drag the primary footage to the Timeline. Select Advanced ▷ Extract Audio (⌘-J) to separate the audio track from the video. The audio appears as a single bright orange line below the video track, regardless of whether it is a mono or stereo track.

3. Select the cutaway footage on the Shelf.

4. With the cutaway selected, turn your attention to the Monitor. Shift-drag just below the scrubber bar to select the entire clip. The crop markers (the white triangles) will split apart to each end of your selection. If you find you've missed part of the clip, drag the right crop marker as needed.

5. Choose Edit ▷ Copy (⌘-C).

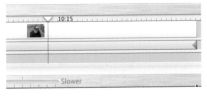

6. Return your attention to the Timeline. Play through the video and determine exactly where you wish to place the cutaway. Move the playhead to that spot.

7. Choose Advanced ▷ Paste Over At Playhead (Shift-⌘-V).

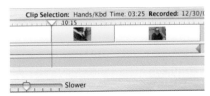

8. iMovie pastes your cutaway material at the playhead, replacing the original video footage and splitting your clip into three parts: the original start, the new material, and the original end. The audio, having been extracted earlier, remains unchanged. iMovie removes the audio from the cut-in clip, allowing for a true cutaway.

cutaway.mov

Enhance the Audio

After extracting the audio (Step 2), you may want to follow the instructions on page 8 to normalize your sound. This offers the perfect opportunity to enhance your audio without affecting the rest of your movie. This step proves particularly important when you use your camera's built-in microphone, which may not provide the best sound quality. As my personal camera does not offer an external microphone jack, I have no option other than the built-in. Therefore, I usually normalize my audio with a sound-enhancement program.

Cutaway for Time

Cutaways do more than maintain visual interest. They can also help you edit overly long material. When dealing with an extended stretch of footage (or a particularly boring main subject), you can use a cutaway to move away from the speaker. Rather than return directly to where you left (as done in the project shown here), clever editing allows you to pick up at a later time. Use this technique judiciously, and make sure to edit your sound carefully.

Transform Other Elements

As far as iMovie is concerned, speed and playback direction are a matter of bookkeeping. Reverse a clip and iMovie changes a single line of text in your project file—it doesn't change the clip itself. Even when you force iMovie to render (select File ▷ Export and click the Render Now button), you just optimize playback without really changing the clip. When you import the rendered clip, you end up with more or less the same clip you started with.

When you want to import a reversed clip and have it show up on your clips shelf reversed, use the Title trick described here. Your new clip will work properly with any overlaid effects, titles, and transitions, and you can open and edit it with QuickTime Pro. The same goes for time warping as for reversing. Lengthen or slow down a clip and apply this method to create a well-behaved clip.

Transform Footage with Empty Titles

A blank title provides a sneaky but very convenient way to combine a few clips together without having to export and reimport footage.

1. Using the Clip Viewer, select those clips you wish to collapse into a single element. Click the first clip to select it. Then Shift-click the last in the series; iMovie automatically selects all the clips between them.

2. Examine the bar on top of the Clip Viewer. It will show that you've selected multiple clips and tell you the combined duration of those clips. Make a note of this number. In this example, the total time selected is 13:05.

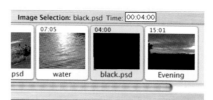

3. Import a blank still—here I use a solid black image, but any still will do—and place it in the Timeline just after the clips you wish to compress. This image provides a buffer between the collapsed clips and the following material so that you will not clip any other footage by accident.

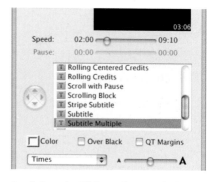

4. Select the Titles palette and choose Subtitle Multiple (from the Apple Plug-In Pack at www.apple.com/imovie). Subtitle Multiple offers a good "empty title" template, offering an arbitrary number of blank lines to extend the title duration. This trick will work with any blank title format other than Stripe Subtitle, which adds a semisolid line to the image.

5. Select each line of default text and press the Delete key on your keyboard to clear it. Make sure to clear every line. Use the slider on the right side of the palette to scroll through the entire list of subtitles.

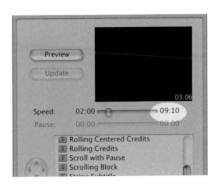

6. Note the maximum clip length for the current title. You'll find this number on the right side of the Speed slider just below the preview area.

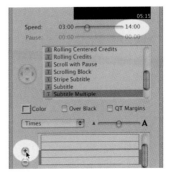

7. Click the + button, adding another blank subtitle, until the maximum clip length just exceeds the length of your clip, but not more than the clip length plus your still length. In this example, after inserting multiple blank title tracks, I get 14:00.

8. Move the Speed slider to the maximum, and drag your title to the front of your first clip in the Timeline. (Make sure that Over Black remains unselected before you drag.)

9. Wait as iMovie renders your title—the small red line that creeps across your clip in the Timeline indicates iMovie's progress. Rendering time will vary based on the length of your clip (this example uses 420 frames) and the speed of your computer. Expect to wait up to a minute or two as needed.

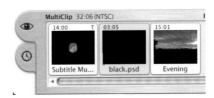

10. Select that portion of the blank still that remains as a separate clip. Press the Delete key on your keyboard to remove it.

Combine QuickTime Tracks

As with iMovie, you can combine footage into a single clip in QuickTime Pro. QuickTime's "simple export trick" is similar to iMovie's "empty title trick." QuickTime Pro collapses multiple tracks into one when you export a movie, rather than when you save. Keep these tips in mind:

- Before exporting to a QuickTime Movie, turn off any output functions. Typical functions include conversion to black and white or automatic blurring. Click Options and look to see if a Format: line is listed. If so, click Filter and select None. If you don't see a Format: line, then you're fine.

- While any export to a movie format collapses your tracks, exporting to QuickTime Movie format preserves your current video quality. You'll need this if you will continue working in QuickTime Pro. When you export to DV, you're likely to lose fine details because of the recompression. (DV uses a 5-to-1 compression format.) Delay exporting to DV until you're ready to return to iMovie.

Transform Footage with Empty Titles *continued*

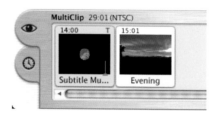

11. Select the combined clip.

12. Examine the Monitor. Move the playhead along the scrubber bar until you find the end of your original clip. If the preview shows the last frame of your clip, press the Right arrow key once to move to the start of the incorporated padding-still.

13. Hold the Shift key and drag below the scrubber bar to select the remaining frames to the right of the clip.

14. Delete the selected frames (⌘-X or Edit ▷ Cut). Although you can use Clear here instead of Cut, I recommend against it. Clear can inadvertently undo the text effect you worked so hard to create.

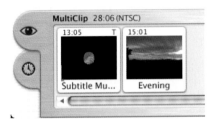

15. Now you have successfully combined your original elements into a single clip. The clip duration should match the length from Step 2.

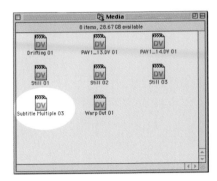

16. (Optional) You can find your combined clip in your project's Media folder, called Subtitle Multiple. This clip will have a number appended to the end, as shown here. You may want to reimport this file (⌘-I) as a new clip if you want to add more titles or effects on top of the combined clip.

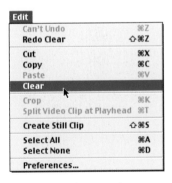

17. (Optional) To undo your work, select your clip and choose Edit ▷ Clear.

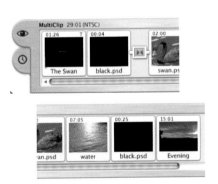

18. (Optional) After clearing, iMovie restores the entire set of materials used to create the clip—including, in this case, the black, padding still. Select the still and press Delete to restore the original set of clips. File ▷ Empty Trash permanently removes these clips.

The Clear Trick

Edit ▷ Clear removes titles from any clip labeled with a small **T** in the top-right corner. Clearing undoes the titling and returns you to an earlier state of editing. If the title extended over multiple clips, combining them, the individual clips will return. If adding the title split any clip in two, this trick will restore the original without the split.

Other clear tricks include the following:

Undo Selecting Undo (Edit ▷ Undo, ⌘-Z) offers the simplest way to restore your clips to an earlier state. iMovie supports 10 levels of Undo. Beware of emptying the trash; when you do, most clip changes become permanent. The state of the restored media will only go back in time to the last time the trash emptied.

Remove a transition When you delete a transition, you restore the clip material that was used to create the transition. The restored material will last twice as long—a transition gathers frames from both sides when it's created.

Restore Clip Media Choose Advanced ▷ Restore Clip Media to return a clip to its original state—at least the latest state available since the last time you emptied the trash. Take care when extracting audio. You won't be able to recombine the audio with the original clip with this command (although you can with Undo).

Snapping Audio to the Playhead

Whenever you resize or move audio, you can take advantage of a special feature that allows you to snap to the playhead's last location. To use this feature, set the playhead in the Timeline before you begin your move or resize. As you move the audio, you'll see a small, ghosted playhead where it was last placed. As you approach the ghosted playhead, use iMovie's built-in snapping behavior to precisely set your audio at that location.

Snapping also works when your audio lasts longer than your movie. Drag the dangling end of your audio to the left. As you shorten the clip, allow iMovie to snap it to the precise end of your final clip.

Note: iMovie offers many snapping behaviors. Whenever you need exact selection placement, iMovie usually allows you to snap to some major feature or another. Not sure if iMovie offers one type of snapping or another? The best way to find out is to try. You might be pleasantly surprised.

Cut Footage Precisely

At times footage must fill an exact gap. Here, we'll trim a black still to pad the start of a movie to match the audio exactly.

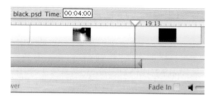

1. Add the padding clip to the end of your movie.

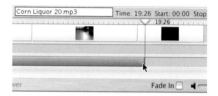

2. Click the small triangle on the right end of your audio clip. The playhead jumps to the end of the audio. Importantly, the playhead moves in parallel in two locations: on the Timeline and in the Monitor.

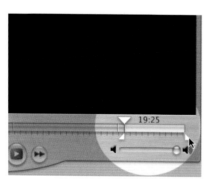

3. Turn your attention to the Monitor. While holding the Shift key, drag under the scrubber bar until you've selected all the frames from the playhead to the end of the still clip.

4. Select Edit ▷ Cut (⌘-X) to remove the excess frames. Your clip will now coincide exactly with the end of the audio.

Positioning Tricks

Move the playhead to the start of a clip Select any clip in the Timeline to move the playhead to the beginning of that clip.

Move the playhead to the end of a clip To move the playhead to the end of a clip, start by selecting the clip. The selected clip appears in the Monitor. Drag the scrubber bar's playhead all the way to the right.

Dismiss the crop markers Choose Edit ▷ Select None (⌘-D) to dismiss the crop markers from the scrubber bar.

Find the ghost crop markers To find your "ghost" crop markers, make sure you have no current selection in the scrubber bar. Move your mouse to the bottom of the Monitor and slowly move the mouse upwards towards the scrubber bar. When your mouse approaches about a cursor-width away from the scrubber bar, the ghost markers will appear. Once the ghost appears, click and drag to create a selection.

Move to the start or end of the movie Pressing the Home and End keys on your keyboard will move the playhead to the start or end, respectively, of your movie.

Add Sounds

You can easily expand the built-in library of sound offered in the Audio palette. OS 9.*x* users, just drag a compliant AIFF sound file to the Sound Effects folder in your iMovie Resources folder. It takes a few more steps for OS X users: Select iMovie in your Applications folder. Right-click and choose Show Page Contents. Open the Contents folder, then the Resources folder, and drag your file into the Sound Effects folder you'll find there.

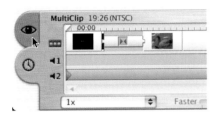

5. Click the tab with the eye icon to switch from the Timeline view to the Clip Viewer.

6. Drag the remaining, trimmed padding clip into its proper place at the beginning.

🔊 Crowd Clapping	04:26	
🔊 Dog Bark	01:24	
🔊 Drum Roll	03:12	
🔊 ExtraSoundsAreEasy.aif	03:01	
🔊 Footsteps	06:24	
🔊 Forest Rain	05:04	
🔊 Glass Breaking	02:07	

2

iMovie Stills

Special Effects with Stills

Stills can create a range of special effects that are hard to match with live-action footage. You can build stills and import them into iMovie, or use iMovie to build stills from your actual footage. Modified and reimported, these altered images produce eye-catching effects that liven up your videos. In this chapter, you will see how to create, edit, and reuse stills to produce a wide variety of effects. You'll learn how to create stills from video clips and use them inside and outside of iMovie. You'll see how to apply filters to stills and discover how to add iMovie transitions to produce visually appealing results.

Basic Stills

Export and Modify Stills

Still Effects

Basic Stills

Still clips play many roles. A still in the right place changes your movie's flow to produce tension and visual interest; a still can draw out a scene or make a unique transition possible. In this section, you'll see how to create still clips from your video footage and use them in your iMovies. You'll learn how to change the way your videos play back, moving between live action and still clips. Stills let you add a new rhythm and variety to your videos yet help ensure that all the elements of your movie work together.

Note: When you add a transition to a clip or a still, be aware that the transition's time comes out of the clip's time. In Step 7 here, for instance, your 5-second still shortens to 3:00, because the inserted transition was set to 2:00.

Add Stills Around a Clip

When you want to add transitions without altering core clip footage, use stills. In these steps, you'll see how to create stills from your footage and use stretching to size those stills perfectly.

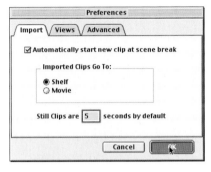

1. For many of these still projects, it helps to use longer clips rather than shorter ones. In this project, long length serves a tutorial rather than a practical purpose. Select Edit ▷ Preferences (in OS X, iMovie ▷ Preferences).

2. Select the Import tab. Enter 5 (the default still clip length) and click OK. All newly created clips will use this length. Existing clips remain unaffected.

3. Select your clip; it will appear in the Monitor. Move the playhead to the far left on the scrubber bar. Select Edit ▷ Create Still Clip (Shift-⌘-S). iMovie creates a still clip of this first frame. Your new clip appears in the first free slot on your clips shelf.

4. Select your video clip again. Then move the playhead to the very right on your scrubber bar. Select Edit ▷ Create Still Clip (Shift-⌘-S). iMovie creates a still from this final frame. Again, this clip appears in the clips shelf in the first available slot.

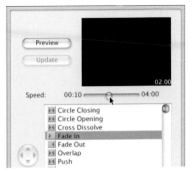

5. Drag your newly created still clips down to the Clip Viewer. Place the clips in order: the first still, your video clip, and the second still.

6. Select the Transitions palette. Choose the Fade-In transition. Move the Speed slider to 2 seconds. The small window at the top of the palette shows the current speed setting. Make a note of this number as you move the slider.

7. Drag your Fade-In transition into place, in front of your first still clip. iMovie will render (calculate) the transition. A small red bar follows the rendering progress. It moves from left to right, under the transition. When rendering is complete, the red bar disappears.

8. Return to the Transitions palette and select Fade-Out. Leave the speed set to 2 seconds. Drag the transition into place after your last still clip. Wait as iMovie renders the transition.

9. Click the clock icon at the left of the Clip Viewer to change to the Timeline presentation. Select the right-side (Fade-Out) transition and drag it to the left. As you drag, your right-most still clip will compress. Continue dragging until the still clip collapses, leaving the fade-out but little else.

10. Select your main video clip. Drag it to the left to collapse your first still clip. Drag as far as you can, leaving just the fade-in portion. After following these steps, you'll be left with your original, unaltered video clip and a pair of fade-in and fade-out effects.

Myrdraal.mov

Removing a Still's Background in Photoshop Elements

Creating a still without its background involves several steps. These instructions are specific to Photoshop/Photoshop Elements, but the overall technique should work with most quality, Mac-based image editors. After you save your still in iMovie (File ▷ Save Frame As, ⌘-F), follow these steps in Photoshop Elements:

1. Carefully select your subjects. Use the magnetic lasso tool to make your preliminary selection. Adjust that selection using the freehand lasso tool—use Option-drag to remove areas from your selection and Shift-drag to add.

2. After you've finished your selection, soften your edges by choosing Select ▷ Feather (Option-⌘-D). Specify 2 pixels and click OK.

3. To remove the background, choose Select ▷ Inverse (Shift-⌘-I) and Edit ▷ Clear.

4. Set your foreground color to black (press Shift-D) and use the paint bucket tool to fill the background.

5. Save your file to disk and import this modified image into iMovie.

Still Variations

Removing the background while retaining your subjects can add a splash to a fade-out still. These steps repeat the general fade-out technique from the previous project but import a modified still for an extra effect.

1. In iMovie, press the End key to move the playhead to the last frame of your movie. Select File ▷ Save Frame As (⌘-F). Navigate to where you wish to save a copy of this frame, enter a name, and click Save.

2. In Photoshop Elements, remove the background from your image. Replace the background with black, and save to disk. If you're unsure on how to proceed, refer to the sidebar on this page.

3. Return to iMovie. With the playhead on the last frame of your movie (press the end key again if needed), select Edit ▷ Create Still Clip (Shift-⌘-S). iMovie creates a still of your last frame, placing it on the clips shelf.

4. Select File ▷ Import File (⌘-I). Navigate to your modified picture and click Open. A still clip of your modified picture appears on the clips shelf.

5. Drag these stills, in order, down to your Clip Viewer. Place them after the current end of your movie. The order goes: movie, last-frame still clip, imported no-background still clip.

6. Move to the Transitions palette. Select Cross Dissolve and set the speed to 2 seconds. This timing offers a nice leisurely transition without boring (or jarring) your viewer.

7. Drag a Cross Dissolve transition down to the Clip Viewer. Place it between the last-frame still and the background-removed still. Wait for iMovie to finish rendering the transition. The moving red line monitors the progress of this operation.

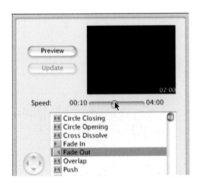

8. Return to the Transitions palette. Select Fade Out and set the speed to 2 seconds. You'll use this transition to blend away your background-free still clip into simple black.

9. Drag the Fade Out transition to your Clip Viewer. Place it to the right of your final clip. Wait as iMovie renders the transition.

10. Click the clock icon to switch from the Clip Viewer to the Timeline. Select each transition and drag it to the left to collapse any remaining still frames. Play back your movie to confirm that it works as expected. Save your work.

ladies.mov

Still Types

iMovie allows you to create stills in several ways. Each offers a different solution and is produced differently:

From footage Derive a still directly from your DV footage. Move the playhead to any frame, select Edit ▷ Create Still Clip (Shift-⌘-S), and iMovie copies that frame to a new still clip and places it on the clips shelf.

From disk When you import an image from disk, iMovie opens it, scales it as needed, and copies it to your project media folder. This still then appears in your clips shelf, ready for use.

From each other You can copy existing still clips to create new ones. Option-drag any still clip to duplicate it. You can perform this copy in the clips shelf, in the Clip Viewer, or between the two.

The "secret" black still clip

iMovie offers a built-in black still clip. Select any clip that does not have a transition to its left. In the Timeline, drag it to the right. A black bar appears. You can add titles to this black still or use it to create a transition, just like any other clip.

Intermingle Stills

In these steps, you'll slow your video to a complete stop to create a striking movie effect. Your video can pause for a message—or for a full examination.

1. Import your source footage into iMovie. This example uses a silent black-and-white video clip of a welder. This clip provides eye-catching opportunities to pause while sparks fly into the air. When you select your clip, try to pick one with good visual moments. To begin, move your clip down to the Timeline.

2. In the Monitor, move the playhead to find a particularly dramatic frame. Take your time looking through your footage. You may wish to use the arrow keys to move frame-by-frame to find the one that best suits your visual tastes. I chose this frame for its splashy, sparks-in-the-air effect. Choose a frame that captures an interesting moment.

3. Press the Right arrow key once to move forward one frame. Select Edit ▷ Split Video Clip At Playhead (⌘-T). This splits your clip into two. The first clip ends with the frame you found exciting and interesting. This splitting operation always places the selected frame into the first clip.

4. Because your clip was on the Timeline, both portions remain selected although the playhead is now at the start of the second clip. Press the Left arrow key once to return to your frame of interest. Choose Edit ▷ Create Still Clip (Shift-⌘-S) to build a still from this frame. This project uses 2-second stills, but any length will do.

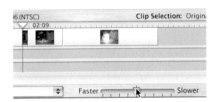

5. Drag the newly created still clip from the clips shelf to the space you just created between the first and second portions of your footage. This new clip duplicates the final frame of the first section and extends it for the length of the still.

6. Press ⌘-D (Edit ▷ Select None) to unselect the still clip while retaining the playhead position. Press Shift-Left arrow to move the playhead ten frames to the left. Choose Edit ▷ Split Video Clip At Playhead (⌘-T) to create a 10-frame clip that precedes your still.

7. Select this new, small clip. Move the toggle on the Faster/Slower slider (at the bottom-middle of the Timeline) a few notches to the right, slowing down this clip.

8. Find a second, third, or fourth point of excitement and repeat Steps 3 through 7 to create additional stop points.

9. Choose the Titles palette. Design a bright, colorful, large title. Match the timing to the length of your first still clip, and drag the title just before the still.

10. Repeat the titling step to add visually striking titles to each still clip. If your video includes sound, click the Mute check box to the right of the video track; this project will distort your sound track. Play back your movie to see that it works as expected. Save your work.

FullStop.mov

Export and Modify Stills

When iMovie effects and titles do not offer the full range of production values you need, consider turning to stills. Exporting a still allows you to modify it in an image-processing program like Photoshop Elements while preserving visual context. This way, you can be fairly certain, upon reimport to iMovie, that the image will work with the original footage surrounding it. In this section, you'll see how to export and modify stills to create a variety of effects, from thought bubbles to a painting that comes to life.

Note: You may experience slight color shifts and variations when you export a still, modify it, and reimport to iMovie. This usually occurs because your image-editing program uses a different color model than iMovie. Most compressed formats (including DV) trade color information for space. When this occurs, try saving to a different format (such as JPEG, TIFF, PICT, PSD, etc.) and reimport.

Thought Bubbles

What really lies behind smiles and laughter? In these steps, you'll see how to add thought bubbles to stills and reimport them into iMovie.

1. In iMovie, choose a clip to work with. Select it and it will appear in the Monitor. Move the playhead back and forth until you find a frame you wish to modify. (I picked this one because it shows the man smiling while the woman's eyes are shut.)

2. Choose File ▷ Save Frame As (⌘-F). When the dialog appears, navigate to where you wish to save your file. Name it and click Save. This saves a copy of the current frame to disk in the format you specify: either JPEG or PICT.

3. Choose Edit ▷ Split Video Clip At Playhead (⌘-T). iMovie splits your clip, just before the frame you used to create the still. This gap allows you to insert your altered still in Step 7.

4. In Photoshop Elements, open your frame. Select the thought-bubble shape tool and add a thought bubble to your image.

5. Use the various shaping and text tools to add a message to your thought bubble. Here, our subject thinks "Football," as a contrast to the more (supposedly) feminine thought of "Relationship!" that will follow. Save your altered image back to disk and return to iMovie.

6. In iMovie, select File ▷ Import File (⌘-I). Navigate to your modified still, select it, and click Open.

7. iMovie creates a still clip from the modified still and stores it in your clips shelf. Drag this still clip into place, between the first and second portions of your already-split clip.

8. Select the second portion of your split clip. Move the playhead along the scrubber bar to find a position for the second still, then select Edit ▷ Save Frame As (⌘-F) and save a copy of that frame to disk. Again choose Edit ▷ Split Video Clip At Playhead (⌘-T) to split your clip in two.

9. In Photoshop Elements, open the second frame and add the thought bubble for your second subject. Save to disk and return to iMovie.

10. Again, select File ▷ Import File (⌘-I) and open your second modified frame. Drag the new still clip into place in the split you created in Step 8. Play back your movie to test that it works as expected. Make any needed adjustments and save your work.

relationship.mov

Total Transformations

When you use filters to transform a still—as you do in the steps on this page—make sure you retain sufficient similarity to your original footage. Your cross-dissolve shouldn't jar your viewer. Instead, it should blend smoothly back into the video. When you over-edit your image, adding too many new details, you end up with a picture that doesn't fit into your overall presentation. This project works because there's actually little difference between the "painting" and the still it was derived from. The only change involves the artistic filter in Step 9.

Restrain Your Image Editing

Although image-editing skills give a decided edge when customizing stills, simplicity goes a long way. A single effect (as seen in this example of a "painting come to life") adds an important mood to your videos without pro-level manipulation. Digital video relies more on big changes than small subtleties. A few broad strokes with an image-editor can create a striking iMovie impression.

Still Life

Follow these steps to create a "painting" that transforms itself into a moving video.

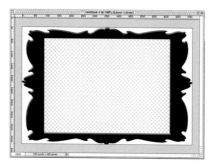

1. In Photoshop Elements, create a new, transparent, QuickTime-sized RGB image (720x480 NTSC, 720x576 PAL). Use the shape tool to create a black picture frame. Fill the outside of your frame with a solid white color, leaving the inside blank. Save your frame to disk.

2. In QuickTime Pro, open your frame image. Select All (⌘-A), copy (⌘-C), and close the image (⌘-W).

3. Still in QuickTime Pro, open your source video. Select All (⌘-A) and choose Edit ▷ Add Scaled (Option-Shift-⌘-V)

4. Open the Movie Properties window (⌘-J). Select Video Track 2 from the left pull-down menu and Graphics Mode from the right. Choose Straight Alpha.

5. Choose File ▷ Export (⌘-E) and export your video to a DV stream.

6. Create a new project in iMovie. Select File ▷ Import File (⌘-I) and import your framed video. It will appear on your clips shelf. Drag the new clip down to the Timeline.

7. Press the Home key to move the playhead to the start of your clip. Select File ▷ Save Frame As (⌘-F). Navigate to where you wish to save the frame, name it, and click Save.

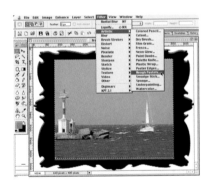

8. In Photoshop Elements, open your saved frame. Use the rectangle selection tool to select the center portion of your image. Choose Filter ▷ Artistic ▷ Rough Pastels.

9. Set the filter options as desired and click OK. Here, I use a Stroke Length of 4, a detail of 6, the Sandstone texture, 100% Scaling, 16 Relief, and lighting from the bottom. Feel free to vary your settings—I've included these just as a starting point. Experiment to discover the exact visual style that works for you.

10. After applying the filter, examine your results. Your central image should appear to be drawn by a pastel artist. The frame and surrounding white space should remain unaltered.

continues on next page

Portrait.mov, Portrait2.mov, Frame.PSD

Return to a Framed Image

Instead of simply fading away, as we do in the steps on this page, you may wish to return to a framed image at the end of your movie. To produce this effect, export your final frame and repeat Steps 8 through 11. Import your file, place it at the end of your Timeline, and use a Cross Dissolve to return from the live action to the pastel still. You'll find an example of this finishing touch in portrait2.mov on the accompanying CD.

Note: At times, you may find yourself unable to view all your clips on the Timeline at once. To help with this, use the Timeline Zoom pop-up menu. You'll find it on the bottom-left of your screen, under the audio tracks and to the left of the speed slider. Select 1x zoom to reduce your Timeline display to its most compact setting.

Still Life *continued*

11. If you are satisfied with your image, save it to disk. If not, select Edit ▷ Step Backward and reapply the filter with different settings.

12. In iMovie, select Edit ▷ Preferences. With the Import tab selected, enter 5 for the default still clip length. Click OK. As with the example on page 38 (☞ "Add Stills Around a Clip," step 1), this length deliberately exceeds the time we need in order to allow better still manipulation.

13. Select File ▷ Import File (⌘-I). Navigate to where you have stored your "pastel-ized" still. Select it and click Import.

14. iMovie opens your image, creates a still clip, and stores it in the Shelf. Drag this clip down to the Timeline and place it to the left of your clip.

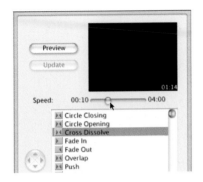

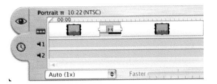

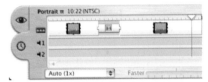

15. Select the Transitions palette. Choose the Cross Dissolve transition. Set the speed to about a second and a half. Any shorter and your viewer may miss the transition; any longer and you may blend too much with your still, destroying the "come-to-life" effect.

16. Drag the Cross Dissolve transition down to the Timeline between the two clips. Watch the progress of the small red bar as it renders.

17. Determine where you want your clip to end. Move the playhead to this position. In this example, I want my movie to last exactly ten seconds.

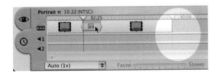

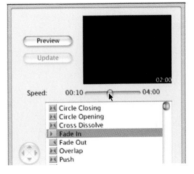

18. Drag the transition to the left, shrinking the still clip. While dragging, keep an eye on the end of your rightmost clip. Drag until that right end roughly approximates the position of the ghosted playhead.

19. Return to the Transitions palette. Choose Fade In. Set the speed to 1 or 2 seconds. Drag this fade-in to the start of your sequence, in front of your now-resized still clip. If desired, add a similar Fade Out transition to the end of your movie.

20. Play back your movie to ensure that it works as expected. Save your work (⌘-S) and, if desired, export a copy to disk or to your camera (⌘-E).

Still Effects

Transitions and effects can transform simple stills into animated scenes that enliven your iMovie productions. iMovie excels at creating transitions between similar pictures. As a transition replaces one still with another, judicious editing can fool your viewer into thinking that only a portion has changed. In this section, you'll see how to transform a yellow flower into a pink one, create a jar out of nothing, and bring a static image to life.

Note: For the Color Blends project, make sure to pick a transition that simply replaces a picture without changing placement; Cross Dissolve is a good candidate. Avoid transitions, such as Push or Warp, that move or resize the images. For this example, I use the Fluid – Drip transition from the GeeThree Spice collection. Don't own that transition? Try Radial for this project instead.

Color Blends

In these steps, you'll use Photoshop Element's Replace Color feature to turn a yellow flower into a pink one, creating before and after stills for your iMovie transitions.

1. In Photoshop Elements, open your original image. Select Enhance ▷ Color ▷ Replace Color.

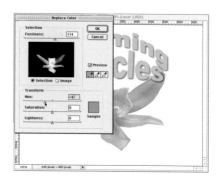

2. Use the eyedropper to select your key color. Adjust the Fuzziness slider to control how much of your image you wish to select—a higher number selects more areas. Slide the Hue bar until the selected areas take on a new color that pleases you. Click OK and save a *copy* to disk—don't overwrite the original!

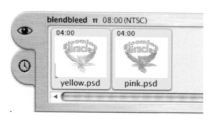

3. Import your "before" and "after" pictures into iMovie. Place them in order on the Timeline. Use nice long stills, 4 or 5 seconds each, to allow plenty of room for your transition.

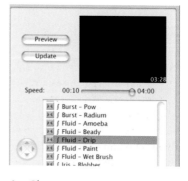

4. Choose your transition. (☞ See the sidebar for some guidelines on which transition to use.) Set the transition speed to the longest possible interval that your stills will support (usually 4 seconds). You'll trim the transition down later.

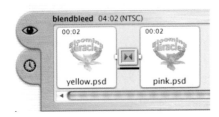

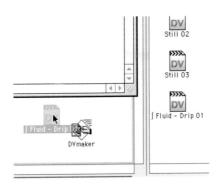

5. Drag the transition into place on the Timeline between the two still clips. Wait for it to render. This may take a minute or two to complete. The small red bar lets you monitor iMovie's progress as it calculates this transition.

6. After rendering, recover the transition footage from your Media folder: Locate the transition and copy it to your main project folder using Shift-drag. Drag this copy onto the DVmaker utility to change its file type. In iMovie, select File ▷ Import File (⌘-I). Open this file and wait for it to appear on your clips shelf.

7. Select the newly imported transition. Move the playhead forward along the scrubber bar until the transition just begins to affect your subject. Drag under the scrubber bar from the start to this location. Adjust the crop markers (the white triangles) to correct any selection errors.

8. Choose Edit ▷ Clear to remove this nothing-much-happens section from your transition clip. Next, move the playhead to the end of the color-change effect. Select from here to the end of your clip and choose Edit ▷ Clear to eliminate dull and extraneous material from the end of your clip as well.

9. Select the original transition (the small box with the arrows) on the Timeline. Press the Delete key or choose Edit ▷ Clear. This removes the transition and restores your original clips. Drag your newly edited transition from the clips shelf to the Timeline between the two stills. Adjust the length of these stills as needed.

10. Test your movie to see that it works as expected, then save it. The pink color should bleed down into the yellow, eventually reshading the flower.

 blendbleed.mov, yflower.psd, pflower.psd

Mind the Length

A good introductory transition, like the one shown in this project, must balance time against interest. The duration should not be so short that the viewer misses the entire point and not so long that it bores. Instead, the transition should last just long enough to be compelling and bring the main subject into the visual story without distracting. All too often, video designers fall in love with their effects to the detriment of their movies. Use this, and all the effects in this book, judiciously.

Use Strong Contrasts

To make this project effective, use images with strong—rather than subtle—contrasts. Pick dissimilar subjects, colors, and textures for your background and foreground elements. You need sharply changing features to present to your viewer as the transition progresses.

Presto! A Jar Appears!

In these steps, you'll see how to use iMovie transitions to introduce a main subject over a still background image.

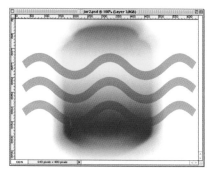

1. In Photoshop Elements, design your foreground and background. Here, I created supporting features to surround and augment the main image (the jar). Place each feature in a separate layer. Save this fully realized image to disk.

2. Hide the main image feature, revealing the background elements. (In the Layers palette, click the eye to the left of the layer holding your main object.) Save a copy of this altered image to another file (File ▷ Save As, Shift-⌘-S). Do not overwrite the original.

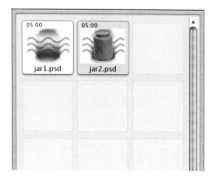

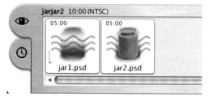

3. In iMovie, select File ▷ Import File (⌘-I). Navigate to your background-only image and click Open. iMovie creates a still clip of this image and places it on the clips shelf. Repeat to import your full image.

4. Drag the two clips down to the Clip Viewer. Place the two clips in order—the one without the subject followed by the one with.

5. Move to the Transitions palette. In this example, I use the Baked Earth effect from GeeThree to introduce my subject over the background. (Any number of other transitions will work as well. The sidebar to the right details several alternatives.) Set the speed to several seconds and drag the transition into place on the Timeline.

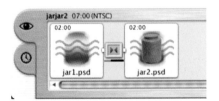

6. Wait for iMovie to finishing rendering. Watch the small red progress bar to get an indication of how far the transition has proceeded. After it finishes, test your effect. If you've done this correctly, the foreground item will seem to crumble onto the background until it appears completely.

Introducing the Main Subject

As you can see in this project, a transition between two stills offers a great way to introduce a main subject over a static background. Available transition sets include the iMovie built-ins, the Apple Plug-In Pack, and the various GeeThree effects. Here are a just few of my favorite transitions that provide subject-over-background introductions.

Spin In (GeeThree) With the spin-in effect, your subject appears to spiral in from nowhere. Use this transition when your subject rests on a solid-colored background. A blank background still blends with your subject still and hides the fact that you're working with two different images.

Cross Dissolve (iMovie, built-in) When working with complicated backgrounds, the Cross Dissolve transition allows you to introduce your subject with flair. (If you like, you can make your subject disappear instead.) You need not design your subject in the top layer. Allow yourself to experiment with removing elements that lie behind or are partially obscured by other objects. Watch a sample of this on the accompanying CD, harrytpotter.mov.

Vapor (GeeThree) GeeThree offers four different "Vapor" effects—Billo, Emit, Evaporate, and Fog. Use these to introduce different parts of your subject at a time, rather than the all-at-once.

Warp In (iMovie, built-in) The Warp In effect provides a compelling trick. The secret is to apply it and then reverse the clip so your subject explodes onto the screen.

jarjar.mov, jar1.psd, jar2.psd, harrytpotter.mov

Utilize Layers

Any experienced user of Photoshop (or Photoshop Elements, or similar programs) quickly becomes familiar with layers. These experts use layers to stack visual effects and visual elements to create more striking presentations. Illustrations made with layers naturally lend themselves to iMovie animation. When you use iMovie to separately change foreground and background elements, you end up producing some very interesting effects. Allow yourself to animate each separately, and you'll create even more stunning results.

See Early Versions

The curious reader will find several variations of this effect on the accompanying CD in the Early Movies section. I built these test versions while developing this chapter before settling on the procedure seen in these steps. Variations include a progressive blend (transback.mov), a background-only blend (straight-back.mov), the baked-earth transition (earth.mov), and a basic cross-dissolve (dissolve.mov).

Background Animations

Go beyond a static background when blending elements. In these steps, you'll animate your background before adding the main subject in front.

1.   In Photoshop Elements, design an image with foreground and background features. Save your image into two files: background only and full presentation. Also save a blank image filled with your primary background color.

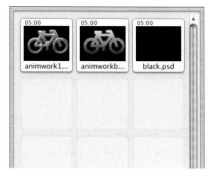

2.   In iMovie, choose Edit ▷ Preferences. Set your default still length to 5 seconds and click OK. Select File ▷ Import File (⌘-I). Navigate to your three files, select them, and click Open. iMovie converts these files to still clips and places them on your clips shelf.

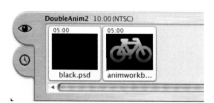

3.   Before blending the foreground and background elements, you'll create a background animation. To start, move the black still and the background artwork still to the Clip Viewer. Place the black still first.

4.   In this example, I use the GeeThree Rolling Fog effect. If you do not own a copy of this effect, use the Radial effect instead (for a slightly different emphasis). Set the speed to 4 seconds, the maximum time allowed for an iMovie transition.

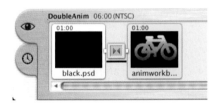

5. Drag the transition into place between your two stills on the Clip Viewer. Wait for iMovie to compute the transition. The small red bar that creeps along under the transition indicates how far iMovie has proceeded.

6. After iMovie finishes rendering, prepare to recover the transition from your Media folder. Leave iMovie for the moment. Open your project folder and the Media folder within. You should find three clips (Still 01, Still 02, Still 03) and one transition there. Option-drag the transition file to copy it to the Desktop.

7. Drag the copied transition onto the DVmaker utility (on the companion CD-ROM). This changes the file's type to dvc! so you can import it into iMovie. Return to iMovie; select File ⊳ Import File (⌘-I), navigate to your transition file, and open it. Wait for it to load and join the full artwork still on your shelf.

8. Empty your Clip Viewer. Select your two stills and the transition between them. Delete them all. Recall that a clip of this same transition awaits you on your shelf. Drag that transition clip and the full artwork to the now-empty Clip Viewer. Place the transition clip before the artwork still.

9. In the Transitions palette, choose Cross Dissolve. Select a speed between 1 and 2 seconds. Here, I use about a second and a half. Allow your viewer to observe some of the background animation before you blend with the foreground. This range of speeds does exactly that.

10. Drag the Cross Dissolve transition to the Clip Viewer between the transition clip and the foreground still. Wait for iMovie to render. If everything works as designed, your background will "blow in" while it blends with the foreground. Don't forget to save your work (⌘-S).

 bike.mov, bike2.mov, bike.psd, bikebg.psd

3

Overlays

Learn the Tricks of Picture-in-Picture

iMovie with its single video track can't overlay movies with other video material, a considerable difficulty when you want to place logos, insets, and so forth over your clips. Fortunately, QuickTime Pro jumps into the fray. In this chapter, you will learn how to create and combine overlays, from simple to complex, that place videos and stills on top of your movies.

Basic Picture-in-Picture

Picture Grids

Hide and Seek

Adding That iMovie Touch

Basic Picture-in-Picture

Placing one video on top of another lies out of the bounds of iMovie, with its single-track video, but falls well within QuickTime Pro's capabilities. This layering feature allows you to combine videos into a single presentation, each playing simultaneously.

In this section, you'll discover how to add stills and video clips onto your imovies. You'll also learn the secrets to single, multiple, and even non-rectangular overlays. After working through these projects, you'll be confident using QuickTime Pro to layer your movie with multiple video tracks.

Note: Pay special attention to clip timing when adding video overlays. A clip that lasts too long will finish after the other footage runs out. Too short, and it disappears before anyone can take notice. Plan this timing in detail and make note of when the overlay clip should start, when it should finish, and whether you need to stretch, trim, or otherwise alter its timing in any way.

Single Overlay

A video clip superimposed over a simple video background can create a more exciting presentation. In these steps, you'll use QuickTime's Add function to build basic overlays.

1. Open your base video in QuickTime Pro. Move the playhead to the location where the overlay will start. As the background movie lasts 9 seconds in this example and the overlay lasts 7, move the playhead to the 1-second mark. This leaves a gap of 1 second on either side.

2. Open the overlay video in QuickTime Pro. Select all (⌘-A), copy (⌘-C), and close the video (⌘-W). This sequence of commands copies all the tracks from your overlay video (including audio, if it exists) to the system Clipboard. For this example, this assumes you copy a single video track from your overlay.

3. Return to the base video and select Edit ▷ Add (Option-⌘-V). QuickTime adds the overlay as an additional track to your video at the location of the playhead, without distorting or scaling the video in any way.

4. Move the playhead backward into the gray zone where the two videos overlap in playback. Bring up the Movie Properties window (⌘-J).

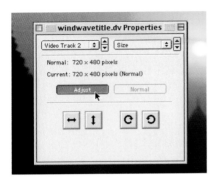

5. Select Video Track 2 from the left pull-down menu and Size from the right. Then click the Adjust button.

6. Use the red resizing handles to shrink your overlay down to about a third or so of its original size. That's 240x180 pixels for this NTSC example. Examine the Normal and Current values in the Movie Properties window to help resize more precisely. (To revert your overlay back to its full, default size, click the Normal button.)

7. Move your overlay into position. Drag from within the middle of the overlay, avoiding the central circle. Here, place the overlay in a central, but slightly raised, position. Click Done (on the Size palette in the Movie Properties window) to finish.

8. Play your movie and make sure that it works as expected—the overlay appearing at the proper point, and disappearing when you think it should. To create a final, merged video, export your work to a new QuickTime movie. (Only export to a DV stream when you're ready to return to iMovie.)

QuickTime Pro Overlays

All QuickTime Pro overlays work more or less the same way: You layer new tracks on top of your existing footage. Layered tracks allow multiple clips to play back at the same time, offering a wealth of presentation possibilities.

Taxing QuickTime Pro

Do not be surprised if QuickTime stutters somewhat during playback. Playing multiple video tracks at once can overtax your computer, particularly older and less powerful CPUs. Add more video tracks, and the problem just gets worse—hesitations all over the place. Fortunately, there's an easy solution. The stuttering problem disappears when you export your work to a merged video. The new video, with a single audio and video track, can play back at full speed without placing extra demands on your computer. This holds true whether you're exporting to a DV stream (intending to return to iMovie) or exporting to a new QuickTime movie.

3overlays.mov

Planned Entrances

When overlaying multiple items, make sure to plan their start points. Sometimes you'll want to start everything at once, where each video clip begins at the same time as the others. This creates a unified presentation and gives equal weight to each piece.

At other times, you may want to stagger entrances as seen in the example here. Staggered entrances allow relative importance to move between each item, changing their prominence as the video progresses and providing a starker contrast with the continuous background clip.

The Gray Background

On occasion, you will run across a track that lasts longer than the others in your movie. When this happens, you may discover a gray background behind your video clip. By default, QuickTime Pro fills any non-video regions of your movie with a solid gray color.

Multiple Overlay

In these steps, you'll use staggered timing, introducing one overlay clip at a time to your video.

1. Begin with the video created in the preceding project, with one overlay in place. Move the playhead into place to begin the second overlay.

2. Open the video for the second overlay. Select all (⌘-A), copy (⌘-C), and close the video (⌘-W)

3. Return to the main video and use Edit ▷ Add (Option-⌘-V) to add the second overlay as the third video track.

4. Move the playhead backward into the middle of the gray bar to see your overlay in context. Open the Movie Properties window (⌘-J), choose Video Track 3 (the track you just added) from the left pull-down menu, and choose Size from the right. Click the Adjust button to reveal the red resizing handles.

5. Resize your second overlay and move it into place. Here, I deliberately overlap the two clips to provide a visual connection between them. Click Done to conclude this step.

6. Play the movie to test your work and make any needed adjustments with the Size palette. When satisfied, move the playhead into position to add the third and final overlay.

7. Open the third overlay video, select all (⌘-A), copy (⌘-C) and close it (⌘-W).

8. Return to the main video and use Edit ▷ Add (Option-⌘-V) to add this third and final overlay. This becomes the fourth video track of your movie. Again, move the playhead back into the gray bar and open the Movie Properties window (⌘-J).

9. Select Video Track 4 and Size from the pull-down menus. Here's a little trick to perfectly align the final two overlays. Click Adjust, resize your third overlay as before, and move it directly over the second. Holding the Shift key, drag the overlay left or right. Shift-drag constrains movement to either horizontal or vertical.

10. Click Done after moving your overlay in place. Your movie is ready for export. You may want to add further titles or other effects back in iMovie.

Don't Stop with Ovals

Overlay shapes may vary as widely as your imagination. You can use wild and exciting shapes. They can have holes in them. They don't have to be continuous. You can even use a stencil look where parts don't connect. Here are some important points:

- For simple masks, don't use any colors other than white and black. (You can use gray, for partial masking, but that lies outside this topic.)

- Anything drawn in white gets masked. QuickTime Pro crops away masked areas, reducing the size of your image.

- Use black to define the areas you *will* be able to see.

- QuickTime will save your entire masked video until you export to a new file. You can restore the overlay to its original size and shape by clicking the Clear button in the Mask palette.

Oval Overlay

Use a QuickTime mask to create more exciting overlays. Masks allow you to specify which portions of your movie remain visible and which are hidden (that is, "masked"). Here you'll mask a video to create an oval overlay.

 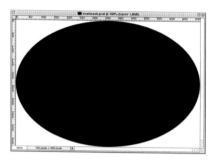

1. Open your base video in QuickTime Pro. Move the playhead to the location where the overlay will start.

2. In your image-processing program, create a new 720x480 pixel image for NTSC (720x576 for PAL). Draw a black oval on a white background. This black oval defines the ultimate shape of your overlay. QuickTime Pro crops away the white areas and retains any video that falls within the oval. Save this file and exit the program.

3. In QuickTime Pro, open your overlay video. Here, I reuse the one from the previous project to provide a better basis for comparison.

4. Open the Movie Properties window (⌘-J); select Video Track from the left pull-down menu and Mask from the right. Click the Set button. This opens a file dialog window that allows you to choose your mask.

5. Navigate to your mask and click Open. QuickTime Pro loads the mask and resizes your video accordingly. The program crops away content from the white areas of your mask, leaving behind an oval-shaped video.

6. Close the Movie Properties window. Select the entire video (⌘-A), copy (⌘-C), and close the video (⌘-W). You've now copied your masked video to memory.

7. Return to the base video. Add the masked video as an overlay by choosing Edit ▷ Add (Option-⌘-V).

8. Move the playhead backward into the gray area until you see both tracks at once. Press ⌘-J to bring up the Movie Properties window, and select Video Track 2 from the left pull-down menu and Size from the right.

9. Click Adjust and use the red handles to resize the image. Move the resized image into place and click Done.

10. (Optional) You can, if desired, change the mask—in place! Open the Movie Properties window (⌘-J); select Video Track 2 and Mask. Then click Set to set a different mask. Your overlay automatically updates to reflect this new mask, while retaining the same position and proportional size as previously set.

 OvalMovie.mov, OvalMask.psd, OvalMask-PAL.psd

Adding Scaled with Moving Video

You may not like the results when you use Add Scaled to add a moving video to your project. Unlike the Add operation, scaling will stretch or squash your results. This can make action in your video look unnaturally fast or slow, depending on the scaling involved. Add Scaled will scale any video, whether synthetic or natural, a single frame or many minutes, to the duration of the current selection.

Audio tracks will almost certainly scale oddly. The sound will appear low and slow (if stretched) or unnaturally high and squeaky (if shrunk). Unlike Adding, Adding Scaled will not preserve the intrinsic sound characteristics of the original audio.

Some people want the expanded or contracted effects that scaling produces. Using a scaled overlay may prove to be exactly what you're looking for, but then again, it may not. Make sure to always play back your movies to determine precisely how the scaling affected the overlay and if it works as you hoped.

Still-Picture Overlay

When adding a still to your movie, you must scale it to fit some duration; otherwise it will appear for only one frame. Here, you'll use Add Scaled instead of Add to place your still over all selected frames.

1. Open your base movie in QuickTime Pro. Use the crop markers to select the frames that will receive the overlay. In this case, we select those frames showing the forward-facing weather reporter.

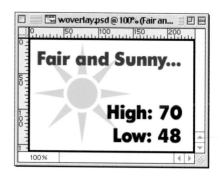

2. Design your overlay in Photoshop Elements. Here, I create a simple forecast illustration of 240x180 pixels. You can make your overlay any size, although it helps to keep it smaller than a standard QuickTime frame.

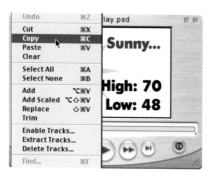

3. Open this illustration in QuickTime Pro. Select all (⌘-A), copy (⌘-C), and close the overlay (⌘-W). You have now copied the illustration to memory in a way that QuickTime Pro can use.

4. Return to the base movie. Select Edit ▷ Add Scaled (Option-Shift-⌘-V). This overlays each selected frame with your copied picture.

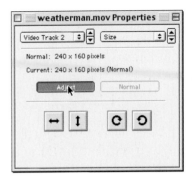

5. Move the playhead back into the gray selected area to see the overlay in context. When the playhead enters the gray area, the overlay should appear.

6. Open the Movie Properties window (⌘-J); select Video Track 2 from the left pull-down menu and Size from the right. This reveals the Size palette that allows you to resize and move your image.

7. Click the Adjust button on the Size palette. QuickTime Pro places red resizing handles on your overlay.

8. Move the overlay into place. If desired, make any size adjustments—although it's not recommended to increase the size much, or the image will distort and pixelate. When you're satisfied with the overall placement, click Done.

9. Play back your movie and make sure it works as expected. Pay special attention to when the overlay appears and disappears.

10. Export your movie (⌘-E, File ▷ Export) to create a video that merges the overlay directly into the video track. If you intend to continue working in QuickTime Pro, make sure to export to a fresh QuickTime movie. Otherwise, export to a DV stream when you're ready to return to iMovie.

Weather.mov, woverlay.psd

Picture Grids

Picture grids offer a creative and sometimes novel way to assemble multiple clips within a single movie. These presentations work because of the underlying regularity of layout. They provide this regularity by combining similar elements. These elements—similar in terms of size and/or shape, but sometimes also content—provide a well-structured context, allowing diversity of the visual story without jarring the viewer.

In this section, you'll see how to design your grids and bring them to life within QuickTime Pro. Here, we'll cover variations including a basic *n*-by-*n* setup (bringing back memories of "The Brady Bunch" TV show) and a fancier freestyle version.

Note: EyeWire's Triangle Images (www.eyewire.com/products/motion/triangle/) offers a wide range of business and lifestyle stock footage. The clips used here are from their Business Portraits, Volume 2. Triangle sells both individual clips (at lower sizes and resolution) and CDs with full NTSC 720x486 DV footage.

Basic Grid

Whatever grid you use—two-by-two, three-by-three, or four-by-four—the method remains the same. In these steps, you'll add each video as a new track, resize and reposition, and then export. Here you'll create a two-by-two presentation.

1. Select four videos that work well together and open them in QuickTime Pro.

2. Because you'll add each extra track to the first video, bring the second video to the fore. Select the entire track of the second video (⌘-A), copy (⌘-C), and close it (⌘-W). This copies the entire track to memory.

3. Return to the first video, move the playhead to the start (use Option-Left arrow to skip back quickly), and choose Edit ▷ Add (Option-⌘-V). This adds the material from the second video as a new track.

4. Repeat the previous two steps with the third and then the fourth video. After doing so, your first video will contain four tracks in total. Bring up your Movie Properties window (⌘-J).

5. Select Video Track 4 from the left pull-down menu and Size from the right. Click Adjust and resize your first track into place. When working with four videos, use Option-drag to snap the videos exactly to ¼-size. Click Done when finished.

6. Select Video Track 3 and do the same: click Adjust, resize the track into place, and click Done.

7. Repeat for the remaining two tracks.

8. Each track may last for slightly different times. If so, these next few steps will help you trim them. Move the playhead carefully along the scrubber bar until you locate the first frame where one track "disappears." Use the arrow keys to move frame by frame to pick this location exactly.

9. Holding down the Shift key, drag your mouse to the last frame of your video. Do not be surprised if one or more of the remaining tracks disappears by the last frame.

10. Select Edit ▷ Clear to remove these extra frames. This trims your movie to the length of the shortest track—all four tracks should reappear after the cut. Export your work to disk: To continue working in QuickTime Pro, export to a QuickTime movie. Otherwise, export to DV stream when you're ready to return to iMovie.

Gridwork.mov

Do the Design Work

Keep proportion in mind when designing a grid layout. Try not to alter the ratio between height and width (3:2 NTSC, 5:4 PAL), unless you're specifically looking for distorted presentation. Retaining the relationship between these two measurements ensures that your scaled video appears properly proportioned in the final result.

Use your built-in calculator (you'll find it on the Apple menu) to determine the exact scale you need. For example, if you're designing a one-fifth-scale insert, divide your original frame height and width by five. Then use your image editor's "fixed size" selections to duplicate these measurements within your layout. A careful attention to detail provides the best layout results.

Note: Make sure to pick clips of a sufficient length. You will, of necessity, trim your videos down to the size of the shortest clip. For these effects to work, you'll need at least several seconds of footage to allow viewers sufficient time to properly view any visual detail.

Designer Grids

Designing grids grows harder as your layout becomes more complex. In these steps, you'll use an image editor to create a layout reference to guide your video placement in QuickTime Pro.

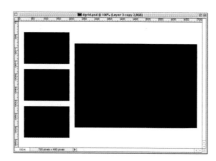

1. Design a reference layout in Photoshop Elements and save it to disk. Here, you'll use a layout with a single main subject to the right and three identical smaller subjects to the left. Keep your layout simple. Let white space work for you rather than against you.

2. Open your first video in QuickTime Pro. Select all (⌘-A), copy (⌘-C), and close the video (⌘-W). This copies the entire track to memory.

3. Open your second video. With the playhead in the far-left position, select Edit ▷ Add (Option-⌘-V). Repeat this twice more—making sure to reset the playhead each time—to add a total of three copies of the first video. You'll place these three copies onto the three small rectangles on the left of our layout reference.

4. Open your layout image in QuickTime Pro. Select all (⌘-A), copy (⌘-C), and close it (⌘-W). This copies the image in a format that QuickTime pro can use.

5. Return to the open video. Select all (⌘-A) and choose Edit ▷ Add Scaled (Option-Shift-⌘-V). QuickTime Pro adds the reference grid to the entire video. If you don't see the grid, make sure you chose Add Scaled (not Add). If you still do not see it, move the playhead to the left to update the display.

6. Bring up the Movie Properties window (⌘-J). Select Video Track 1 from the left pull-down menu and Layer from the right. Click the small down-arrow until Video Track 1 reappears in front. (☞ Read more about ordering layers in the Chapter 1 project "Know Your Tracks.")

7. Select Size from the right pull-down menu and click Adjust. Resize and move this track until it fits perfectly in place on the large, right rectangle. Then click Done.

8. Select Video Track 2 from the left pull-down menu and Layer from the right. Click the small down-arrow until Video Track 2 appears in front.

9. Select Size from the right pull-down menu, click Adjust, and fit the track in place on one of the small, left rectangles. Repeat to resize and position the remaining two tracks. Don't forget to click Done after finishing each resize and move.

10. If needed, trim any extra frames from the end of the movie, as per the previous project. Export your work to disk.

Skiset.mov, refgrid.psd, refgrid-PAL.psd

Hide and Seek

Overlays provide the perfect opportunity to hide a bit of unwanted detail from your picture. This method works by placing a masking element—one that "masks," that is, hides—over a portion of your video. The overlay hides the detail and blends in with the rest of your image background.

To make this effect work, you select a part of your image that does not ever change—nothing must move over it, not even shadows. The overlay simply stays there, blocking view of your unwanted element. In this project, you'll see how to make a proper selection and manipulate it to create an effective patch.

Note: Creating the overlay can prove to be an art. Your experience with and expertise at digital image manipulation provides the key. The more comfortable you are using cloning stamps, the better your cover-up will be.

Note: When you feel that the cure is worse than the disease, do not hesitate to skip the patch— you may be better off without.

The Cover-Up

In these steps, you'll hide a mistake by covering a portion of your video with a simple overlay.

1. Open your flawed video in QuickTime Pro. Export a typical still to a bitmap (BMP). You'll need this still to create your overlay.

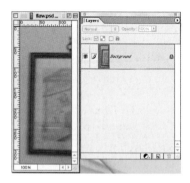

2. Open the still in Photoshop Elements. Crop away (Edit ▷ Crop) all but the flawed area and a bit of surrounding material.

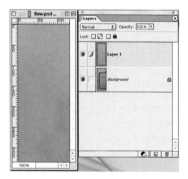

3. Use your favorite technique to clone and smudge away the detail to create a fake "wall." Here, I use the clone tool to select areas of the wall and copy them to cover the picture. Save this file to disk in any standard format.

4. Open the image in QuickTime Pro. Select all (⌘-A), copy it (⌘-C), and close the file. The Clipboard now contains a version of your image that QuickTime Pro can use with your main video.

5. Return to the flawed video, select all (⌘-A), and add the patch over the entire file with Edit ➢ Add Scaled (Option-Shift-⌘-V).

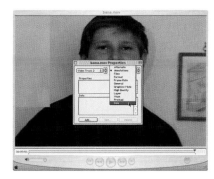

6. Open the Movie Properties window (⌘-J). Select Video Track 2 from the left pull-down menu and Size from the right. This selects the Size palette that allows you to resize and move your overlay.

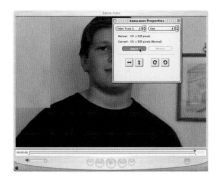

7. Click Adjust to reveal the red moving and resizing handles around the patch.

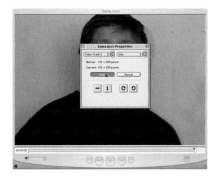

8. Carefully move your patch over the flaw—you shouldn't have to resize. Click Done to finish. Use File ➢ Export (⌘-E) to merge the patch with your original video.

Weigh the Merits

Take time to evaluate your results. Does the patch stand out too much from the original video? Does it completely hide your flaw? Have you covered all the shadows and other secondary features of your flaw? Making a good patch depends more on artistic skill rather technical know-how.

If you remain unsure, try several patches. One might work better than the others. And try different techniques. Consider blending gradients to match the natural background colors. Or copy a piece of wall from another part of the picture, adjusting the brightness to match. You may also want to use feathering to better hide your edges.

Note: Advanced users working with more dynamic footage may want to use several masks, changing them as needed for various portions of your video. While, in theory, you could make a separate mask for each frame of your video, practical experience shows that you can get away with far less work for most cover-up projects.

CoverUp.mov

Adding That iMovie Touch

Bring your iMovies back home after resizing and merging them in QuickTime Pro. iMovie offers elegant ways to join your clips together and turn them into works of art. Although QuickTime Pro offers many of the same features, it lacks iMovie's friendly interface and ease of use that makes assembling your movies such a pleasure.

In this section, you'll find a couple of examples intended to whet your appetite and demonstrate with broad strokes some techniques you can expand upon. Work through these projects to create your own virtual photo album and portrait gallery.

Note: You can purchase the GeeThree Slick Transitions and Effects used in this book from the GeeThree website: **http://geethree.com/p_slickboth.html**. The Page Peel transition is part of Volume 1.

The Family Photo Album

"Page turns" help create a virtual photo album with moving pictures. In these steps, you'll use the GeeThree Slick effects' Page Peel transition to produce an album with pages designed in Photoshop Elements.

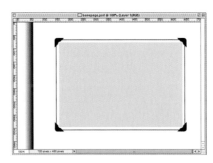

1. Design your basic page layout in Photoshop Elements. Although you can design a variety of pages for different layout styles, here you'll just use the one.

2. Follow the directions from "Designer Grids" to add your first movie on top of your layout in QuickTime Pro. Keep in mind that you're using only one copy of your video. Add the layout, move it behind your video, and then resize your video into place. Pay special attention to both sizing and placement.

3. Export your work to a DV file, suitable for import to iMovie. Repeat these steps for each video page of your "album."

4. Import your "page" files into iMovie and drag them, in order, onto the Clip Viewer.

5. Open the Transitions palette. Select Page Peel and choose the left arrow from the direction control. (If you do not own a copy of Slick Transitions and Effects, I recommend you use a left Push transition instead.)

6. Thoughtfully set the duration of your transition and drag it in place between each pair of "pages." I like a nice slow turn, about a second and a half. Experiment with a single transition until you're happy. Depending on the number of clips, rendering all the transitions at once will take a significant amount of time.

Lowdown on Page Peel

Your Page Peel transition may not work exactly as you expect. With Slick Transitions and Effects, the page does not turn to one side or the other. Instead, it moves diagonally until it leaves completely.

Hopefully, someone will develop a more album-like transition in the future, but for now the Slick Page Peel does a fine job without distracting too much from the photo album metaphor.

Note: Late-breaking news! As this book was about to go to press, GeeThree announced a new collection of transitions and effects including a true page-turn transition. Nicely, this new transition turns the page around an entire side that you select.

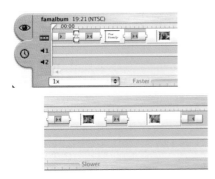

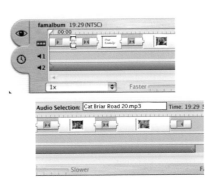

7. Add a fade-in and fade-out transition to the beginning and end of your movie, to enter and depart more gently.

8. Your album contains material from a variety of video sources. Adding a sound track brings your production together and offers a unifying theme. Use iMovie's Audio palette to import music from your favorite CD or select File ▷ Import to open an AIFF or MP3 sound file.

photoalbum.mov, pages.sea, pages-PAL.sea

Plan the Tour

Plan in advance how your "pictures" hang on your virtual wall and how your viewer should traverse that wall.

- Make sure that the "walk" feels natural, and ensure that more than one picture does not occupy the same virtual "space" on the wall.

- Test your movie before saving. I often make mistakes with the counterintuitive "pushes" with unexpected results.

- Don't plan a wall that's too "high." Even though there's no real wall, people often adjust their neck muscles as they watch. As the video goes up, so do most people's heads. Too high and a simple video can put an unconscious strain on neck muscles.

Note:

Ulead (**rfm.ulead.com**) provided the animated video clips used in this example. Their CG series offers computer graphic stock footage on various topics. To use these, open the movies in QuickTime and export them to DV streams. Other royalty free video titles include outdoor shots, nature images, and a variety of seasonal and themed sets. Stop by the Ulead site for a more complete list of their latest offerings.

Virtual Art Gallery

In these steps, you'll combine your overlay technique and iMovie's Push transitions to create a virtual art gallery walk-through.

1. Design your frames using two layers. First, create a black-and-white template for your video. Then add a picture frame on top in a new layer. To work properly, you must design these elements together. Use a full RGB image to design both mask and frame, then save each layer to a separate file.

2. In QuickTime Pro, open your frame art, select all (⌘-A), copy (⌘-C), and close the window (⌘-W). QuickTime copies your art to the Clipboard as a video track.

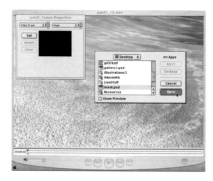

3. Open a movie in QuickTime Pro. Bring up the Movie Properties window (⌘-J) and select Video Track from the left pull-down menu and Mask from the right.

4. Click the Set button, navigate to your mask, and click Open. QuickTime Pro opens your mask and shrinks your video to match the black portion.

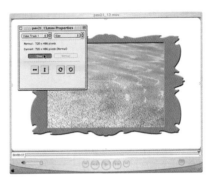

5. Select your entire movie (⌘-A) —the one you just added the mask to. Scale the picture frame (it's on the Clipboard) over the entire track (Edit ▷ Add Scaled, Option-Shift-⌘-V). Your display window returns to full size, matching the size of your picture frame image. This does not affect the size of your masked video track.

6. Bring back the Movie Properties window (⌘-J) and select Video Track 1 from the left pull-down menu and Layer from the right. Click the small down-arrow until your video appears in front of the picture frame.

7. Because you designed your frame at the same time as your mask, your overlay will appear exactly where it should, on top of the picture frame. If you want to make any small size or placement adjustments, select Size from the right pull-down menu. Click Adjust and make any needed changes. Click Done to finish.

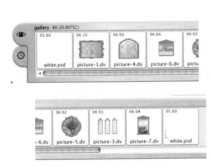

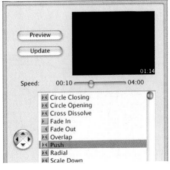

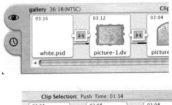

8. Export your work to a DV stream, then repeat these steps to create the remaining pictures in your art gallery. Import them into iMovie and lay out the clips on your Clip Viewer.

9. Select Push from the Transitions palette. Set the time to a leisurely transition—at least a second and a half. Deciding the directions to push can be difficult. Here, I imagine a person walking left to right, their eyes traveling up and down. To create a right movement, Push left; for looking up, Push down; and looking down, Push right.

10. After designing your transitions, drag each to the Clip Viewer. Expect to wait a good long time as they render.

4 Transparency

Add Blending and Holes to Your Videos

QuickTime Pro offers ways to see through parts of your video to reveal underlying layers. Transparency and translucency create more complex and interesting presentations. This chapter presents the merges, blends, overlays, and holes offered by QuickTime Pro. You'll experiment with different techniques and learn which contexts support which transparency choice.

The Grand Tour

Overlays and Basic Transparency

Focus Attention

Merging with Transparency

The Grand Tour

QuickTime Pro offers so many transparency methods, it quickly becomes confusing. To fight this confusion, take this short tour of QuickTime Pro's various graphic modes. In this section, you'll explore the way many of these graphics modes operate. The hands-on nature of this tutorial allows you to discover exactly what each feature does. After working your way through these options, you'll gain a better understanding of how these modes transform overlays and the video beneath them by seeing them in action. While not exhaustive, the examples shown here highlight the most common and most useful of the graphics modes available for your use. Use this tour as a stepping stone—after working through these steps, go back and experiment and push the boundaries. The best way to learn the nature of QuickTime transparency is to try things yourself.

Take the Tour

In these steps, you will use the demonstration overlay (included on the CD that accompanies this book) to explore overlay and transparency features.

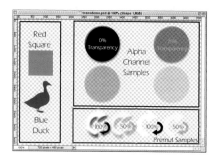

1. Using Photoshop Elements, I created this sample overlay using a variety of transparency and color settings. Notice how the checked background bleeds through at places and some elements are more visible than others.

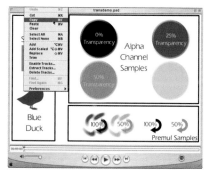

2. Open TransDemo.psd in QuickTime Pro. (PAL readers, use TransDemo-PAL.psd instead.) Select all (⌘-A), copy (⌘-C), and close the overlay (⌘-W).

3. Choose a movie and open in QuickTime Pro. Nearly any movie will do for this tour. Select the entire movie (⌘-A) and add the overlay to each frame of that movie (Edit ▷ Add Scaled, Option-Shift-⌘-V).

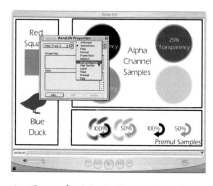

4. Open the Movie Properties window (⌘-J). Select Video Track 2 from the left pull-down menu and Graphics Mode from the right.

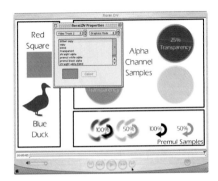

5. Notice how your overlay (Video Track 2) defaults to Dither Copy. In this mode, QuickTime Pro presents a complete overlay without any transparency. It copies the contents of each pixel to the display, using dithering (color approximation) when a monitor cannot display enough colors.

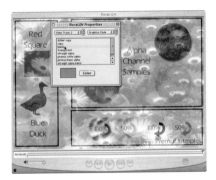

6. Select Blend from the list of options. With Blend, QuickTime Pro combines the overlay with the underlying video, blending them together (as the name implies). This creates a kind of translucency, but no real transparency—at least as shown here with the initial settings.

continues on next page

TransDemo.psd, TransDemo-PAL.psd

Know Your Modes

Here is a quick run-down of the modes covered in this tour. The other modes offered by QuickTime Pro are rarely used and left as an exercise for the reader.

Dither Copy Draws a layer without transparency. Use this graphics mode (it's the default) for all non-transparent situations. It is more robust than its little brothers, Copy and Composition, both of which may not work as well on displays with limited color.

Blend Creates a blended presentation where you can partially see through the top layer to the layer beneath. Choose a "color" to balance the degree of translucency: the darker the color, the more translucent your layer. Choose black and your layer turns completely transparent. Choose white to make your layer opaque.

Transparent When you choose a color, changes all pixels of that color to complete transparency, revealing any layers beneath.

Straight Alpha Although they can be part of video or image files, alpha channels don't store information about color and light levels. Instead, they store transparency information. Some programs (like Photoshop Elements and MakeEffectMovie) save these alpha channels along with the rest of your data. Straight Alpha uses alpha channel levels to determine the opaqueness or transparency of each pixel.

Premul White Alpha Works like Straight Alpha, but removes the white component previously combined ("mul"tiplied) into your overlay.

Premul Black Alpha Works like Straight Alpha, but removes the black component previously combined into your overlay.

Straight Alpha Blend Combines Straight Alpha with Blend.

Planning in Photoshop Elements

To create the effects you see in the sample overlay, I relied on two techniques. First, I created an image with a transparent background; and second, I used layer opacity. These techniques combine to provide QuickTime Pro with the transparency information it needs.

When starting my new image, I chose Transparent from the Contents option in the New File dialog. Select this mode to instruct Photoshop Elements to create an image with a transparent, rather than a solid-color, background. By default, Photoshop Elements uses a checked grid pattern to show this transparent background.

Create each shape in a separate layer. This allows you to assign transparencies to each object without affecting any other element. You will find the Opacity slider on the Layers palette. Adjust this slider to set the relative translucency of that element. When you save to a .psd file, Photoshop Elements stores the layer opacity information in an alpha channel. QuickTime Pro reads this data and uses it when you set your graphics mode.

Take the Tour continued

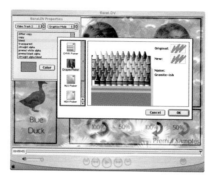

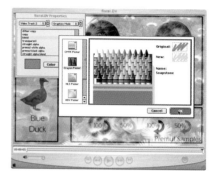

7. Click the Color button below the list of graphic modes. QuickTime Pro opens the color picker. Choose the Crayon Picker tool from the list at the left of the dialog.

8. Select a lighter shade of gray than the Original color shown at the upper right. To do so, just choose a crayon and click OK.

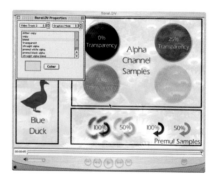

9. QuickTime Pro uses the color you select to adjust the overlay transparency. By selecting a lighter color, you instruct QuickTime Pro to increase the opacity associated with this blended layer. The graphical layer now appears more prominently.

10. Click the Color button again. Now choose a dark color from the Crayon Picker. (I use the Crayon Picker here in order to select a color with a single click. You may set your color with any of the pickers offered by your system.)

11. This time, QuickTime Pro increases the transparency to the point where you can barely see the overlay over the background. Use this method to regulate your blends to the degree needed. Choosing black hides your overlay completely; white shows it fully opaque.

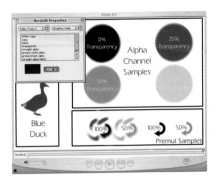

12. Select Transparent from the list of graphic modes on the palette. This mode chooses a color that will become transparent. Many people refer to this mode as "chroma key." Click the Color button.

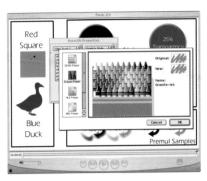

13. QuickTime Pro displays the color picker. Press and hold the Option key to select the eyedropper tool. This tool allows you to select a color from any open QuickTime Pro window.

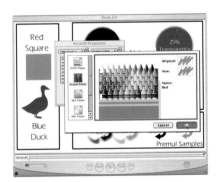

14. Move the eyedropper to the red square and click the mouse. The color picker samples this red and loads it as the New color. Click OK to finish, selecting red for the transparency tool.

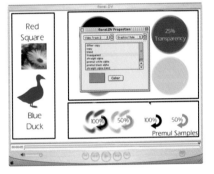

15. When you set your transparent color, QuickTime Pro looks for any pixel displaying that color. It hides these pixels from the overlay, allowing the video underneath to show through. Here, the red square disappears, revealing the flowers below.

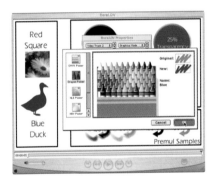

16. Color, not shape, matters. Click the Color button again. This time, use the eyedropper (Option-click) to select a pixel from the blue duck. Click OK.

continues on next page

Picking Colors

Sometimes the color you think you picked might not be the color you end up with. Colors change for all sorts of reasons. Layer transparency offers just one explanation for why a color appears differently in Photoshop Elements and in QuickTime Pro. To get around this problem, use the eyedropper tool to select transparency colors directly from your overlay.

When using the system color picker, press the Option key to transform the cursor into the eyedropper tool. Select your colors from any open QuickTime window. Move the eyedropper cursor over the color you wish and click. The color picker samples that color, determines its representation, and reflects that in the chosen picker tool. The descriptions offered by the crayon color picker may amuse you. I particularly like the name Warm Shale-ish to describe a dark reddish-gray color.

Take the Tour *continued*

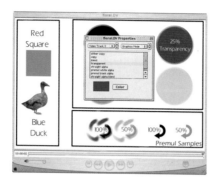

17. Here, QuickTime Pro turns all the blue pixels transparent, again revealing the video track lying under the overlay.

18. Choose Straight Alpha from the graphics modes. QuickTime Pro uses the alpha channel from your graphic file to determine how to display each shape. The circle at 0% transparency (or 100% opacity) appears as expected; the background, created transparent, disappears. Elements at other opacity levels reveal a little, some, or a lot of the video.

19. Take notice of the white cast that affects the transparent elements. Here, a black circle offers a distinct grayish tone. Other elements may show whitish features as well.

20. Select Premul White Alpha. QuickTime may premultiply an overlay's color components with a white pixel. This setting removes the white from the pixel before blending it with the background at its transparency level. You can see this effect most clearly in the Premul Samples on the bottom-right of the overlay.

21. Premul Black Alpha works the same way as Premul White Alpha, removing black color components from the overlay pixels. When applied, however, to an image that has used white premultiplication, you may end up with odd—and not very attractive—results.

22. Select Straight Alpha Blend as your graphics mode. Because the blue color remains from Step 17, the overlay appears quite lightly. Click Color.

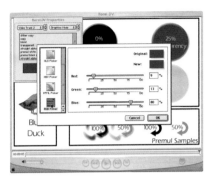

23. Choose the RGB color picker.

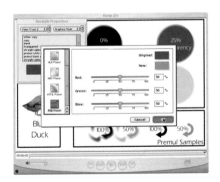

24. Set the red, green, and blue values to 50%, a medium gray color. You may find it easier to type the values than move the sliders. Click in the Red percentage box; enter **50**. Tab and repeat for the Green and Blue percentage boxes. Click OK.

25. QuickTime Pro applies the alpha values, as per Step 18, and then blends your image in a strict fifty-fifty fashion with the underlying video.

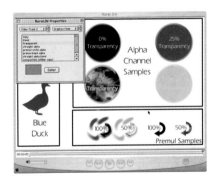

26. Before concluding this tour, recall that you set the current color to a 50% gray in Step 24. Choose Transparent from the list of graphics modes. As expected, the 50% circle disappears, replaced with the flowers from the video underneath.

Overlays and Basic Transparency

I cannot tell you the number of times people have asked how to add a small overlay, or "bug," in the corner of their iMovie. "I just want to add a logo," they say. "Can't I do that in iMovie?"

Fortunately, QuickTime Pro easily handles this task. For thirty bucks, more people have gone away happy with this one feature than any other. But QuickTime Pro overlays do not start or end with logos. With a little creativity, you can do a lot more with overlays than you might have ever dreamed.

In this section, you'll not only learn how to create your bug, but will see how to add simple overlays that lie on top of and open up into the footage beneath.

Simplicity

Follow these steps to overlay your video with a simple picture with transparency.

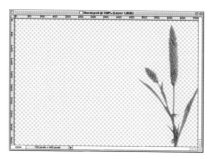

1. In Photoshop Elements, or your favorite image editor, create a new, blank image the exact size of a QuickTime frame (720x480 for NTSC or 720x576 for PAL). Use a transparent background and add a single graphic element on top. Here, place a flower, toward the right of your frame. Save to disk as a .psd file.

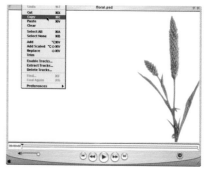

2. Open this image in QuickTime Pro by selecting File ▷ Open Movie In New Player (⌘-O). Select all (⌘-A) and copy the entire track to the Clipboard (⌘-C). Close the image (⌘-W).

3. Open a video in QuickTime Pro. Select all (⌘-A) and choose Edit ▷ Add Scaled (Option-Shift-⌘-V) to overlay each frame of the video.

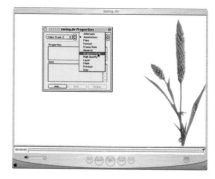

4. Type ⌘-J to open the Movie Properties window. Select Video Track 2 from the left pull-down menu and Graphics Mode from the right.

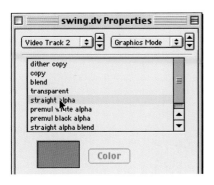

5. Choose Straight Alpha from the list on the Graphics Mode palette. When you're doing basic overlays, with images that use only full transparency and full opacity, Straight Alpha offers your best choice of modes.

6. Move the playhead along the scrubber bar to test your results. QuickTime will have added this overlay to each frame of your base video. To finish, export your work to a new movie. QuickTime Pro will create a new video, where the overlay and the base images merge into a single video track.

SwingOverlay.mov

FreePlay Music

The music used in this sample video, and in most of the other sample videos on the CD that accompanies this book, comes from FreePlay Music (**www.freeplaymusic.com**). You can find this amazing collection of music on their website, and within your Apple iTools account (in /Software/Mac OS X Software/Extras). You'll even discover additional tracks in the iTools account, not found on the FreePlay website.

FreePlay Music offers royalty-free sound tracks that you can use directly in your personal, private usage iMovies without paying a penny. (The use of FreePlay music in any other revenue-generating manner does require the user to obtain a license directly from FreePlay Music. Although not technically free for this type of use, FreePlay Music charges less than competing music libraries.)

Typically, an editor or producer of video for broadcast must choose between commissioning their own music or purchasing a library of music "pre-cleared" of up-front fees before they can submit their work to a broadcaster for public performance. But the use of FreePlay Music in any media destined for broadcast will not result in any additional costs to broadcasters over and above what they already pay the Performing Rights Organization. Instead, this music is made available free of up-front charges if the music will ultimately be broadcast. FreePlay Music has extended this use of their music to all private, noncommercial insertions in any media of any kind.

Besides their website, FreePlay Music has made certain pieces available exclusively on Apple's website. These tracks, as well as access to the complete FreePlay Music suite, are available on your personal iDisk (**www.apple.com/idisk**).

Combine Transparencies

Today's television offers a wide variety of "bugs." Just turn on any channel and watch the bottom-right corner. You're sure to see a bug down there if you look long enough (or imbibe enough alcohol). One popular type mixes translucency, transparency, and opacity. (Typically, this involves a translucent logo with a solid letter in the middle.) Achieve the same effect by combining different transparency levels in your image-editing program. Place your bug elements in separate layers and adjust the Opacity slider for each. When you save, your editor will store separate transparency values for each individual layer. QuickTime Pro understands the layer and alpha values stored in most Photoshop formats.

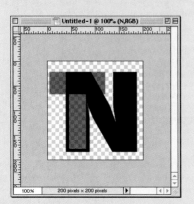

The Bug

These steps show how to use QuickTime Pro to add a small logo to the corner of your iMovie.

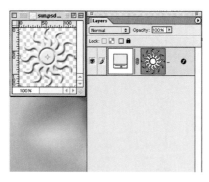

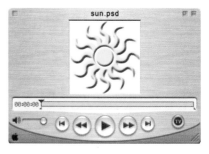

1. Create your bug (logo) in Photoshop Elements or your favorite editing program. Create a solid bug on a transparent—not white—background. A small file works well. The sample shown here uses a 128x128-pixel canvas. Save to disk using a .psd file.

2. Open your image in QuickTime, select all (⌘-A), copy (⌘-C), and close the window (⌘-W). This copies the bug track to the Clipboard in a form QuickTime Pro can reuse.

3. Open the base video to which you'll add the bug. Select all (⌘-A) and Add Scaled (Option-Shift-⌘-V) to add your bug to every frame of the video.

4. Your bug will appear in the top-left corner of your video window, in front of your base video.

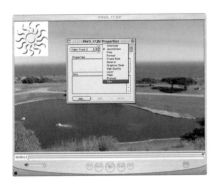

5. Press ⌘-J to open the Movie Properties window. Select Video Track 2 from the left pull-down menu and Size from the right.

6. Click the Adjust button. Red resize handles appear around your bug.

7. Drag your bug into position; drag from the middle of the logo, but avoid the center circle. Keep your logo within your TV-safe zone (☞ sidebar). Stay within the original video boundaries; don't run over the edges, or you'll inadvertently resize your video. Press ⌘-I to check the current size. Click Done to finish your move.

8. If not already there, press ⌘-J to return to the Movie Properties window. This time, select Graphics Mode from the right pull-down menu and choose Straight Alpha. The transparent background of your logo disappears.

9. Many people prefer a translucent overlay to a solid one. Press ⌘-J and select Straight Alpha Blend. The logo will now blend into the background.

10. To blend further, click the Color button. Select a darker color from the Color Picker and click OK. The darker the color, the more the overlay will blend into the background.

SunLogo.mov, sun.psd

Accessorize Your iMovie

After finishing this project, I returned to iMovie to give it a little more flair before exporting it to the movie you see on the CD. Here are a few changes to make:

Add sound effects It doesn't matter how "lion-ish" your actor sounds, a few realistic growls will "sell" your movie.

Enter and leave gracefully I can't enthuse enough about "fade-in" and "fade-out." They introduce and leave a movie without jarring the viewer.

Add the real still Use a cross-dissolve to move between the original still and your animated lips at both the start and the end. This trick creates a better continuity with the original picture and adds more verisimilitude (not that we're talking about much "reality" here, with a talking lion).

Note: Commercial televisions don't handle bright colors well. Bright reds provide a particular hazard; they tend to bleed across the TV screen. To handle this, broadcasters use "safe colors" that are sure to work on most TV sets. These colors, which use RGB levels below 240, are duller than the bright primaries that work so well on computer screens.

Your Lion Lips

With these steps, you will create an image cutout to reveal talking lips behind your favorite feline (or other animal) friend.

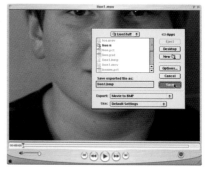

1. Film your subject talking. Make sure to use a tripod so the footage remains steady. Import from your camera into iMovie, and export to a full-quality QuickTime movie. Open this movie in QuickTime Pro.

2. Export a typical still from your movie. Choose File ▷ Export (⌘-E). Select Movie To BMP and save to a bitmap. You will use this still as a reference, to locate your subject's mouth.

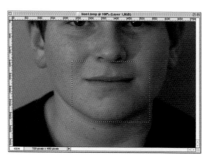

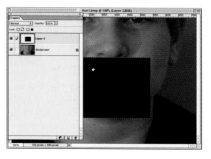

3. Open the still in Photoshop Elements (or your favorite image editor). Using the rectangle selection tool, select the area around the mouth of your subject.

4. Use the paint bucket tool to fill the selection with black.

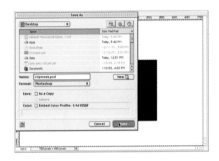

5. Choose Select ▷ Inverse to invert your selection. This selects the remaining part of your image. Fill this inverted selection with white. Save this file out to disk as a .psd file; give it a name such as clipmask.psd.

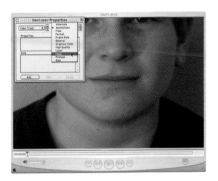

6. Return to QuickTime and your original movie. Bring up the Movie Properties window (⌘-J). Select Video Track from the left pull-down menu and Mask from the right.

7. Click Set. Navigate to the mask you created in Step 5. Click Open. QuickTime Pro opens the mask and resizes your video, clipping it to the mask.

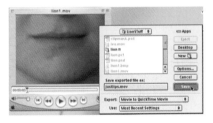

8. Export (⌘-E) your clipped movie to a new QuickTime movie file.

9. Return to your image editor. Open the still you will use as an overlay. Here, we use an image of a standing lion. Use the oval selection tool to select the area around its mouth.

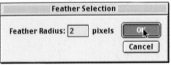

10. Choose Select ▷ Feather. Enter a small value, such as 2, and click OK. This command softens the edges of your selection, allowing it to blend better as an overlay.

continues on next page

leo.mov, lion.psd, lion-PAL.psd

Set the Mouth

Be aware of the full range of motions within your video, particularly when placing the mouth behind the oval opening. Move the playhead back and forth to scan through the entire movie.

Take note of how wide the mouth will open and which features—nose and chin—may appear without proper resizing. Don't be lulled by a single perfect still at the start or end of your movie. Imperfections may be hiding just out of view.

Test your video and make any needed adjustments before you export to disk.

Note: QuickTime Pro cannot see hidden layers in your Photoshop Elements .psd files. When you hide a layer (by clicking the small eye icon in the Layers palette), it becomes invisible to QuickTime Pro, too.

Note: Nearly every television "overscans," losing a little picture information on each side of the screen. This problem gets worse as a TV ages. To compensate for overscanning, broadcasters use "safe zones"—basically, the center 80%–90% of the image—to ensure that important image elements appear correctly, even on older TV units. This provides clear viewing of your material, no matter how poorly adjusted a TV set may be.

Your Lion Lips *continued*

11. Choose Edit ▷ Cut (⌘-X) to remove the picture material within your feathered selection. Make sure you can see through your cut to the transparent background, otherwise this effect will not work.

12. Save your image to disk as a new .psd file. (Be sure to avoid overwriting your original artwork.) Return to QuickTime Pro and open the file there.

13. Open the Movie Properties window (⌘-J). Select Video Track from the left pull-down menu and Graphics Mode from the right.

14. Choose Straight Alpha from the list. Notice how the lion's mouth turns from white to gray.

15. Close the Movie Properties window and return to your lion video. Select all ((⌘)-A), copy ((⌘)-C), and close the image ((⌘)-W). When asked, do not save. You have now copied your image and it's associated graphics mode to the Clipboard.

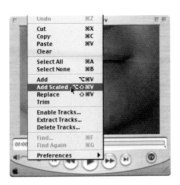

16. Open the movie you saved of your subject's lips. Select all ((⌘)-A) and paste the animal image over every frame of the video (Edit ▷ Add Scaled, Option-Shift-(⌘)-V).

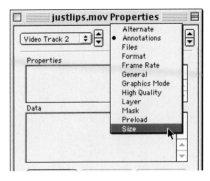

17. Open the Movie Properties window ((⌘)-J). Select Video Track 1 from the left pull-down menu and Size from the right.

18. Click Adjust. The red resizing handles will appear around the smaller video, still hidden behind the main image.

19. Drag the mouth into place. Resize it as needed to make the human mouth fit within the transparent area.

20. Play the movie to make sure everything works as desired. Make any tweaks and adjustments needed. Then export your work to combine the video—lion and lips—into a single, merged track. Make sure to export to a fresh QuickTime movie to keep working in QuickTime Pro; otherwise, export to a DV stream when you're headed for iMovie.

Cropping

Using masked videos allows you to overlay parts of your image without worrying much about size.

Unlike alpha channels and transparent colors, a masked video actually changes its dimensions when hiding cropped areas. This limits your concern about bits that might stick out from the original 720x480 (or 720x576) frame and cause unsightly resizing. (Keeping proper dimensions is vital when working with digital video.) Smaller overlays can better move around your frame without extending beyond those edges.

Note: QuickTime Pro's Info window can help when you're concerned about overlays that may extend too far. Click ⌘-I to open the information window. The Normal Size and Current Size lines will help you catch overlays that have strayed out of bounds. In addition, you'll find other useful information, including your video's format, frame rate, data rate, size, and more.

The Ghost

In these steps, you will build a mask in Photoshop Elements and use it to crop your video down to a more manageable size. After, you'll see how to use it to create a "ghostly" effect.

1. Open your "ghost" video in QuickTime Pro. Use the playhead to move back and forth through the video to find a fairly typical frame. You'll need this frame as a reference for laying out your cropping mask. Try to use an overlay video whose background, lighting, and camera conditions roughly match your base video.

2. When you have selected a typical frame, export it (⌘-E) to a bitmap (BMP).

3. Open the bitmap image in your image editor. Create a new layer and, using the image beneath as a guide, select around your subject. The portion you pick will form your new image; everything outside will be cropped. Fill this selection with the color black. Click the eye icon next to your original layer to hide it.

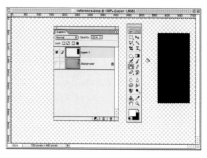

4. Invert your selection (Select ▷ Invert Selection or Shift-⌘-I) and fill the rest of the image with the color white.

5. Delete the image reference layer (drag it to the garbage can at the bottom of the Layers palette) and save the mask file to disk as a new .psd file.

6. Return to QuickTime Pro and to the video you opened there earlier. Open the Movie Properties window (⌘-J). Select Video Track from the left pull-down menu and Mask from the right.

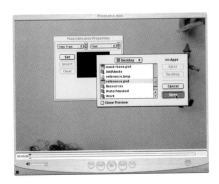

7. Click the Set button on the Mask palette. Navigate to your cropping mask file and click Open. QuickTime Pro will open your mask file and use it to crop your movie. As the movie resizes, it matches the shape you laid out in Step 3.

8. Export to a new, high-quality QuickTime movie. Then, close your original video, and open the new, smaller one. Select all (⌘-A), and copy (⌘-C).

continues on next page

That Export Thing

In many of these projects you're instructed to export your file, open the new version, copy it, and then close it. The reason is this: In most cases, adding masks or other special effects only affects one video layer. When you export, you force QuickTime Pro to collapse the file, combine all the layers and effects, and produce a single video track in the new version. Then, when you open and copy, you're copying not all the original layers, but only one, new, merged one.

Saving As...

In QuickTime Pro, when you choose File ▷ Save As, you're offered two options. You can save to a new, self-contained file or save normally with references. Each option offers benefits. The first allows you to create a fully portable movie. You can upload it, e-mail it, or whatever without having to send along a collection of supporting files. The downside is size: A self-contained movie takes up a lot more space than a reference movie. The second option allows you to produce a very small movie indeed. But you must keep all your source materials in the same folder as the reference movie. Lose one, and your movie will no longer work.

doggy.mov

The Blend

When you select Blend as your graphics mode, you create a presentation that combines the top video layer with the one beneath it. The result usually looks a bit washed out and light, as you can see in this project. This proves perfect for the ghostly, washed-out effect we're looking for here.

You can further wash out your blend by adjusting the color below the list of graphic modes. Click Color to open the color picker. Choose a darker color to further minimize your overlay and click OK.

When you return to your video, the overlay will appear lighter and even ghostlier. Avoid picking too dark a color—your "ghost" may disappear completely—or too light a color—you lose the ghostly effect.

As with many QuickTime features, you may want to experiment with several settings before deciding on your final choice.

The Ghost *continued*

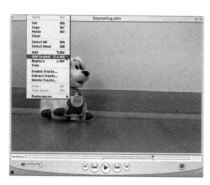

9. Open the video you intend to overlay. Use the crop markers on the Timeline to select the portion where your "ghost" will appear. You may scale the video, as I've done here (Edit ▷ Add Scaled, Option-Shift-⌘-V), or simply add at the playhead (Edit ▷ Add, Option-⌘-V) if you want to preserve the overlay's timeline.

10. Open the Movie Properties window (⌘-J). Select Video Track 2 from the left pull-down menu and Size from the right.

11. Click the Adjust button and move the overlay into position. Resize if desired. Click Done when finished.

12. Select Graphics Mode from the right pull-down menu. Select Blend from the list presented. QuickTime Pro lightens the overlay and blends it into the layer beneath, creating a ghostly effect.

13. Play back your video and determine whether it provides the effect you're looking for. Pay special attention to when your overlay appears and disappears.

14. Export your movie to disk. Make sure to export to a fresh QuickTime movie if you intend to keep working in QuickTime Pro. If you're ready to return to iMovie, select DV stream instead.

Crop Anything

You can use the method described here to crop any QuickTime movie for any purpose you may have in mind. Sometimes I find myself in receipt of slightly off-sized movies. For example, I've come across movies that are 323x241 pixels when I really wanted one that was exactly 320x240. With the Mask settings, I can easily trim my movies down to the proper size and discard the extra pixels that might line the edges.

This method avoids many problems associated with resizing and scaling your video. Individual pixels remain exactly as they were in the original. There's no need to add, average, or otherwise interpolate pixel values where you lose clarity and crispness.

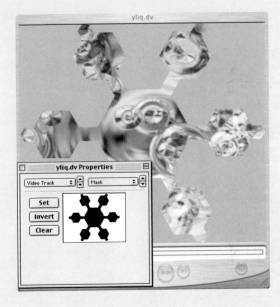

Focus Attention

QuickTime transparency offers tricks you can use to focus attention on a particular item—or hide attention from another. Whether using an arrow, an oval of light, or any other highlighting, you can force your viewer to pay attention to a particular detail within your movie. Similarly, you can use a black rectangle, an out-of-focus block, or something similar to prevent your viewer from seeing part of the frame. Either way, you can use these procedures to control the presentation of information within your video.

In this section, you'll discover the steps needed to add attention-focusing features to your movie. You'll learn how to design, overlay, and merge these items with your movies. Most importantly, you'll see examples in action that may inspire you to step beyond these projects and create your own.

The Arrow

An arrow provides the simplest and most direct way to focus user attention. Follow these steps to add a simple arrow to part of your video.

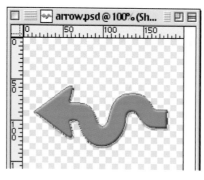

1. Design an arrow in Photoshop Elements. Place your solid arrow on a transparent background. Save your work to disk as a new .psd file and exit the program.

2. Open the movie you wish to highlight in QuickTime Pro. Decide which feature you wish to highlight. Select those frames that display this feature in roughly the same position. There's no use in pointing toward an item that has moved out of range.

3. In QuickTime Pro, open your arrow. Select all (⌘-A), copy (⌘-C), and close the arrow image (⌘-W). QuickTime copies the arrow track to the Clipboard, ready for reuse.

4. After closing the arrow image, return to your main video. With your frames already selected, choose Edit ▷ Add Scaled (Option-Shift-⌘-V).

5. Move the playhead backward into the gray selected area to reveal the arrow on top of your base footage.

6. Open the Movie Properties window (⌘-J). Select Video Track 2 from the left pull-down menu and Graphics Mode from the right.

7. Choose Premul White Alpha from the list of options offered. This graphics mode removes any blended white elements from the shiny red arrow used here.

8. Choose Size from the right pull-down menu. Click Adjust to reveal the red resizing handles around your arrow.

9. Move your arrow into place. Make sure to move the playhead within the selected area to confirm that your arrow works throughout the selection before you click Done.

10. Export your movie to combine the arrow and the underlying footage into a single video track.

arrow.psd, arrow.mov

Dark Images

When you work with dark images, the technique shown here needs a few modifications. These changes help take the low pixel light levels into account and produce better highlights.

Use yellow or white Instead of creating a transparent oval on a black background, create a yellow or white oval on a transparent background.

Adjust the blend White and yellow highlights may over-bleach your target area. Click the Color button after choosing Straight Alpha Blend and select a darker color to lower the overlay intensity.

Create a beam of light Rather than use an oval, you may want to create a triangle or trapezoid shape that mimics a ray of light shining on your subject.

Note: Although ovals work particularly well, there's no need to limit yourself to a particular shape. Use rectangles or stars if you like, or even a one-of-a-kind freeform shape.

The Ellipse of Light

A simple overlay can highlight an important feature within your video. Follow these steps to add an ellipse of light to your footage. In this sample, we answer the simple question, "Has he proposed yet?"

1. Open your video in QuickTime Pro. Select the frames to highlight, then move the playhead to the start of your selection. Select File ▷ Export (⌘-E) and save to a bitmap (BMP)—this is your first reference. Move to the end of your selection (Option-Right arrow). Again, select File ▷ Export (⌘-E) and save to a second bitmap.

2. Open your reference images in Photoshop Elements. Choose the second image window (it doesn't really matter which you choose, but we'll use the second just to clarify this procedure). Select all (⌘-A), copy (⌘-C), and close the image (⌘-W). This copies the second reference image to the Clipboard.

3. Choose the first image window and paste (⌘-V) the second image on top, forming a second layer.

4. Select Layer 1 in the Layers palette. Move the Opacity slider to 50% so you can see both pictures at once. You can now gauge exactly where to place your revealing oval.

5. Click the New Layer icon at the bottom of the Layers palette. You will use this layer to create your mask.

6. Use the oval selection tool to select your feature. Make your selection carefully, using the position of the feature in both reference images.

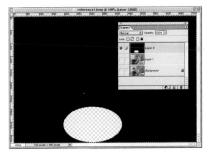

7. Choose Select ▷ Inverse. Fill the inverted selection with black using the paint bucket tool. Hide the two reference images (click the eye icon next to each layer) and save the file to disk with a new name, such as overlaymask.psd. QuickTime Pro cannot see hidden layers in .psd files.

8. Open the overlay in QuickTime Pro. Select all (⌘-A), copy (⌘-C), and close it (⌘-W). With these steps, QuickTime Pro copies the overlay track to the Clipboard. Return to your main movie and choose Edit ▷ Add Scaled (Option-Shift-⌘-V). QuickTime Pro adds the overlay to those frames you selected in Step 1.

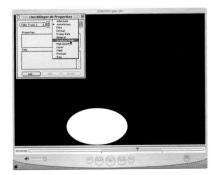

9. Move the playhead back into the gray selected area. This reveals the overlay, in context. Press ⌘-J to bring up the Movie Properties window. Choose Video Track 2 from the left pull-down menu and Graphics Mode from the right.

10. Choose Straight Alpha Blend. Your ellipse disappears entirely and the remaining black background blends into your footage. If desired, adjust the blend color (↩ "The Grand Tour" earlier in this chapter) to darken your overlay. Export your work to disk.

didhe.mov, overlaymask.psd, overlaymask-PAL.psd

Other Ways to Hide

Although I used Edge Detection as a simple expedient in this example, you may want to use any number of other techniques to obscure your subject.

Blur While the blurring filter offers the best results for this procedure, you probably need to apply the filter to your footage several times to actually hide your subject's features.

Shrink After applying your cropping mask, use the Size palette to shrink your video by half or more. Export this to disk. In Step 10, don't just move your overlay into place. Resize it at the same time, back to the original dimensions. The quality loss will obscure facial features, while you retain the colors from the original movie.

Emboss The emboss filter offers one more interesting choice for this method.

Note: Please note that the small, sample video does not show the animated lines as well as the full 720x480 DV version. In the full version, you see a moving outline of the subject's face, while details remain hidden.

Hide a Face

Follow these steps to hide a face from your footage. You can use this technique to someone's identity whether protecting your informant or dealing with a missing permission/release slip for your video.

1.   Open your video in QuickTime Pro. Choose a clip where your subject's face does not move too much. As in the previous example, export two reference clips from the start and end of your video.

2.   Load your references into Photoshop Elements, as described in the previous example, and adjust the opacity so you can see both images at once. Select the area around your subject's face, taking movement into account, but avoiding overlap with other subjects.

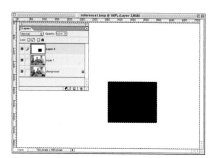

3.   Add a new layer and fill the selection with black. Invert your selection (Select ▷ Inverse) and fill with white. Save this mask to disk.

4.   Return to QuickTime Pro and your video. Open the Movie Properties window (⌘-J). Select Video Track from the left pull-down menu and Mask from the right. Click Set and choose the mask you just created. QuickTime resizes your video, reshaping it down to show your subject's face but little else.

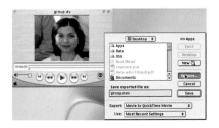

5. Choose File ▷ Export (⌘-E). Select Export To QuickTime Movie and click Options.

6. Click Filter. Choose Edge Detection from the list of filters. Click OK to return to options and click OK again to return to the file export. Enter a name, such as oneface.mov, and click Save. Wait for QuickTime Pro to create and export a new movie of your filtered subject's face.

7. Close the original movie without saving! Then open the original movie and the filtered face movie in QuickTime Pro.

8. Select the entire face-only video (⌘-A), copy it to the Clipboard (⌘-C), and close it (⌘-W).

9. Move the playhead to the start of your main video and choose Edit ▷ Add (Option-⌘-V).

10. Open the Movie Properties window (⌘-J). Select Video Track 2 and Size from the pull-downs. Click Adjust. Carefully move the overlay into position until it masks the video beneath it. Unfortunately, there's no better way to do this than just "eyeing" it, but small errors won't throw off your final video. Click Done and export your work.

FaceHide.mov

Merging with Transparency

I recently watched a TV show that showed two scenes, side-by-side on the screen. Neither portion was distorted, and each was clearly as originally filmed. It just so happened that half the action took place on the right part of the screen and half on the left.

I thought it was very cool and set out to re-create the effect on my own. It didn't take long. QuickTime transparency allows you to merge footage in all sorts of novel and innovative ways.

Here are a couple of examples of the way you can use transparency to merge several video sources together into a coherent whole.

Side-by-Side Masking

A mask with two halves helps create a side-by-side, "split screen" presentation of your footage. In these steps, you'll learn how to perform side-by-side masking in your own videos.

1. Choose two movies whose principle action takes place on opposite sides of the screen and does not cross to the other side.

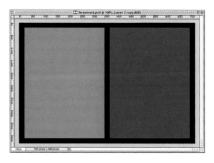

2. In Photoshop Elements, create a layout that divides the screen in two. Fill each cavity with a different solid color. Although I use a fairly simple, rectangular approach here, feel free to vary the design as desired. Save your work to disk as a .psd file.

3. Open this layout image in QuickTime Pro. Select all (⌘-A), copy (⌘-C), and close (⌘-W). Open the left-side footage, select all (⌘-A), and overlay the mask you just copied (Edit ▷ Add Scaled, Option-Shift-⌘-V).

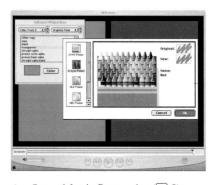

4. Open Movie Properties (⌘-J). Select Video Track 2 and Graphics Mode. Choose Transparent from the list. Click Color and, pressing the Option key, click with the eyedropper to sample the color from the left portion of your mask. QuickTime removes all instances of that color from the overlay.

5. You should now be able to see the leftmost footage through your mask. Select File ▷ Export (⌘-E). Choose Movie To QuickTime Movie and click Options. You're about to set these options to ensure that your video retains the highest quality during export, so that you'll be able to reuse it when revealing the rightmost footage.

6. Under Video, click Settings; ensure that you've chosen Best Quality and 29.97 frames per second (NTSC) or 25 fps (PAL) and click OK. Then if you see a Filter: line, click Filters, select None, and click OK, to remove the filter. Click OK to return to the Save dialog. Save your movie to a new file, such as lefthalf.mov.

7. Open the newly saved movie, select all (⌘-A), copy (⌘-C), and close it (⌘-W). Then open your source video for the right-side footage. Select all (⌘-A) and add this video (Edit ▷ Add, Option-⌘-V). (Don't use Add Scaled, as it may distort your video.)

8. Open the Movie Properties window (⌘-J). Select Video Track 2 and Graphics Mode from the pull-down menus. Choose Transparent from the list. Click Color and, while pressing the Option key, use the eyedropper to sample the color from the right portion of your mask. You should be able to see the right half of the movie as well.

9. Check that your movie works as expected. You should see one movie displayed in each half and each should play back independently of the other. At this point, don't be surprised if the movies lag a little during playback as your computer has a lot of computation to handle.

10. You can now export to either a DV stream, for iMovie, or to a QuickTime movie, as just seen, if you want to continue working on your movie in QuickTime Pro

sidebyside.mov, 2waymask.psd, 2waymask-PAL.psd

An Alternative

When you inset an overlay into your footage, you may blend two different flavors of the same movie into the same presentation. Follow these steps to add this sort of visual emphasis to your film. In this case, I add a focus of color over a black and white background.

If you like, use a mask to crop your inset to the right shape, as seen in "Cropping" earlier in this chapter. Use the image from Step 3 to trim your video down to the proper size.

There's one difficulty with this approach. You must ever-so-carefully put the overlay back in place—and if you miss, even slightly, it shows. The method detailed in the step-by-step instructions, here, avoids this fine adjustment and offers, to my mind, an easier technique.

Note: The high quality settings described in Steps 5 and 6 help whenever you need to export and reuse video, not just for this project alone.

Color Inset

In these steps, you will create a full-color video inset over a black-and-white background video.

1. This effect needs a black-and-white copy of your video to work; follow these steps to create one. Open your movie in QuickTime Pro. Select File ▷ Export (⌘-E) and choose to export to a QuickTime movie. Click the Options button on the Export dialog to invoke the Movie Settings window.

2. In the Movie Settings dialog, click the Filter button. Choose Color Tint from the list of filters, and select Black And White from the pull-down menu. This instructs QuickTime Pro to save your image without color. Click OK, and then click OK again from the settings window. Enter a file name, such as bwversion.mov, and click Save.

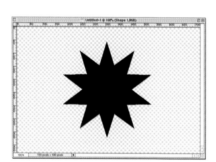

3. Create a mask in Photoshop Elements with a strong central element, like this star on a blank (unfilled) background. This mask defines where you'll place your color inset over your black-and-white video. Save the file, open it in QuickTime Pro, select it (⌘-A), copy (⌘-C), and close it (⌘-W).

4. Open your black-and-white movie, select all (⌘-A), and overlay the mask to each frame of your video (Edit ▷ Add Scaled, Option-Shift-⌘-V).

5. Open the Movie Properties window (⌘-J). Select Video Track 2 from the left pull-down menu and Graphics Mode from the right. Choose Straight Alpha. The areas around your central geometric shape will disappear, revealing your background movie.

6. To export your movie, select File ▷ Export (⌘-E). Click Options. Click Filter and select None to remove the black and white filter you just used. Click OK, and click OK again. Enter a filename, such as overlaid.mov, and save. You've now merged all the layers into a single track in the exported movie.

7. Open your newly created black-and-white overlaid movie. Select all (⌘-A), copy (⌘-C), and close (⌘-W). Open the color version of your movie, select all (⌘-A), and overlay the footage you just copied to memory (Edit ▷ Add Scaled, Option-Shift-⌘-V).

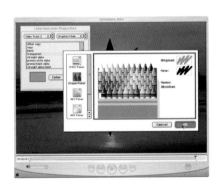

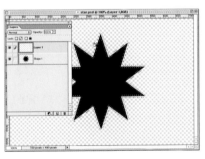

8. Bring up the Movie Properties window (⌘-J). Select Video Track 2 from the left pull-down menu and Graphics Mode from the right. Choose Transparent, click Color, and while holding the Option key, sample the center shape with the eyedropper. Click OK.

9. In Photoshop Elements, select your object, choose Select ▷ Modify ▷ Border, and enter 10. Fill the new surrounding selection with a color, in a new layer. Discard the old layer, and save to a file such as border.psd.

10. Open and copy your border in QuickTime Pro before adding it (scaled) to your movie. After applying the Straight Alpha graphics mode, it will overlay the video as shown here. You can now export this movie as desired.

 inset.mov, border.psd, star.psd, border-PAL.psd, star-PAL.psd

The Reveal

Transparency allows you to reveal parts of your movies while hiding the rest behind a matte. This technique, called masking, creates more artistic presentations of your footage, offering hints without giving away the whole.

I'm very fond of masking, particularly when I want to tie together bits and pieces of video from a variety of sources into an opening presentation or visual collage.

By using a consistent background, I take advantage of visual similarity to combine dissimilar elements into a visual whole. In this project, you learn how to create a see-through title mask that produces striking results.

Note: Be creative with your masks. Don't assume that you have to stick with a single hole in a larger presentation. Allow yourself to experiment with multiple windows, particularly with moving subjects who can travel from opening to opening as the clip plays.

Add a Title Mask

QuickTime Pro masking uses overlay with openings that allow your video to show through. In these steps, you'll create a see-through title that lets you view the footage behind it.

1. Create a new image in Photoshop Elements, using RGB color and a transparent background. Fill this image with the color that will form the background of your title overlay.

2. Choose the selection text tool. In Photoshop Elements, you'll find the selection choice on the options bar, to the right of normal text.

3. In both Photoshop and Photoshop Elements, the background changes color, usually turning red, when you create selections in masking mode. Add your title and commit it (click the check mark in the options bar) to return to normal editing mode. The title will turn into a selection.

4. When your selection appears, choose Edit ▷ Cut (⌘-X) to remove the text from your overlay, leaving behind the empty background. Save your file.

5. Open your mask in QuickTime Pro. Select all (⌘-A), copy it (⌘-C), and close the mask (⌘-W). QuickTime Pro copies the mask track to the Clipboard.

6. In QuickTime Pro, open the video you want to mask. Select all (⌘-A) and Add Scaled (Option-Shift-⌘-V) to copy the mask over each frame of your movie.

7. Open the Movie Properties window (⌘-J). Select Video Track 2 from the left pull-down menu and Graphics Mode from the right.

8. Select Straight Alpha as your Graphics Mode. The letters disappear, revealing the movie beneath.

9. Test your video by pressing Play. You should see the source video through the newly revealed mask.

10. Export your video to DV format (⌘-E). You can now import your custom title into iMovie and use it as desired.

TheWay.mov, textoverlay.psd, textoverlay-PAL.psd

Smooth Transitions

As my shortest clip in this example lasts just over three seconds long, I set the push time to about one and a half seconds, leaving a little hang time in there.

I like to keep the transitions consistent—using the same duration for each push. This provides a more consistent visual presentation throughout the final video.

If your video quality will not suffer, consider slowing down your shorter clips a little to extend them to fit with the larger ones. Keep the push leisurely but moving. Too fast and your viewers will miss a key part of the effect—that the video changes during the push. Too slow, and it's just boring.

Note: You can actually scale overlays onto your entire video in either of two ways. First, you can select the entire track (⌘-A) as I do in most of the examples in this book. Alternatively, you can select nothing (⌘-B). Either way, you continue by selecting Edit ▷ Add Scaled (Option-Shift-⌘-V). QuickTime Pro will scale the data in the Clipboard over your entire track.

Push Your Masks

After masking various bits of your footage, have fun with them. In these steps, you'll use iMovie's Push function to combine masked footage into a coherent whole.

1. Start by adding your masks to your clips as described in the preceding project. Use a variety of mask shapes and clips to create the most interesting materials. A single background color used consistently helps unify your final results. I use white here.

2. Create a new project in iMovie and import each clip. Make sure to include a plain still that is the same background color as your mask. Lay out your clips, padding them on each end with the background still.

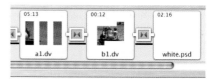

3. Select the Transitions palette. Choose Push, setting the direction to right. Each picture will arrive from left to right, pushing the previous one out of the way. Set the push time as desired.

4. Drag the transition between each set of clips. Kick back and wait as iMovie creates the intermediate frames. This may take a long while.

5. Test out the results in the Monitor and make any adjustments until you're satisfied with the flow of the transitions.

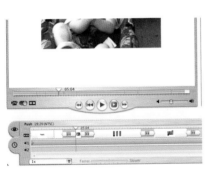

6. Trim the stills at the start and the end and, if desired, add an intro title and a music track.

Odd Shapes and Colored Masks

Don't limit yourself to such simple shapes as squares, rectangles, and circles when unlimited possibilities exist. Instead, consider using unusual shapes like sailboats, starbursts, and airplanes to mask your video. Photoshop Elements offers several dozen via its shape tool. Just draw out a shape in an unused color, import it into QuickTime Pro as you've seen in this chapter, and you can use that shape as a mask—and you don't even have to convert it to a selection and cut it from your matte. Instead, draw as usual with a simple color.

In QuickTime Pro, don't select Straight Alpha (or its variations) from the Graphics Mode list. Instead, choose Transparent. Click the Color button, and choose the mask color. (Press the Option key, using the eyedropper for easy color selection.) QuickTime converts that color into transparent pixels, allowing you to see through your mask to the video below.

Use this trick to add a consistent theme to your work, such as travel (as here), nature, geometry, or so forth. By selecting related shapes, you tie together the whole presentation and make the effect seem less random.

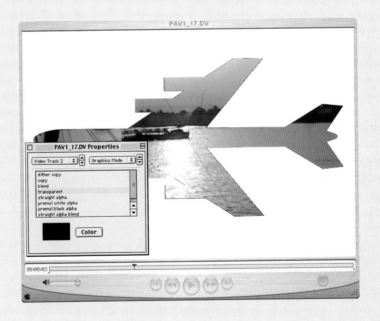

Push.mov, pushmasks.sea

iMovie and the Squashed Circle

Don't worry that your circle appears distorted in iMovie. This common problem becomes more noticeable when you use a regular shape, such a circle, where distortions are more apparent than in regular footage.

As discussed in Chapter 1, iMovie (top image) uses a different aspect ratio than QuickTime (bottom image). When you export your movie out to tape or to a full-quality QuickTime movie, you'll correctly restore the original proportions.

Spin In and Out

GeeThree's Spin transition works particularly well with masked images, creating an unusual presentation where your video twirls in and out. Get the GeeThree Slick Transitions and Effects (http://geethree.com/p_slickboth.html), then follow these steps to create this spinning effect.

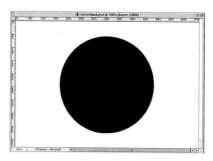

1. Create your core mask in your image editor. Here, I use Photoshop Elements to create a basic black circle on a white background.

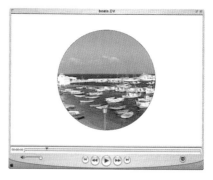

2. Open the mask in QuickTime Pro. Select the entire mask track (⌘-A), copy (⌘-C), and close (⌘-W). Select your video track (⌘-A), and choose Edit ▷ Add Scaled. Open Movie Properties (⌘-J), select Video Track 2 and Graphics Mode, choosing Transparent. Click the Color button and select black.

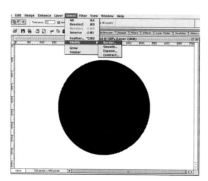

3. Whenever you use this kind of masking, the borders may look rough. Return to Photoshop Elements. Use the magic wand to select the circle. Choose Select ▷ Modify ▷ Border. Enter a reasonably wide border, such as 12 and click OK.

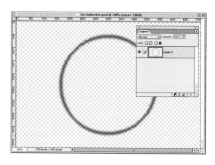

4. Choose Select ▷ Feather ▷ 2 to create a smoother border that will blend with the footage beneath. Create a new layer (click the New Layer button in the Layers palette) and discard the original layers (drag to the palette's trash can). Select a color and fill the selection. Save to a new file, such as CircleBorder.psd.

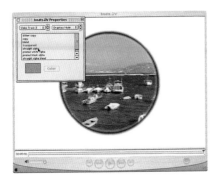

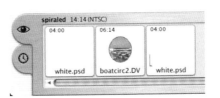

5. Open this new image in QuickTime Pro to add this mask over your footage, this time using Straight Alpha. Export your footage (⌘-E) to a DV Stream for use in iMovie.

6. Create a new iMovie project and import your video and a still that matches your mask's background color—in this case, a blank white still. Move these to the Timeline and duplicate the still (Option-drag) so it appears before and after your clip.

7. Select the GeeThree Spin In transition from the Transitions palette. Drag it between the first still and your clip. Do the same for the Spin Away transition between your clip and the second still. Keep the spin fairly short—about a second. Wait for iMovie to render these transitions.

8. Play back your newly rendered movie to ensure that you're satisfied with the transition times and the overall flow.

9. Trim away the extra portions of your stills, retaining a bit of white before and after each transition.

10. Save your project and export as desired.

swirl1.mov

Better Building Blocks

Using the text combination trick (☞ "Transform Footage with Empty Titles" in Chapter 1) offers several advantages when applying special effects like the double-spin. By combining footage, you can use longer transitions, slowing down so that your audience can better appreciate your special effect. It also allows you to treat each group of modified clips as a single building block, making it easier to move your effect footage around as a whole when you decide to reorder your clips.

Time and Results

Give yourself plenty of time to build the effect in this project. Sometimes it can be maddening how slowly iMovie seems to go when adding several transitions at once. Take heart, though, in that things don't get any better in higher-end software. You can't build this effect any faster in Final Cut Pro or Adobe Premiere. The only answer is faster computers—and we're still years away from computers that are consistently fast enough to produce video effects in real time without special-purpose hardware. If you're a tea or coffee aficionado, consider this the perfect time to take a break and make yourself a cup.

DoubleSpin

Combine spiraled footage to create a very cool double-spin effect. In these steps, you'll build off the previous example to create a movie where one element spirals away as the next one comes into play.

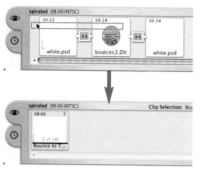

1. Use the combine-with-a-blank-title trick (☞ "Transform Footage with Empty Titles" in Chapter 1) to turn your spiral footage into a single clip. After you've done this, trim your clip down to remove excess frames from both sides of the actual spiral.

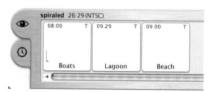

2. Import several other clips, also created with the spiral effect and collapsed with the title trick. Drag these clips into your Timeline/Clip Viewer.

3. Select the Push transition and choose a direction—here, I use up. Set the speed to allow for the two spirals to appear on-screen at the same time. Two seconds provides a nice unhurried transition.

4. Drag the transition down to the Clip Viewer, between each set of clips, and wait for iMovie to finish rendering.

5. After all the frames have rendered, play back the movie and determine whether iMovie has created the transitions to your satisfaction. If not, play with the transition speeds and any remaining padding frames until you achieve the desired results.

6. Save your project and export as desired.

Beyond the Spin

Don't limit yourself to spins when combining animated footage with the push transition. The trick described in this project works equally well with any changing footage. What makes this effect stand out is the elements that transform as they move. Here, I use the GeeThree Pow transition to make my individual clips explode in and out as they push.

iMovie Playback Shortcuts

Use these shortcuts to help you control your iMovie playback.

SHORTCUT	ACTION
Spacebar	Toggle playback on and off
Up arrow or Down arrow	Adjust volume up or down
Home	Reset the movie to the beginning
End	Reset the movie to the very end
Left arrow or Right arrow (video clip selected)	Move playhead by one frame in direction selected
Shift-Left arrow or Shift-Right arrow (video clip selected)	Move playhead by ten frames in the direction selected
Left arrow or Right arrow held down (video clip selected)	Continuous scroll in the direction selected
⌘-] (video clip selected)	Fast forward
⌘-[(video clip selected)	Fast rewind

DoubleSpin.mov

5

Animated Effects

Add Animated Style to Your iMovies (with Just a Few Steps)

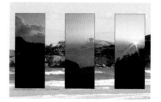

One of Apple's least publicized—and most useful—utilities adds magic to your iMovies. This program, MakeEffectMovie, is free and available for download from the Apple FTP site. With MakeEffectMovie and QuickTime Pro, you'll create effects that move and change, offering seriously cool results, including moving borders, animated icons, flying overlays, and more.

Basic Overlay Animation
A Little Transparency
See Through
Fast and Fabulous

Basic Overlay Animation

Animated borders offer some of the simplest effects you can achieve with MakeEffectMovie. They quickly allow you to surround your video with motion and style. In these examples, you'll see how to build your own. You'll create custom-sized images, add a motion effect, and then import the results into QuickTime, to be placed over your video clips. In just a few steps, these techniques allow you to create simple scrolling effects.

Note: In most MakeEffectMovie examples, you press ⌘-2, ⌘-1 to start building your effect. These shortcuts refer to the Test ▷ Standalone Movie and Test ▷ MakeEffectMovie menu selections. By making a stand-alone effect movie, you'll be able to save and reuse these tracks without having to keep copies of your original artwork on hand at all times.

Note: When animating text, choose a bold, easy-to-read font face and a fairly large size. The DV rendering process can make text hard to read.

Stock Ticker

These steps show how to apply MakeEffectMovie's Push effect to a pair of image stripes. When complete, you'll produce an animated overlay that offers the latest "stock prices."

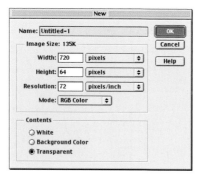

1. In Photoshop Elements, create a new image 720 pixels wide by 64 pixels high. (This size applies to both NTSC- and PAL-system users.) This creates a wide, thin strip that leaves enough room to see most of your video.

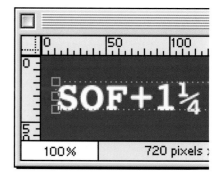

2. Fill the background of the image with any solid color; choose a contrasting color for the text. Add enough text to avoid gaps at the start or end of your animation. When you're satisfied with your layout, save to disk as a .psd file.

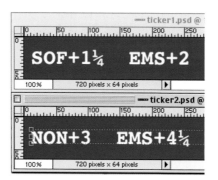

3. Make a copy of your first image file, open the copy in Photoshop Elements, and alter the text. This new file acts as the second half of your scrolling ticker, so use different stocks and prices. For fun, I retained the EMS stock and raised the price to indicate a rapidly moving hot item for my fake ticker.

4. Launch MakeEffectMovie; it begins without opening any other windows. OS 9 users may want to check for the red heart icon in the menu bar to confirm that it's running. Type ⌘-2, ⌘-1. An open file dialog appears. Navigate to your first ticker image file and click Open.

Finding MakeEffectMovie

Version Apple offers a variety of MakeEffectMovie versions. The instructions in this book refer to version 2.1 with a 3 April 1998 (8:31) build date and a 4 October 2000 (3:03 PM) modification date—you can find these dates and version numbers by selecting the application in your Finder and choosing ⌘-I (File ▷ Get Info ▷ General Information). This version comes with source code as well as the application program. Be aware that other MakeEffectMovie versions may open the file selection dialogs immediately upon launch.

Download Download your copy of MakeEffectMovie at this URL:
ftp://ftp.apple.com/developer/Sample_Code/QuickTime/QuickTimeIntro/
MakeEffectMovie.sit

In the event that the Apple site becomes temporarily unavailable, you can also download copies from ZDNet and CNET, although the version may vary slightly.

Documentation You'll find the MakeEffectMovie documentation at this URL:
http://developer.apple.com/quicktime/quicktimeintro/tools/makeeffectmovie.html

In addition, you may view sample effects at
http://www.apple.com/quicktime/samples/effects/

About MakeEffectMovie

Apple developed MakeEffectMovie to showcase the range of effects for QuickTime developers, but it provides a handy utility that outperforms its original purpose. The package I recommend you download actually includes sample source code to demonstrate how the QuickTime calls are used to build your movie. The curious can browse through these files to see how QuickTime programming can be accomplished. The less curious can simply use the MakeEffectMovie utility to build exciting and lively videos.

Note: If you want, you can actually drag movies onto the MakeEffectMovie program icon to launch the program with those movies selected as your choices. As convenient as this drag-and-drop operation is, I find it a little hard to specify which file I want as the first and which as the second.

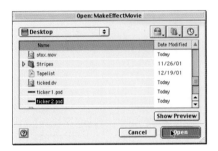

5. A second open file dialog appears. Navigate to your second ticker image and click Open. For a scrolling effect, like the one you're creating here, MakeEffectMovie needs two files to start with.

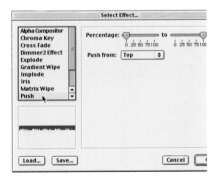

6. MakeEffectMovie displays a Select Effect dialog. Choose Push from the scrolling list of effects on the left side of this window.

continues on next page

  TakeStock.mov, ticker1.psd, ticker2.psd

Why Video Track 4?

MakeEffectMovie blends two images or movies together to create an *effect movie*—a QuickTime movie with a built-in animated transition. It creates three separate tracks: source material from each video and a unifying effect track. Retain these tracks as produced—deleting any of them messes up your effect movie— and do not export before use. Exporting destroys vital composition information; you lose scalability and will export just two or three frames. Those frames cannot scale to produce a smooth, continuous effect. You also lose transparency. Dealing with three (or, occasionally, two or four) tracks at a time is irritating but necessary when working with effect movies.

Note: To build longer scrolling sequences, create more ticker images and follow Steps 4 through 8. You'll build several sequences: image two scrolling to image three, three to four, and so forth. Combine these in order in QuickTime Pro before selecting and copying in Step 9.

Stock Ticker *continued*

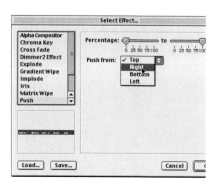

7. To create the ticker-tape effect, choose Right from the pull-down menu and click OK. A File Save dialog appears.

8. Navigate to where you wish to save this effect movie, enter a name (I use stockpush.mov), and click Save. Wait for MakeEffectMovie to build the movie. Open that new movie in QuickTime Pro.

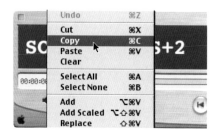

9. Select the entire effect movie (⌘-A), copy it to the system Clipboard (⌘-C), and close the window (⌘-W).

10. In QuickTime Pro, open the movie you wish to overlay. Here, I use an 8-second stock clip from EyeWire's Triangle Images. Select the entire movie (⌘-A) and choose Edit ▷ Add Scaled (Option-Shift-⌘-V) to scale the animation across your entire video.

11. The ticker appears at the top of the screen. To move it into place, open the Movie Properties window (⌘-J). Select Video Track 4 from the left pull-down menu and Size from the right.

12. Click Adjust. Red resize handles appear around your overlay.

13. Shift-drag your ticker into position (restricting your video to move vertically but not horizontally). Position the ticker slightly above the bottom of the screen, about 30 or 40 pixels, to allow some of the footage to appear beneath it. (For reference, your ticker is 64 pixels high.)

14. When satisfied with the ticker placement, click Done. Close the Movie Properties window. Move the playhead back and forth throughout the movie to ensure that all works as planned. The ticker text scrolls from right to left.

15. To merge your four source tracks into one, export your video to disk. Select File ▷ Export (⌘-E).

16. Navigate to where you wish to save your file. If you intend to continue working in QuickTime Pro before returning to iMovie, be sure to export to a QuickTime movie. Otherwise, select DV Stream. Enter a file name and click Save.

SMPTE

Why did Apple choose the set of effects offered in MakeEffectMovie? The answer lies in the Society of Motion Picture and Television Engineers (SMPTE), a body that defines standards for the broadcast industry. Apple used these while designing its own QuickTime standard. In document 258M-1993, for example, SMPTE details a set of official wipes. Select Wipe from the list on the left of MakeEffectMovie's Select Effect dialog, and you'll find those wipes listed in the pull-down menu (on the right portion of the dialog). Apple complied similarly to create many of the other QuickTime effects offered in MakeEffectMovie. Microsoft uses these standards, too. Its DirectX library offers a nearly identical set of wipes, transitions, and so forth in compliance with the SMPTE.

Note: Learn more about the SMPTE on their website at www.smpte.org. SMPTE hosts an online store where you can shop for standards documentation, books, journals, and test materials.

An Animated Border

Two-way animated symmetry can add an extra visual flair to your movies. Follow these steps and add a pair of symmetric animated borders to your video.

1. Create a new 720x64 pixel image in Photoshop Elements. Design it with directional visual elements that lead the eye in one direction or another. Here I place right-pointing yellow arrows on a black background. Save this image to disk.

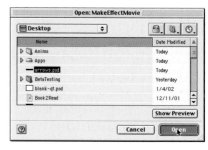

2. Launch MakeEffectMovie. Type ⌘-2, ⌘-1. When the file selection dialog appears, choose the file you just created and click Open. A second file selection dialog appears; choose the *same* image and click Open again. To create this scrolling effect, MakeEffectMovie needs two source files even if they are the same, as seen here.

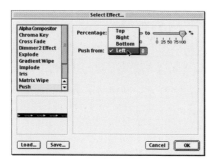

3. Select Push from the scrolling list of effects. As our arrows point right, choose Left from the Push From pull-down menu. Click OK. Navigate to where you wish to save your effect movie, enter a name (I used pusharrows.mov), and click Save.

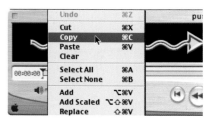

4. In QuickTime Pro, open the movie you just saved (pusharrows.mov). Select the entire movie (⌘-A). Copy the animation (⌘-C) and close (⌘-W).

5. Open the movie you wish to overlay. Select all (⌘-A). Scale your animated overlay over the entire movie *twice* to create two strips: Use the Edit ▷ Add Scaled command (Option-Shift-⌘-V) and then use it again. After this, you will have added six new video tracks.

6. Open the Movie Properties window (⌘-J). Select Video Track 7 from the left pull-down menu and Size from the right.

7. Click the Adjust button. Red resize handles appear around your overlay. Hold the Shift key down and move your overlay straight down to the bottom of the screen. Place it as precisely as possible at the bottom. Too high and you'll see parts of your movie under the overlay; too low and you'll resize your movie. When finished, click Done.

8. Check your Video Size. Select Movie from the left pull-down menu, leaving the right pull-down menu on Size. Confirm that your movie remains the same size as it began. (Normal Size and Current Size should be identical.) If not, make the adjustments needed so it is.

9. After you finish placing and checking your bottom overlay, select Video Track 4 from the left pull-down menu if it is not already selected. Click the left-right double-arrow button; this flips your video track and allows the animation arrows to progress right-to-left.

10. Play your movie to confirm that it works as expected, then export to disk. This collapses all seven (7!) of your video tracks into a single, combined clip.

arrows.psd, followme.mov

Set the Pace

Experimentation, measurement, and a little math help determine the numbers needed for animation repetitions. Use these techniques to decide how many times you want your animation to play during your movie.

Calculate the pixels In general, you'll find that the shorter the distance your animations travel, the more repetitions you will need. In this exercise, your border scrolls just 64 pixels before repeating. In the previous project, it scrolled 720 pixels. By thinking about the pixel distance, you'll gain a better appreciation for the possible duration you'll need.

Play it through by hand
Play through the initial effect movie, manually moving the playhead at different speeds to estimate how long the animation should last. Once you decide on an approximate time, divide the length of your video clip by this duration. You'll end up with the number of repetitions needed for your video.

There's no "right speed"
Adjusting animation repetitions is an art, not a science. When you play back your movie, the animated portions should look smooth—neither hurried nor too slow. Don't be afraid to go back and choose a different repetition number when you don't like the results you've created.

Border Variations

A vertical roll offers a visually interesting variation to the horizontal movement shown in the previous example. Follow these steps to create a "rolling" border.

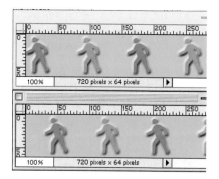

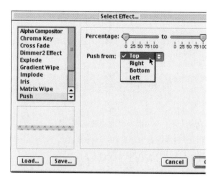

1. In Photoshop Elements, design a pair of "stripes" (short but wide graphics), with the elements in one offset from the other by about half.

2. Launch MakeEffectMovie. Press ⌘-2, ⌘-1. In the two subsequent open-file dialogs, first select stripe1 and click Open, then stripe2 and click Open. Select Push from the scrolling list. Choose Top from the Push From pull-down menu.

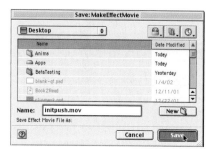

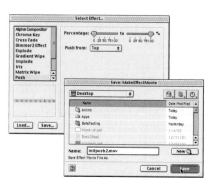

3. Click OK and save your work to disk as initpush1.mov. As each animation provides just half the scroll (the first pushing the second, then the second pushing the first), you must still create the second half of the animation.

4. Press ⌘-2, ⌘-1. This time, select stripe2 first and click Open. Select stripe1 and click Open. Choose Push from the scrolling effects list and Top from the Push From pull-down menu. Click OK and save your work to disk as initpush2.mov.

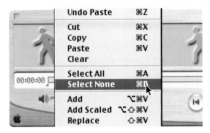

5. In QuickTime Pro, open initpush1.mov. Select all (⌘-A) and copy (⌘-C). Close initpush1.mov (⌘-W). QuickTime copies this portion of your animation to the system clipboard.

6. Open initpush2.mov. Select None (⌘-B). Click the left-most of the five QuickTime control buttons to move the playhead to its far-left position. Paste (⌘-V). QuickTime pastes the animation you copied in Step 5 in front of the preexisting animation. By adding this first half, you've created a complete animated scroll.

7. Select all (⌘-A). Copy the animation to the Clipboard (⌘-C). Select None (⌘-B); QuickTime deselects without changing the playhead location—which should remain at the start or end of your effect movie. For this (9-second) video, we'll add three more repetitions of the complete scroll for a total of four.

8. Paste (⌘-V) three times, then select the entire movie (⌘-A) and copy it to the Clipboard (⌘-C). You're ready to add the copied animation to your video. In QuickTime Pro, open your main video. Select all (⌘-A) and use Edit ▷ Add Scaled (Option-Shift-⌘-V) *twice* to overlay your video with two copies of the animation.

9. Open the Movie Properties window (⌘-J). Select Video Track 7 (which is the second copy of your animation) from the left pull-down menu and Size from the Right. Click Adjust.

10. While pressing the Shift key, drag the second overlay into position at the bottom of your frame. Click Done. Play back the video to test it before exporting to disk.

  Stripe1.psd, Stripe2.psd, Walkers.mov

A Little Transparency

A little transparency can add a lot of Wow! to animations. By eliminating portions of stills or videos, animated elements appear to travel independently around your movies. In this section, you'll see how to make backgrounds disappear while retaining the animated foreground elements. From flying teapots to morphing flowers to wherever your imagination will lead you, your animations will take off on their own and move by themselves.

OS X Note: Some OS X users report inconsistent behavior when adding transparency to their QuickTime movies. If this happens to you, consider doing your work in Classic mode, using the OS 9.x version of QuickTime Pro. Alternatively, you may want to use Transparent rather than the Alpha settings—some of our beta testers reported this option worked more consistently for them. Hopefully, these inconsistencies will disappear when QuickTime Pro 6 is released.

The Flying Teapot

In these steps, you will use a transparent background to make foreground objects "fly" across the screen.

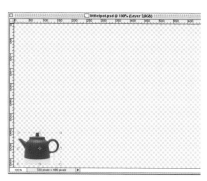

1. Create a new, blank image in Photoshop Elements (720x480 NTSC, 720x576 PAL). Add a single, small image to the bottom-left corner. Here, I place a teapot onto the transparent background. Save your image to disk as a new .psd file.

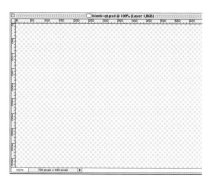

2. Create a completely blank, transparent image in Photoshop Elements and save it to disk. You'll need a blank image like this one for many animation effects. The file adds extra "space," allowing MakeEffectMovie more flexibility when moving around and placing opaque elements.

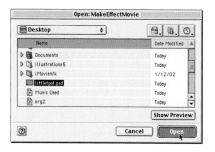

3. In MakeEffectMovie, select ⌘-2, ⌘-1. Choose your blank image and click Open, then choose the teapot image and click Open.

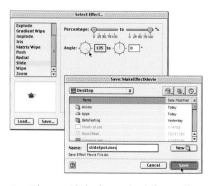

4. Choose Slide from the left scrolling menu. Adjust the first angle to 135, as seen here. Then click OK and save slidetpot.mov to disk.

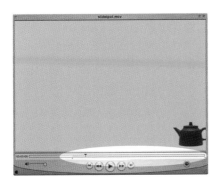

5. In QuickTime Pro, open slidetpot.mov. Move the playhead until you find the teapot's entrance. Select from just before this frame to the end of the movie. This allows you to skip those frames without the teapot. Copy this selection (⌘-C) and close the movie (⌘-W).

6. Open your base movie in QuickTime Pro. Move the playhead to the far left. Shift-drag the cursor along the scrubber bar, stopping a second or two before the end of your movie. (These remaining frames will allow us to add a final still image in Step 14.)

7. Choose Edit ▷ Add Scaled (Option-Shift-⌘-V). QuickTime Pro scales your animated overlay to the selection you just made.

8. Move the playhead back into the gray, selected area in order to see your overlay in place.

9. Open the Movie Properties window (⌘-J). Select Video Track 4 from the left pull-down menu and Graphics Mode from the right.

10. Select one of the Alpha options. Here, I choose Premul White Alpha, to remove any whitish residue from around the edges of my teapot.

continues on next page

 tea42.mov, teastuff.sea

The Linger

A sudden stop is a harsh ending for animations. Take note of how your movement ends and design around it. For many moving effects, you'll want to add a quick linger after the animation concludes, as you do in these steps. By inserting a still for a second or two, you allow your viewer to pause and consider the animation before rushing into the next portion of your movie. Creating a gentle finish to your animations is well worth the extra steps.

If you simply don't have enough footage to allow for a linger at the end of your animation, consider using the fade-out technique shown in Chapter 2, "Add Stills Around a Clip." This allows your footage to slow down to a still, pause for a second or two and then fade away.

No matter how you accomplish your goal, soft endings are desirable features for any animation work you do. Take the extra time to make your work end as beautifully as it began.

The Flying Teapot *continued*

11. You now need to invert the selection in your movie—selecting the unselected frames. Press Option-Right arrow to move the playhead back to the right crop marker. Choose Edit ▷ Select None (⌘-B) to center the crop markers around the playhead.

12. Press Shift-Left arrow to start a selection one frame to the left of your playhead. Then drag the right crop marker to the end of your video.

13. In QuickTime Pro, open your original teapot image—not the animation, but the source picture. Select the entire image track (⌘-A) and copy it to the Clipboard (⌘-C). Close the image (⌘-W).

14. Return to your video. Choose Edit ▷ Add Scaled (Option-Shift-⌘-V) to add the still over the frames of your current selection.

15. The overlay appears on top of your video. If needed, move the playhead slightly to the left in the gray selected area until you see it.

16. Open the Movie Properties window (⌘-J). Select Video Track 5 from the left pull-down menu and Graphics Mode from the right.

17. Choose the same mode as in Step 10. You should be able to play back your image with the following results: The teapot should enter the video shortly after the start and "fly" until a few seconds before the end of the movie. It should then freeze in place until the conclusion.

18. Export your work to disk, allowing QuickTime Pro to meld your animated overlay and the base video into a single video track.

Animation Speed

The speed at which your animation progresses is determined solely by the number of seconds you selected in Step 6: the longer the selection, the slower your animation will proceed. The effect movie animation you create doesn't really have an intrinsic length associated with it. It gains a timing component only when you use QuickTime Pro to scale the animation over your selected frames. If you find your animation proceeds too slowly or too quickly, you may want to reconsider the footage you're using.

Stretching Long

The longer you stretch your animation, the less you need to pad it with any sort of linger effect. A stretched animation will naturally last longer towards the end than one with a shorter duration. Given the extra work and fuss involved in adding a lingering still, you may want to test your movie first with the simple Select-All/Add-Scaled approach before you begin to fine-tune your work with the method detailed here. Sometimes, the simplest and most direct approach works the way you need it to.

Bending Text

I created the text messages you see here in Adobe Photoshop Elements. In order to achieve the "bent" look, I clicked the Create Warped Text button, just to the right of the text-color box and toward the right end of the options bar. This button launches a dialog from which you can select from a wide variety of warp styles, including arcs, shells, bulges, and flags. Simply choose a style, click OK, and allow Photoshop Elements to bend your text into a fanciful presentation.

Add a Three-Dimensional Look

As with Photoshop 6 and later, Photoshop Elements offers layer styles that allow you to create a 3D look for your text overlays. Build your text layer as you normally would. Then choose the layer and select a style from the Layer Styles palette. You'll find this palette in the shortcuts dock. I find that the Bevels styles work best with text. You may want to choose from such styles as Simple Sharp Outer, Scalloped Edge, Simple Inner, or Simple Emboss. Each of these styles transforms your titles, offering a smart and elegant look.

Send a Message

MakeEffectMovie's cross-dissolve allows you to blend overlays in and out of your video. Follow these steps to add messages over your movies.

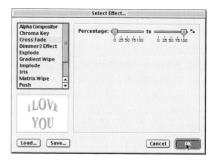

1. In Photoshop Elements, design several related overlays. You can create them in one file for proper positioning and consistent size, but save each to a *separate* .psd file. "I Love You" is the main text; the three translations are additional messages. Also, save a blank, transparent file of the same size under the name blank-qt.psd.

2. Launch MakeEffectMovie. Press ⌘-2, ⌘-1; first open blank-qt.psd and then open the main "I Love You" image. Choose Cross Fade, click OK, and save to ily.mov. This produces an effect movie, in which your message slowly appears on the screen.

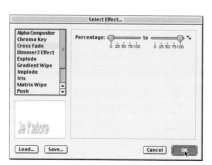

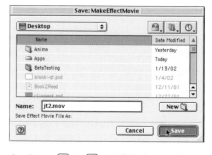

3. For each remaining message, you need to make a *pair* of effect movies. To make the first pair, start by pressing ⌘-2, ⌘-1. Select blank-qt.psd and then the message; click Open after each. Choose Cross Fade, click OK, and save to the first of the paired movies (here, jt1.mov).

4. Press ⌘-2, ⌘-1. This time, select the *message* first and then the blank file, clicking Open after each. Choose Cross Fade, click OK, and save to the second of the paired movies (thus, jt2.mov).

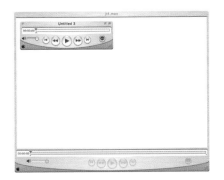

5. In QuickTime Pro, create a new movie. Open the first message movie (here, jt1.mov), select all (⌘-A), copy (⌘-C), and close it (⌘-W).

6. Paste the copied material into your new movie (⌘-V). The movie window resizes to fit, and the play-head moves to the end of the track. Leave it there.

7. Open the second movie of the pair—here, jt2.mov. Select all (⌘-A), copy (⌘-C), and close (⌘-W). Return to your new movie—the playhead still in place on the right—and choose Edit Paste (⌘-V). QuickTime pastes the second animation after the first.

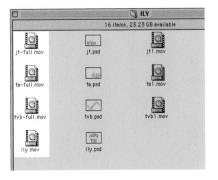

8. Move the playhead back and forth to confirm that the effect works as expected, with the message fading in and then out. Choose File ▷ Save As and save this movie to disk, naming it so it's clearly the complete, paired effect (I used "full": jt-full.mov).

9. Now, repeat Steps 3–8 for the remaining overlays. When they're all done, check your inventory. You should have a single "I Love You" movie and, for each subsequent overlay, a complete message movie. Each "full" movie should both fade-in and fade-out; the "I Love You" movie just fades in.

10. In QuickTime Pro, open the "I Love You" movie. Select the entire video (⌘-A), copy it (⌘-C), and then close the window (⌘-W).

continues on next page

ilytruly.mov, loves.psd, loves-PAL.psd

Alpha vs. the Blend

In the steps detailed in this section, I instruct you to use Straight Alpha Blend on your secondary messages. This choice allows you to create a softer, more blended presentation. I like this look because it hints the messages rather than showing them outright. This soft blend, however, is by no means mandatory. You may prefer to use bolder text in your movies. If so, choose Straight Alpha or Premul White Alpha instead.

The Photoshop Elements Alternative

If you like, you can adjust your transparency in Photoshop Elements rather than in QuickTime Pro. To do so, just adjust the Opacity slider in your Layers palette before saving your title to disk. When you take this approach, you'll more exactly control the degree of transparency associated with your title. This helps when you want to use specific ramped opacities for different overlays (for example, 30%, 40%, 50%, etc.). I don't use this method very much myself, because I prefer to see the overlaid title with the video when adjusting my blending characteristics.

Send a Message *continued*

11. Now, open your base video. Select all (⌘-A) and scale the main "I Love You" overlay onto your movie (Edit ▷ Add Scaled, Option-Shift-⌘-V).

12. Open the Movie Properties window (⌘-J). Select Video Track 4 from the left pull-down menu and Graphics Mode from the right. Choose Straight Alpha.

 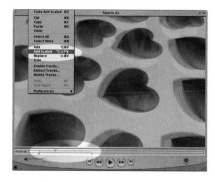

13. Open your first full message movie. Select it (⌘-A), copy it (⌘-C), and close it (⌘-W).

14. Select some portion of the base video where the message will appear and fade away. The location does not matter. Be sure, however, to select at least several seconds' worth. Scale your copied effect movie over this portion. (Edit ▷ Add Scaled, Option-Shift-⌘-V).

15. Move the playhead back into the selected gray area until the new overlay appears.

16. Open the Movie Properties window (⌘-J). Select Video Track 7 from the left pull-down menu and Graphics Mode from the right. Choose Straight Alpha Blend.

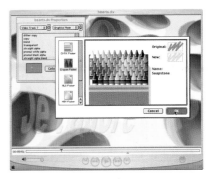

17. Click the Color button. Choose a lighter color from the color picker. I particularly like Soapstone from the Crayon Picker. It blends the text overlay while it brings out the color just enough to be noticeable.

18. Repeat Steps 14–17 for each remaining message, picking random locations. Try to overlap messages so that one appears while another is disappearing. To determine your video track, add 3 for each new message: The next track is 10; the one after that 13, and so forth.

19. Test out your video and see if it works in the way you wish. To change message placement or duration, remove the message, change the selection of frames in your base video, and add again. Just remember: you have three tracks to remove for each message.

20. Assuming that everything works the way you want, export your work to disk (⌘-E). You may also want to save (⌘-S) a copy of your movie (saving normally, using dependencies) so that you can return and make minor tweaks as needed.

Small and Sweet

Overlays can make a statement without being large. Design your overlays with placement and resizing in mind. Although transparency allows you to hide an image background in favor of your opaque foreground, it does not allow you to move your overlay outside the bounds of your base video without resizing. Choose and use smaller overlays that allow you greater placement flexibility.

In this project, you'll use very small overlays indeed—just the size of a flower. I chose a 240x240-pixel canvas for this exercise, because it balances the need for clear visual with a smallness that allows it to be placed at nearly any point on your video.

Note: If you own a scanner, you can scan your flowers directly into Photoshop Elements. Simply lay your favorite blooms on your flatbed scanner, close the lid, and scan. Be sure to clean your glass and lid carefully after use.

Flower Power

Follow these steps to create a rotating overlay that swaps between flower varieties.

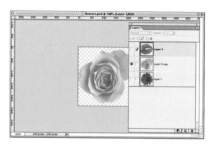

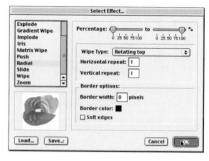

1. In Photoshop Elements, design your flowers on separate layers of a common document. Here, I create a 240x240-pixel canvas for my work. Center all flowers with respect to the others. When you're satisfied with both size and placement, save each flower out to a separate .psd file.

2. Launch MakeEffectMovie. Press ⌘-2, ⌘-1. Select your first flower and click Open. Select your second flower and click Open. Choose Radial from the list of effects. Choose Rotating Top from the pull-down list to the right. Click OK. Save your effect to flora1.mov.

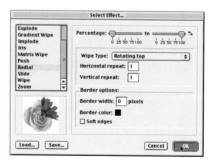

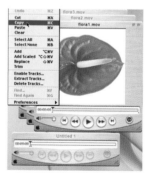

3. Repeat Step 2 (⌘-2, ⌘-1, open both, Radial/Rotating Top, save) for the remaining pairs of flowers (second and third, then third and fourth if you've made more, and so on), naming the movies in sequence. When you reach the last flower, choose that file and then choose the first to finish the loop.

4. In QuickTime, open a new player to create a new movie, which will become your full animated overlay. Open all your flower movies at once, and process them in sequential order. For each, select all (⌘-A), copy the tracks to the Clipboard (⌘-C), close the window (⌘-W), and paste at the end of the new movie.

5. After pasting all the animations, in order, select the entire new track (⌘-A), copy (⌘-C), and paste several times (⌘-V). This adds repetitions of your animation to your overlay. Select your entire track again (⌘-A) and copy the repeating animation to the Clipboard (⌘-C). Save your completed overlay (⌘-S).

6. In QuickTime, open a base movie of your choice. Select all (⌘-A) and scale your animation over the entire video (Edit ▷ Add Scaled, Option-Shift-⌘-V).

7. Open the Movie Properties window (⌘-J). Select Video Track 4 from the left pull-down menu and Graphics Mode from the right. Select an alpha graphics mode. Here, I use Premul White Alpha to remove the slight white halo around my flowers.

8. Select Size from the right pull-down menu. Click Adjust, move the flower overlay into place, and click Done.

9. Repeat Steps 6–8 to add several more overlay copies to your video. Move and resize each one into position. To adjust the proper video track, add 3 for each subsequent paste—Video Track 7, Video Track 10, etc.

10. Test your movie, then export your file to disk (⌘-E).

flowers.psd, flowerpower.mov

Flattened Circles

Whenever you deal with QuickTime circles, don't be surprised when they look more oval than circle in iMovie. They should look fine when you export to a TV or camera.

If you want your circles to look just right in iMovie, however, design them in a standard iMovie frame (640x480 pixels NTSC, 768x576 pixels PAL) and then resize the image in Photoshop Elements (Image ▷ Resize ▷ Image Size) to the QuickTime size before use. QuickTime sizes are 720x480 pixels for NTSC and 720x576 for PAL.

Note: Some effects, like the one detailed here, are meant more for background pizzazz than foreground presentation. It often helps to overlay them with a title or image. In the sample movie (found on the CD that accompanies this book), I've added a title to draw attention away from the circles and better blend them into the background imagery.

Bull's-Eye!

Circles rotating in opposite directions come together to form a bull's-eye in this example. In these steps, you'll layer a series of radial effects, reversing some to produce an interesting merge effect.

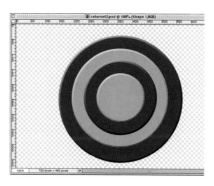

1. In Photoshop Elements, design concentric circles using a standard DV-sized window with a blank, transparent background. Use a separate layer for each circle and, after saving your complete design, also save each circle to a separate .psd file. Also save a transparent still of the same size.

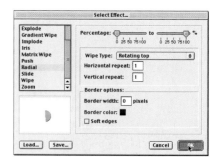

2. Launch MakeEffectMovie. For each circle, do the following: Press ⌘-2, ⌘-1. Open the blank still, then open the circle. Choose Radial from the scrolling list and Rotating Top from the pull-down menu. Click OK and save to a uniquely named effect movie file (I've used XC1.mov, XC2.mov, etc.).

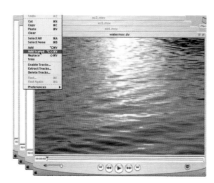

3. After creating all your movies, open them—and a base video—in QuickTime Pro. In order, largest circle to smallest, do the following: Select the entire circle video (⌘-A), copy (⌘-C), and close (⌘-W). Select your entire base video (⌘-A), and Add Scaled (Option-Shift-⌘-V).

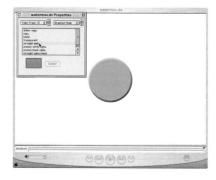

4. Open the Movie Properties window (⌘-J). Select Video Track 4 from the left menu and Graphics Mode from the right. Choose Straight Alpha. Repeat for Video Track 7, Video Track 10, and so forth—adding 3 to the track number each time—until you've set the mode for every circle.

5. In the Movie Properties window, select Video Track 4 from the left pull-down and Size from the right. Click the left-right "mirror" button on the bottom-left of the palette. Repeat for *alternating* circle tracks, adding 6 to the video track number each time—10, 16, etc.

6. For whatever reason, some radial sweep effects never look quite right at the end; many show slight gaps as seen here.

7. To correct the gap, select a few frames at the end of your video. In QuickTime, open the .psd file showing all the concentric circles. Select the entire file (⌘-A), copy (⌘-C), and close (⌘-W). Return to your base video and use Add Scaled (Option-Shift-⌘-V) to add that image over the final frames.

8. Bring up the Movie Properties window (⌘-J). Choose the very last video track from the left pull-down menu. What its exact number will be depends on how many circles you've added to your project. Here, I select Video Track 14.

9. Choose Graphics Mode from the right pull-down menu. Select Straight Alpha from the list. The background disappears, revealing a fully closed set of circles at the end of your video.

10. Test your video, then export it to disk.

LordOTRings.mov, colorset.psd, colorset-PAL.psd

See Through

You can do more with animated overlays and transparency than just place animated items on top of a base video. When you add "holes" to your effect movies, you can add see-through windows that let you peek from one video into the next. These flying windows add a new effect that differentiates itself from other animated transparency techniques. In this section, you'll learn how to create basic moving gaps as well as more advanced two-source video combinations. In all cases, you'll create a *mask*—an image that hides some parts of your video while revealing others.

Note: If you like, you can substitute an oval or a square for the rectangle used in this exercise without otherwise changing any of the steps. Want to create an even bolder video? See the opposite sidebar for some ideas.

Basic Mask Animation

In these steps, you'll create a moving window that flies across your footage.

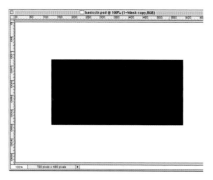

1. Create your mask in Photoshop Elements. Here, I design a very basic rectangle for my revealed area, using black on white. Remember to use QuickTime image sizes for your image (NTSC: 720x480, PAL: 720x576).

2. Create a blank image with the same background color as your mask (in this case, white) using the QuickTime sizes, and save it.

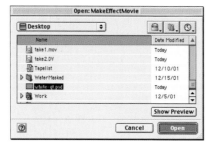

3. Launch MakeEffectMovie. Press ⌘-2, ⌘-1 to begin creating a stand-alone effect movie. Select your blank image and click Open.

4. Select your mask image and click Open.

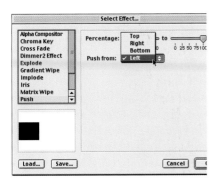

5. Select Push from the list of effects. Choose a direction; in this case, we'll use Left so our "window" travels from left to right. Click OK.

6. Save your movie to disk: I've saved to a new movie called Push1.mov, but you may want a more descriptive name if you plan on reusing this effect in the future. Click Save to finish saving.

continues on next page

FlyByMask.mov, CarGo.mov, MaskPkg.sea

Be Bold

Don't feel limited to simple geometry or even a plain background. Consider adding a funky frame around your mask or using an unusual presentation. So long as you have a large central object, you can animate and mask with it. Here, I make the car's red color become transparent. You can watch the car video on the CD that accompanies this book.

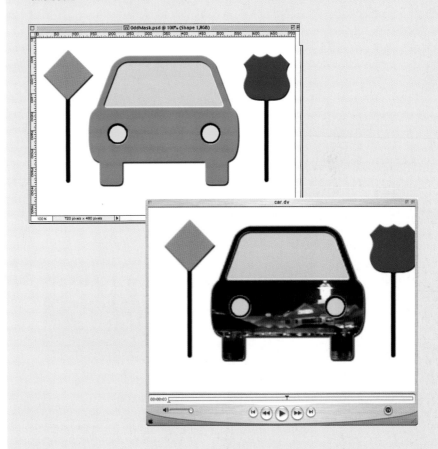

Reverse the Effect

In Step 14, you select a transparent color. In this case, I chose black. If you like, however, you may choose white instead to reverse the effect and create a moving black block over your footage. Later in this chapter, in "Flying Stripes," you will learn how to combine moving elements like this to produce a clever and eye-catching video.

Variations on the Effect

When creating your moving mask in Steps 3–10, you use the Left push effect in MakeEffectMovie. You can easily change the push direction to vary the effect built in this project. You can design your moving window to move down, right, or up. Alternatively, you can use the Slide effect to create a window that wiggles around your video using a trajectory you pick in MakeEffectMovie. When using Slide rather than Push, make sure that your first effect movie ends and your second effect movie begins at the same angle.

Basic Mask Animation *continued*

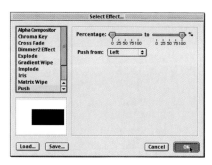

7. Staying in MakeEffectMovie, press ⌘-2, ⌘-1 again. This time, open your mask image first and your blank image second. Again, select Push and Left before clicking OK.

8. Save this second movie to disk. For this example, we'll call it Push2.mov.

9. Quit out of MakeEffectMovie and launch QuickTime Pro. Open Push2.mov. Select All (⌘-A), copy (⌘-C), and close the movie (⌘-W).

10. Open Push1.mov. Move the playhead to the very end of the movie and then paste the copied portion from Push2 (⌘-V). Save the Push1 movie (⌘-S). You're now ready to use the complete animated mask. Select all (⌘-A), copy (⌘-C), and close the movie (⌘-W).

11. In QuickTime, open the movie you want to mask and select all (⌘-A).

12. Choose Edit ▷ Add Scaled to paste the mask over your footage (Option-Shift-⌘-V). The mask obscures your video entirely, as seen here. Move the playhead until you can see some or all of the black rectangle.

13. Bring up the Movie Properties window (⌘-J). Choose Video Track 4 from the left pull-down menu and Graphics Mode from the right.

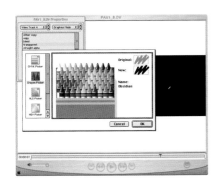

14. Choose Transparent from the list and click Color. Press the Option key and click to sample the black of your mask with an eyedropper. Click OK to set your color. If the Color Picker window covers your black rectangle so you cannot use the eyedropper, dismiss the dialog, move the window with your video in it, and try again.

15. After setting the transparent color, you should be able to see footage through your mask. Play the movie to ensure that all works as expected.

16. Export your movie. If you've finished with it in QuickTime, export it to a DV Stream so you can use it with your iMovie project. If not, export it to a high-quality QuickTime movie so you can work on it further in QuickTime. Avoid the DV format until you're sure you're ready to work in iMovie.

Pick Unusual Colors

It's not that uncommon to accidentally mask out part of your image when you don't mean to. Black and white are fairly common colors in digital video. You find them most often, obviously, in deep shadows and in very bright areas (when the camera's image detector receives enough light to reach maximum saturation). To avoid accidental masking, stick to less common colors—ones that you don't tend to find in videos. Pure colors, like green, red, and blue, are fairly rare. Planning and careful examination are the keys to avoiding accidental masking.

Don't Be Afraid to Try Again

When you pick a wrong color, as in Step 6, don't be afraid to go back and correct your work as I do in Step 7. Your videos are meant to last a very long time. Put in the extra effort now, and you'll be rewarded throughout the years as you go back to view your work. A fixable mistake can haunt you. A well-done video can be a joy forever.

Overmasking

Snazz up your animated masks. You can reuse movies made with the preceding project ("Basic Mask Animation") as a mask for another video.

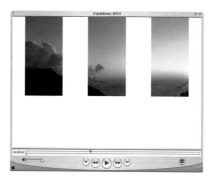

1. Follow the steps in "Basic Mask Animation" to add a three-windowed mask that moves vertically down the screen. Export your movie to QuickTime; you cannot save a movie to DV and retain enough quality to use it as a mask in this fashion. Select the entire movie (⌘-A), copy it (⌘-C), and close it (⌘-W).

2. Open the base movie that you intend to overlay.

3. Move the playhead to the start of your movie and choose Edit ▷ Add (Option-⌘-V). Here, the overlay runs shorter than the base movie. Move the playhead to the end of the overlay, drag to the end of your movie, and trim the excess footage (Edit ▷ Clear).

4. Open the Movie Properties window (⌘-J). Select Video Track 2 from the left pull-down menu and Graphics Mode from the right.

Adding Scaled

You can, if desired, use Add Scaled to match your video overlay to the length of your base video rather than clip as we do in these steps. On the up side, this allows you to stretch or compress the overlay to an exact length.

Take care, though. If your video contains human figures or any other natural action, the distortion in time may prove distracting. On the other hand, sometimes time distortion offers the exact effect you're looking for. Your mileage can and will vary.

Use Add Scaled with care when adding video rather than masks. And use it only when you're really looking to achieve a particular time flow for your video.

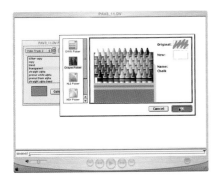

5. Select Transparent and click the Color button. Press the Option key and click with the eyedropper to sample the background color from your overlay.

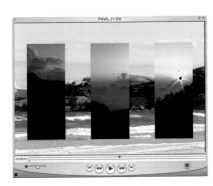

6. Play your movie to make sure everything works as expected. Occasionally you'll find errors, like this one where the bright sun had white pixels that were masked out. In a situation like this, you can either start over from scratch—as we do in the next step—or just live with results and hope that no one will notice.

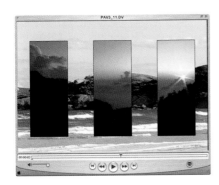

7. Here, I've gone back and redone the masks using a red and black mask rather than a black and white one. You'll find both masks on the CD that accompanies this book. After repeating Steps 1–6, the sun now appears as it should.

8. Export your work to disk. (⌘-E)

tripleplay.mov, 3Maskpkg.sea

MakeEffectMovie Blurs?

You may wonder why these steps use QuickTime Pro for blurring rather than MakeEffectMovie. After all, using QuickTime Pro forces you to set a filter during export—a filter that you must remember to remove later. In contrast, MakeEffectMovie allows you to set a blur with fewer steps, and you don't have to worry about leaving the filter turned on.

The answer is this. MakeEffectMovie doesn't seem to work consistently when applying an effect to an effect movie. Because this project requires a series of blurs, you can better rely on QuickTime Pro to get the job done.

Other Lens Shapes

Although I use a rectangular lens in this exercise, do not feel that you must limit yourself to the same shape. Experiment with other geometries. You may want to use round or oval lenses, or even create a matched twosome of circles to emulate a pair of glasses. Keep your framing edges small with respect to the main lens area so the frame doesn't overwhelm the video. Otherwise, be creative and add framing elements that augment the lens illusion.

The Moving "Lens"

In these steps you'll build a moving lens that seems to focus the video beneath it. Here, you'll use two copies of your video—one blurred, one not—and an animated mask.

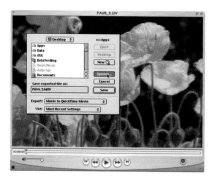

1. Start by blurring your video as follows. Open it in QuickTime Pro. Select File ▷ Export (⌘-E), and choose Export To QuickTime Movie. Click the Options button on the Export dialog to open the movie settings window.

2. Click the Filter button on the Movie Settings window. (This button will not appear unless you chose to export to a QuickTime movie in Step 1.)

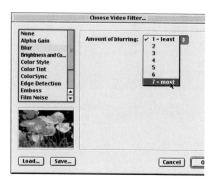

3. Choose Blur from the list of filters offered. Select level 7, the most blurring, from the pull-down menu on the right. Click OK to set the filter and then OK to close the settings window. Enter a file name, and click the Save button to finish.

4. Close your movie and open the blurred version. Repeat Steps 1–3 and save. Then open the re-blurred version and repeat another two or three times until your video is pretty blurry.

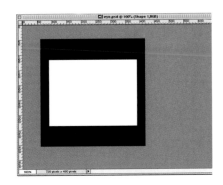

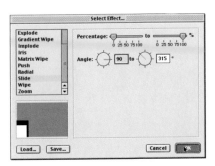

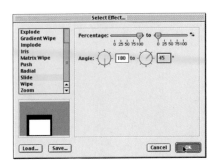

5. Create a new QuickTime-sized image in Photoshop Elements. Draw a black rectangle with a smaller, white, rectangular insert. Fill in the rest of the image with a solid red color for later masking. Save this to disk as a .psd file. Also save a plain solid-red image—you'll need this for MakeEffectMovie.

6. Launch MakeEffectMovie. Press ⌘-2, ⌘-1. Open your solid red image first, then your lens image. Here, I use the Slide transition to add a loose, loopy slide to my mask: Select Slide from the list; set the first angle to 90 degrees and the second to 315. Click OK and save your movie to disk as slide1.mov.

7. Remaining in MakeEffectMovie, press ⌘-2, ⌘-1. Choose your lens image, click Open, then choose the solid red image, click Open. Again select Slide. Set the first angle to 180, the second to 45. Drag the first percentage slider to 100 and the second to 0. Click OK. Save as slide2.mov.

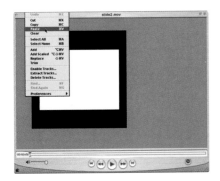

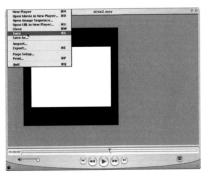

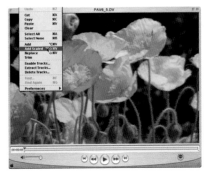

8. In QuickTime Pro, open slide1.mov and slide2.mov. Select the entire video of slide1.mov (⌘-A), copy (⌘-C), and close (⌘-W). Move the playhead, in slide2.mov, to the far left of the scrubber bar. Select Edit ▷ Paste (⌘-V). Doing so adds the first half of your animation in front of the second, creating a continuous moving lens.

9. Save this full animation to disk. Then select all (⌘-A), copy (⌘-C), and close the animation (⌘-W).

10. In QuickTime Pro, open your original, in-focus movie. Select All (⌘-A) and add the mask scaled (Edit ▷ Add Scaled, Option-Shift-⌘-V).

continues on next page

Focus.mov, eyepkg.sea

No Alpha?

This project uses solid colors—white inside the lens, red outside. You might wonder whether you could use transparency and alpha channels instead. In fact, you could skip the white center and use a transparent center for your first set of overlays. When you merge the in-focus movie with your lens, it doesn't matter whether you do so with a transparent color or an alpha channel. You cannot, however, use such a trick for the outside of the lens. You need a solid color to use for the second masking.

To create the first merged video, you export it. Whenever you export rather than save, you not only create a single track from many, but you also lose any alpha-channel information associated with those tracks in the exported results. Instead, you must use a solid color to ensure that you create a mask that supports the transparent color option.

The Moving "Lens" *continued*

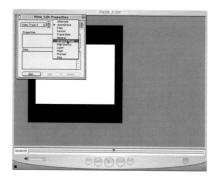

11. Open the Movie Properties window (⌘-J). Select Video Track 4 from the left pull-down menu and Graphics Mode from the right.

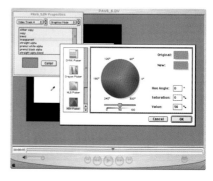

12. Choose Transparent, click the Color button, and Option-click to sample the white color from the center of your lens.

13. Export your work out to withlens.mov, a fresh QuickTime movie, using the highest quality settings. This merges your in-focus footage with the moving lens, producing a single track that you can reuse with transparency.

14. Open withlens.mov. Select all (⌘-A), copy (⌘-C), and close (⌘-W). Open your blurred movie, select all (⌘-A), and add (Edit ▷ Add, Option-⌘-V). Blurring does not change the length of your movie, so both the blurred and lens footage should remain the same length.

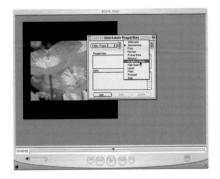

15. Open the Movie Properties window (⌘-J); select Video Track 2 from the left pull-down menu and Graphics Mode from the right.

16. Choose Transparent, click Color, and use the eyedropper tool (Option-click) to sample the red color that surrounds your lens. Click OK.

17. Choosing your transparent color reveals the blurred movie outside your lens. Play the movie and test to see that everything works as expected.

18. Export your work to disk (⌘-E). If you wish to save to a QuickTime movie, take special care that you've unselected the blur filter. To check, click Options; if you see Filter: Blur listed, click Filter and select None before saving.

Variations on a Theme

You can use this moving-lens effect in many other ways—don't limit yourself to in-and-out-of-focus. Consider these variations:

Moving Ellipse Revisit the ellipse-of-light project (☞ Chapter 4) with a moving version that travels over your video.

X-Ray Add a moving "X-ray" effect with the Color Tint ▷ Black & White filter.

Color in a Colorless World Let your lens add color into a black-and-white rendition of your movie.

The Han Solo Effect QuickTime Pro's Emboss effect creates an eerie look, as if the contents were embedded in metal. Use a moving eye to look through the "metal" to the true colors beneath.

Rose Colored Glasses Take a look through a pair of tinted "lenses" to a rose-hued world. Use Color Tint ▷ Other and add a light pink overlay to your video.

Fast and Fabulous

When you combine animation with transparency, you can easily build some dazzling effects. In this section, you'll see just a sampling of the styles and effects available to you with MakeEffectMovie and QuickTime Pro. Here, you'll learn how to fly stripes around your movie, explode a duck, and create a series of zooming still overlays. And, while the examples are specific, the methods are not. Reuse these techniques in your own projects with your own subject matter to create your own fabulous iMovies.

Note: This project is actually a tribute to one of my favorite BBC America programs, "Monarch of the Glen." If you receive this show on your television, make sure to watch the opening sequence. You can reproduce nearly every effect used in QuickTime Pro.

Flying Stripes

In these steps, you'll learn how to design and animate a series of flying stripes that overlay your movie.

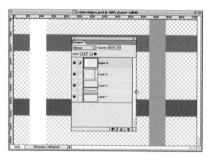

1. In Photoshop Elements, I design stripes that I'll use to overlay my images. Although you should design them together, save these into separate QuickTime-sized .psd files, using a transparent background for each one. Also save a completely empty transparent image of the same size as well.

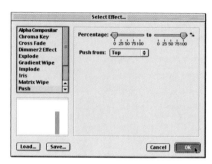

2. To animate the first stripe, open MakeEffectMovie; type ⌘-2, ⌘-1. Open the stripe file and then the blank file. Choose Push, a direction, click OK, and save the file to a helpfully numbered name—e.g., yellowstripe1.mov. Repeat, but select the blank file first and then the stripe file. Push the *same* direction and save to yellowstripe2.mov.

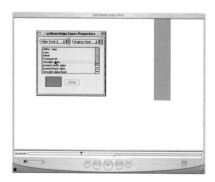

3. Open the first file in QuickTime. Select all (⌘-A), copy (⌘-C), and close (⌘-W) the movie. Then open the second of the pair. Move the playhead to the very end of the movie and paste (⌘-V). Open the Movie Properties window (⌘-J). Select Video Track 3 and Graphics Mode from the pull-downs; choose Straight Alpha, close the window, and save.

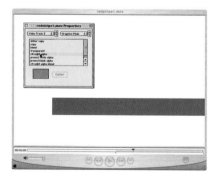

4. Now, to build more stripes, repeat Steps 2 and 3 as many times as you like, picking a different stripe/direction combination each time.

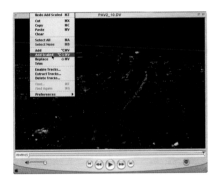 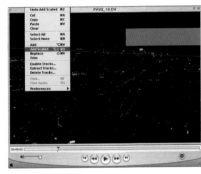

5. After creating your moving stripes, open your base video in QuickTime. We will now add each stripe one at a time. Open your first stripe movie, select all (⌘-A), copy (⌘-C), and close the stripe movie (⌘-W). Select your entire base movie (⌘-A), and add the stripe scaled (Edit ▷ Add Scaled or Option-Shift-⌘-V).

6. Move the left crop marker a bit to the right to set the stripe's entrance. Open up your next stripe. As before, copy the entire track, close the movie, and Add Scaled to the base movie. Notice that by moving only the left crop marker, all your stripes will finish at the same time, producing an elegant, coordinated ending.

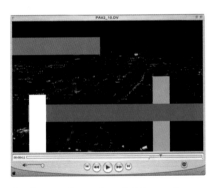 

7. Repeat Steps 5 and 6 for each stripe, moving the left crop marker more for each additional stripe so that each stripe begins at a later time than the last one.

8. After adding all your stripes, play the movie back to test that you're satisfied with the overall flow. Export your movie to a DV Stream (for iMovie) or to a QuickTime movie for further work.

MakeEffectMovie and Alpha

One of MakeEffectMovie's best features is that it preserves any transparent parts of an image. It doesn't alter alpha channels when you combine stills from Photoshop Elements. (Alpha channels store transparency information in a image file.) By using Photoshop Element's alpha channels, you avoid the "pick the transparent color" step. You can also preset your graphics modes in the movies that MakeEffectMovie creates. Just select Straight Alpha for Video Track 3 and save your movie. Your overlay will be ready to copy and use with preset graphics-mode-enabled stripes.

JPEG 2000

Although not yet supported by either QuickTime Pro or Photoshop Elements, JPEG 2000 promises to revolutionize transparency. Combining great compression features with transparency channels, JPEG 2000 offers a great alternative to cumbersome and large .psd images. With luck, you'll be seeing this file format supported in QuickTime Pro 6 and Photoshop Elements 2, although it might take slightly longer than that. The excitement surrounding JPEG 2000 with its expanded feature set continues to grow.

 FlyStripes.mov, ColorStripes.psd, ColorStripes-PAL.psd

Creating the On-Time Appearance

You can easily create a duck that appears immediately rather than one that shows up about halfway through your movie. The secret lies in using just part of your explode-duck movie track. Instead of selecting the entire video (as you do in Step 5), move the playhead along the scrubber bar until the duck just starts to appear. Select from this point to the end and copy. Continue with Step 6, as detailed here. In your final movie, the duck will explode from the very start.

Use this trick whenever you work with animated elements. Don't just select and copy. Instead, inspect the effect movie first. Identify the interesting portions and select just those rather than the whole movie. In some videos, you may want to cut down even further, selecting only a sub-portion of the object animation.

The ÜberDuck

Follow these steps to explode a duck with MakeEffectMovie's implode effect.

1. Design your duck and a title as two separate files in Photoshop Elements. Use a full QuickTime-sized image for each (720x480 NTSC, 720x576 PAL). Save these to disk in .psd format. Also create and save a blank, transparent image of the same size.

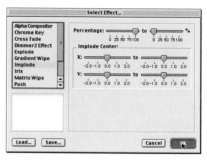

2. Create the exploding duck effect movie as follows: Launch MakeEffectMovie. Type ⌘-2, ⌘-1. Select your duck, click Open; select the blank, click Open. Choose Implode from the effects list. Move the percentage sliders so the first reads 100% and the second 0%. Click OK.

3. Save the effect movie as explodeduck.mov.

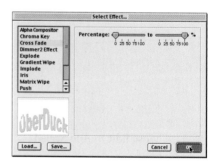

4. Remaining in MakeEffectMovie, type ⌘-2, ⌘-1. This time, select the blank image, click Open then select your title, click Open. Choose Cross Fade from the effects list. Click OK. Save this second effect movie as titleuber.mov.

5. In QuickTime Pro, open explode-duck.mov. Select all (⌘-A), copy (⌘-C), and close the file (⌘-W). QuickTime Pro copies the entire effect movie, including all tracks, to the Clipboard.

6. Open your base video. Select all (⌘-A) and choose Edit ▷ Add Scaled (Option-Shift-⌘-V). QuickTime scales your effect movie over the base video.

7. Open titleuber.mov. Again, select all (⌘-A), copy (⌘-C), and close (⌘-W).

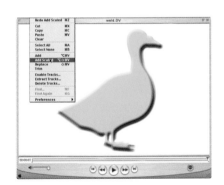

8. Return to your base video. Everything should still be selected, but if not, choose Edit ▷ Select All (⌘-A). Choose Edit ▷ Add Scaled (Option-Shift-⌘-V) to scale your title video over both the base video and the exploding duck track.

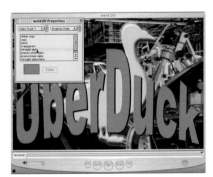

9. Open the Movie Properties window (⌘-J). Select Video Track 4 from the left pull-down menu and Graphics Mode from the right. Choose Straight Alpha. Select Video Track 7 from the left pull-down menu and again choose Straight Alpha.

10. Test your video to make sure that it works as expected, then export to disk.

uber.mov, uberpkg.sea

Shapes vs. Pictures

Although the example here demonstrates this animated effect using drawn shapes, there's no reason you cannot use real pictures instead. The zoom-within-zoom effect provides a great way to combine digital photos into a sequence and incorporate them into a video. And although photos do not offer the convenience of transparency (as these shapes do), you can easily resize your animated sequence down to produce a live-action border around your images.

Pay Attention to Detail

The most tedious part of this effect involves assembling your movies and stills together to create a complete effect movie. To do so, you'll need to paste a number of files in order in Step 5. *Make sure you follow the sequence exactly.* Miss a file or change the order, and your animation will not work correctly. In each case, the image graphic goes before its movie version.

Fruit of the Zooms

One fruit exploding out of another can create a visual punch. Follow these steps to create a series of zooms, overlaying your video.

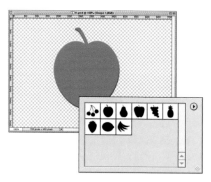

1. In Photoshop Elements, design a series of multicolored fruits. Use the built-in shape tools, such as this cherry. Save each image in its own file: f1.psd, f2.psd, and so forth. For this example, I've created five. For each pair of fruits, you'll make an effect movie where the second fruit zooms out of the first.

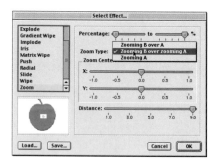

2. Launch MakeEffectMovie. Select ⌘-2, ⌘-1. First open f1.psd, then f2.psd. Choose Zoom from the list of effects. Select Zooming B Over Zooming A from the Zoom Type pull-down menu. Move the distance slider all the way to the right (9.0). Click OK.

3. Save to a new effect movie. Here, save to mf1.mov. (As you make the remaining fruit movies, number them consecutively.)

4. Repeat Steps 2 and 3, choosing the next pair of fruits, until you have made all your effect movies. Don't forget to close the "circle" from the last image back to the first—for five fruits, you'll make five movies: f1/f2, f2/f3, f3/f4, f4/f5, and f5/f1.

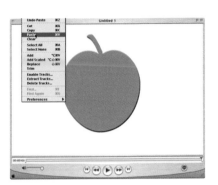

5. Create a new movie in QuickTime Pro. Paste the following files in order: f1.psd, mf1.mov, f2.psd, mf2.mov, f3.psd, mf3mov, f4.psd, mf4.mov, f5.psd, mf5.mov, f1.psd.

6. In turn, open each file, select all (⌘-A), copy (⌘-C), close (⌘-W), and paste into your new movie (⌘-V). Do this in the order shown in Step 5. After each paste, the playhead advances to the new end of the movie. Make sure not to touch the playhead between each paste.

7. When you've finished assembling your animation, save it to disk. Save normally (with dependencies).

8. Select your entire animation (⌘-A), copy it (⌘-C), and close it (⌘-W). As you've saved your work, you can easily return to this movie if needed.

9. Open your base video. Select the entire track (⌘-A), and scale your copied animation over it (Edit ▷ Add Scaled, Option-Shift-⌘-V).

10. Open the Movie Properties window (⌘-J). Select Video Track 2 and Graphics Mode from the pull-downs; choose Straight Alpha. Select the next video track, Video Track 3, and again choose Straight Alpha. Continue until you've selected Straight Alpha for every video track *except* Video Track 1. Test the movie and then export to disk.

fruits.psd, fruits-PAL.psd, fruitzoom.mov

Other Animation Tools

Although MakeEffectMovie offers an easy way to create animations for your videos, you can use many other programs and approaches to develop animated material. Any number of software titles spring to mind—Adobe After Effects, Macromedia Director, Macromedia Flash, Adobe Live Motion, and so forth. The key lies in portability. If you can export to a video format that QuickTime can read, then you can export from QuickTime to DV format. This allows you to use animated sequences from these terrific tools in iMovie.

Overlap Your Feet

The key to this effect lies in overlapping your overlay placement in the timeline, to provide visual continuity from one to the next. In this project, each new foot appears before the previous foot disappears. This allows your eye to track from one foot to the next and better allows the animation to proceed.

Moving Feet

Follow these steps to create an animated series of footprints that walk across your video. The key to this effect lies in overlapping your overlay placement in the timeline, to provide visual continuity from one to the next.

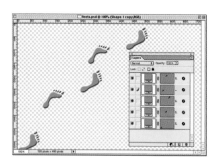

1.   Create your overlays in Photoshop Elements, storing each one in a separate layer. Adjust as desired, then save each layer to a separate file. Here, I saved each one to f1.psd, f2.psd, etc.

2.   Determine how long each overlay element should appear. For this example, I want each foot to linger for about ½ second and overlap with the next foot for about ¼ second. Open your base video. Select ½ second's worth of video, a bit after the beginning. Place the playhead at about one second in, for reference.

3.   Open the first overlay in QuickTime Pro, select all (⌘-A), copy it (⌘-C), and close the overlay (⌘-W).

4.   Add the overlay onto the selected frames with Edit ▷ Add Scaled (Option-Shift-⌘-V). The playhead will jump to the end of the added selection.

Sounds

Although your movie will work fine as-is, I found it useful to add small footstep sounds to each print as it appears. Often when working this kind of discontinuous animation, it helps to add sound effects to delineate the appearance of each overlay. Small sounds work best. Avoid sounds that last too long or that overwhelm your main soundtrack. Be subtle, and you'll be rewarded by better movies.

Note: You'll find a great collection of royalty-free sounds at www.alcljudprod.se/eng/huvudsida_a_e.html. ALC designed these sounds over the last 15 years of film production and now offers them free of charge for personal use.

5. Without touching the playhead, move the right crop marker to ½ second to the right of the playhead and the left crop marker about ¼ second to the left of the playhead.

6. Open the second overlay in QuickTime Pro, select all (⌘-A), copy it (⌘-C), close it (⌘-W), and add it (scaled) over the selected frames (Option-Shift-⌘-V). Again, the playhead jumps to the end of the added selection.

7. Repeat Steps 3–6 for each of the remaining feet. When all the overlays are Added in, open the Movie Properties window (⌘-J). For each video track except Video Track 1, set the Graphics Mode to Straight Alpha.

8. Play back your movie to see that everything works as desired. Then export to disk (⌘-E).

footsteps.mov, feets.psd, feets-PAL.psd

6 Titles

Make the Most of iMovie Titling

One hears the complaints again and again: iMovie titles are weak… limited… small… ugly. Don't let those negative voices dissuade you from editing your videos in iMovie! There's a lot more you can do with iMovie titles than you might first think. In this chapter, you'll see how to create larger, bolder, and more interesting titles and discover how to add special effects and artistic title presentations. Let these projects inspire you to build your own titles with better iMovie text effects.

Big Text

Manipulate Titles

Artistic Titles

QuickTime Title Tricks

Big Text

At times, the biggest iMovie titles can seem pretty small. You drag the font size slider as high as it goes and still feel cheated by the results. Your text looks tiny, and it's hard to read, even on a big television screen.

Don't settle for small titles in your iMovies. In this section, you'll learn how to ramp up the size and pump up your text. You'll use both built-in iMovie features and external programs to build the results you need. These techniques will allow you to create the title size you're looking for, as big as you want. You'll design the title that best works with your movie—not just the titles that the Titles palette allows you to create.

Note: Watch out for the extra frame! Experience shows that iMovie often adds an extra frame to Zoom's introductory animation. In this project, Step 3 uses 11 frames rather than 10 to take this into account.

The Zoom Trick

In these steps, you'll use and then edit the Zoom title style to add a large-sized title to your iMovie clip. Use this trick to replace your too-small Centered Title–style with a title that uses much larger text.

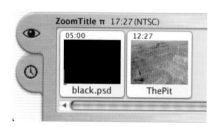

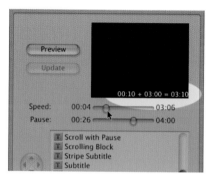

1. In iMovie, import a plain, black still clip and place it in front of your clip in the Clip Viewer. NTSC users can import black.psd from the companion CD. PAL users should import black-PAL instead.

2. Select the Zoom title style in the Titles palette. Zoom offers two controls, Speed and Pause. As you move either slider, watch the black preview area. The first number corresponds to the Speed slider, the second to Pause. Set the Speed to 10 frames, as shown here. Set Pause to the title length desired—this example uses 3 seconds.

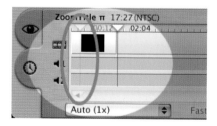

3. Click the clock icon on the Timeline to switch from the Clip Viewer display. Move the playhead to frame 12. You're about to add space for the first 10 frames of your Zoom (the Speed you set in Step 2) plus another frame for good measure—a total of 11 frames.

4. Drag your clip to the left. As you do so, your black still shrinks. Allow the playhead to snap to the ghosted playhead at frame 12 to set your still length exactly.

Over Black

Selecting Over Black in the Titles palette creates a large-sized title on a black background. Simply drag your Zoom-style title to the Timeline or Clip Viewer. Wait for iMovie to render the frames and then edit away the first few frames. (These frames contain the zooming animation.) Removing them leaves a simple title over a plain, black background. If you want your title to fade in as well as out, add a cross-fade to the start with a black still clip.

5. Use the same options you selected in Step 2 when choosing your font and title text in the Titles palette. Adjust the Text Size slider. The preview window in the palette offers an excellent idea of how your title will fit on the screen.

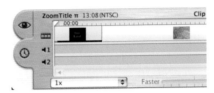

6. Drag the Zoom title in front of the black still on your Timeline. Wait as iMovie builds your title. If you've set things up correctly, iMovie will add the smaller, introductory portions of your Zoom onto the black still, leaving just the full-sized title on your actual clip.

The Built-in Black Clip

The curious will be happy to know that you can use iMovie's "secret" built-in black clip to perform the effects described in this project. To find the secret clip, select any clip in the Timeline without a still or a transition to its left. Drag that clip to the right; iMovie adds the black still to the left as you drag. Read more about iMovie's black clip in Intermingle Stills, Chapter 2.

Note: Meet the Titles! You can view all the iMovie title types in action. Watch TitleGallery.mov on the accompanying CD.

7. Select your new Title clip. In the Monitor, use the crop markers to select those frames with a black background. (If needed, drag the cursor under the scrubber bar to make the crop markers appear.)

8. Select Edit ▷ Clear (or press Delete) to remove these unwanted introductory frames. Your title should appear full-sized, starting with the first frame of your clip, and last for the time specified in Step 2 before fading away.

BigTitle.mov, black.psd, black-PAL.psd

Easy Title Shadows

Photoshop Elements makes it easy to create a title shadow like the one seen in this project.

First, copy your title layer—just drag it down to the "page" New Layer icon at the bottom of the Layers palette. Choose this new layer, select the text within it, and change the color to black. Use the color swatch in the Options bar to change colors, rather than the swatches in the Tools palette.

Next, fuzz your title with these steps: Choose Layer ▷ Simplify Layer, then Filter ▷ Blur ▷ Gaussian Blur. Enter a small number, such as 4 pixels, and click OK. This blurs your title to create a more realistic shadow.

Choose the move tool (V). Press the Down arrow key five times, then press the Right arrow key five times. This offsets your title by five pixels in each direction, creating a more realistic shadow effect.

To finish, drag your shadow layer into place, under your title layer.

Big Photoshop Elements Titles

Photoshop Elements offers a quick and easy way to add titles to your iMovies. In these steps, you'll discover how to create images that work well with iMovie transitions to produce the large titles you want.

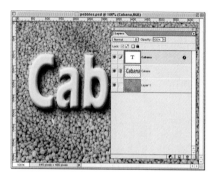

1. In Photoshop Elements, design your iMovie-sized title. Here, you see a title created with three layers—a base layer, a title layer, and a shadow layer. Save this image to disk, but do not close it. After saving, hide the title and optional shadow layers. Save a copy of the background-only image.

2. In iMovie, choose Edit ▷ Preferences (iMovie Preferences in OS X) and set your default still length to 5 seconds. Import your background and title images, and drag the newly imported images down to your Clip Viewer. Place the background still to the left of the title.

3. Select the background still. While holding the Option key, drag to the right of the title still. This creates a copy of your background on the right side of the title still.

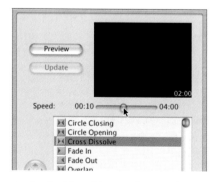

4. In the Transitions palette, select Cross Dissolve. Set the Speed to 2 seconds. Drag this transition between the first and second stills on your Clip Viewer. Repeat to add this transition between the second and third stills. Wait for iMovie to finish rendering.

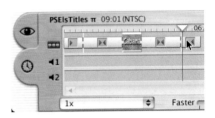

5. Return to the Transitions palette. Select Fade In. Move the Speed slider to 1 second, and drag this transition in front of the first still. Then select Fade Out, leaving the speed at 1 second; drag this transition after the last still. Again, wait for iMovie to render your transitions.

6. Click the clock icon to switch from the Clip Viewer to the Timeline. Select the first two-way transition (the Cross Dissolve), just after the first still clip. Drag this transition to the left, collapsing the still clip completely.

7. Select the final one-way transition (the Fade Out) and repeat the drag to the left. Completely collapse the third still clip.

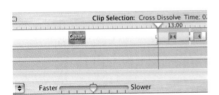

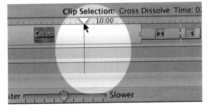

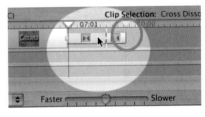

8. Drag the second of the two-way transitions (Cross Dissolve) to the right. Lengthen the still clip by a good bit.

9. Decide how long you want your title to last. Move the playhead to that time. Here, I set the playhead at 10 seconds.

10. Select the second two-way transition from Step 8 and drag it back to the left. Carefully watch the final transition. Use the ghosted playhead to exactly position the end of this transition at the 10-second mark. Save your work to disk.

PshopTitle.mov

Control the Pause

When you create a title in iMovie, you control both the overall speed of the title—how quickly it appears and disappears—as well as the pause time. When you bypass iMovie to add titles in QuickTime Pro, you must spend more time and effort to control this pause.

The way I structured this project allows you to adjust your speed pretty easily. In Step 4, you create title2.mov, an effect movie with an unchanging title. You can create a longer pause in Step 6 by duplicating this movie. Instead of adding one copy of title2.mov, add two or more. The more copies you add, the longer the pause will be with respect to the time allocated to the entrance and exit of your title.

Each copy lengthens your pause but cuts back the relative speed of the title entrance and exit. Edit ▷ Add Scaled instructs QuickTime Pro to stretch your movie over a selected area. With the steps shown in this project, the introduction, pause, and exit each last for one third of the time. When you add three copies of the title, the introduction and exit each last for one fifth of the selected time; the title lasts for three fifths. Choose your repetitions with care so that your entire effect works exactly as you wish.

Large QuickTime Titles

With QuickTime Pro and MakeEffectMovie, you can add large, funky titles to your iMovies. In these steps, you'll create an animated title and lay it over your footage.

1. In Photoshop Elements, create a new, transparent, RGB image using QuickTime sizing (720x480 NTSC, 720x576, PAL). Design your title over a blank background and save it to disk as a .psd file. Also save a full-sized completely blank image.

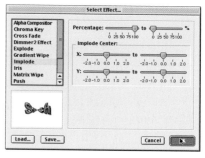

2. Launch MakeEffectMovie. Press ⌘-2, ⌘-1. First open your title, then open the blank image. Choose Implode from the list of effects. Set your first percentage slider to 100 and your second to 0. Click OK and save to title1.mov. Your movie will contain a sequence in which your title explodes (reverse-implodes) onto the screen.

3. Remaining in MakeEffectMovie, press ⌘-1. Select your title and click Open. Select your blank image and click Open. Choose Cross Fade, click OK, and save to title3.mov This creates an effect movie where your title fades away.

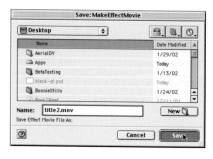

4. In MakeEffectMovie, press ⌘-1. Select your title and click Open. Select the same title again and Open. Choose Cross Fade and click OK; save as title2.mov. This extra step allows you to create a three-track video of your title, to create a pause in your animation. This three-track effect movie will blend perfectly into the surrounding movies.

5. In QuickTime Pro, open all three title movies and create a new, blank movie.

6. Bring title1.mov to the front. Select it (⌘-A), copy (⌘-C), and close it (⌘-W). Paste this into your new movie (⌘-V). Leave the playhead at the end of the new movie. Bring title2.mov to the front. Select all, copy, and close, and again, paste this into your new movie. Repeat for title3.mov, adding it after title2.mov.

7. After adding all three segments to your new movie, choose File ▷ Save As and save to disk. Make sure to select Make Movie Self-Contained. This saves a complete copy of your title animation in a reusable form.

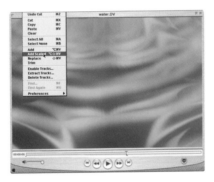

8. Select your entire effect movie (⌘-A), copy it (⌘-C), and close (⌘-W). This copies the entire effect—including all three subeffects—to the Clipboard.

9. In QuickTime, open your base movie. Use the crop markers to select the part of your movie where you wish to add your title. This may include all or just part of your video. Choose Edit ▷ Add Scaled (Option-Shift-⌘-V) to scale your animation over these frames.

10. Move the playhead backward, into the gray selected area, so you can see your overlaid title. Open the Movie Properties window (⌘-J). Select Video Track 4 from the left pull-down menu and Graphics Mode from the right. Choose Straight Alpha. Test your movie to see that it works as expected and then save or export your work to disk.

Snurch.mov, Snurch.psd, Snurch-PAL.psd

Manipulate Titles

Did you know that you could edit footage *after* applying a title? Treat title clips just like any others. You can split them, trim them, create still clips, add further titles, and so forth. These next few tricks produce some great results. By applying a title and then modifying the results, you alter the way the title flows and introduce new points of interest.

In this section, you'll learn how to adapt the Drifting and Scrolling Block titles to add extra dash of style. You'll see how layer effects over title clips to add extra pizzazz. You'll also discover how layering titles can produce results that defy linear layout. These are just a few examples out of a realm of possibility. Go beyond these projects and use the title-manipulation technique to create better and more interesting titles of your own.

A Paused Drift

In these steps, you'll add a pause to iMovie's Drifting title to create a title that hesitates while it introduces.

1. In iMovie, select Edit ▷ Preferences (OS X: iMovie ▷ Preferences). Set your still length to 10 seconds; click OK. Import a still image and drag it to the Timeline. This effect does not work over moving footage. (You can use Over Black; the effect works just as well on a black background as over a still image.)

2. In the Titles palette, select Drifting. Set the speed to 8 seconds. Choose a color, a font, and enter your text. Make sure you have deselected Over Black when adding your title over a still clip. Your still length deliberately exceeds the title length to allow for the stray frame or two that often crops up in iMovie.

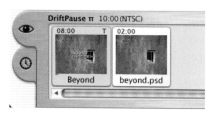

3. Drag your title down to the Timeline and place it in front of your clip. Wait as iMovie renders the title. The small red bar monitors the progress and offers an indication of how far your title has progressed.

4. Click the Eye icon to choose the Clip Viewer. Select the title clip, which is marked with a *T*. It should be the first clip within your Clip Viewer.

5. Select Edit ▷ Preferences (iMovie ▷ Preferences in OS X). Set your still length to 2 seconds and click OK.

6. Turn your attention to the Monitor. Move the playhead along the scrubber bar to find the brightest moment of your title. If you've used the settings outlined in these steps, this should occur at exactly 4 seconds, as shown here.

7. Select Edit ▷ Split Video Clip At Playhead (⌘-T). iMovie splits your footage into two 4-second clips.

8. Without moving the playhead, now select Edit ▷ Create Still Clip (Shift-⌘-S). A still clip of this frame appears in your clips shelf.

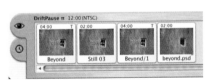

9. Drag the newly created still clip between the first and second portions of your title. This still adds the pause to your title drift.

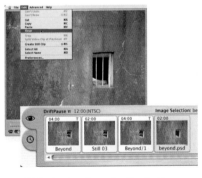

10. If desired, select the final clip—the remaining portion of your original still—and discard it (Edit ▷ Clear). Test to see that your movie works as expected, then save to disk.

 DriftPause.mov

Scrolling Capitals

iMovie only allows you to select one font in its Titles palette. This may be a problem when you use scrolling title effects. Often you want to differentiate some parts of your title from others. One obvious way to accomplish this is to alternate uppercase title elements with mixed case. Another, sneakier way to approach this problem involves using the Capitals font. This font offers two sizes of text based on whether the Shift key is used or not. Select the Capitals font and enter your text, using uppercase for main titles and lowercase for secondary titles. To see this effect in action, watch scrollcaps.mov on the accompanying CD.

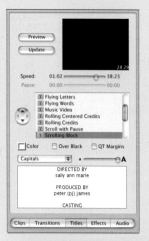

A Tumbling Scroll

In these steps, you create a title that pauses to tumble mid-scroll. To add some finishing touches, you'll export your work to QuickTime Pro, add a themed overlay, and return to iMovie.

1. In iMovie, select the Titles palette. Choose Scrolling Block and enter your text block. Here, the Courier font gives the feel of an old-fashioned computer terminal, and a bright green reinforces this imagery. Choose Over Black, adjust the font-size slider to its largest setting and set the speed to about 10 seconds.

2. Drag your title down to the Clip Viewer and wait for it to render.

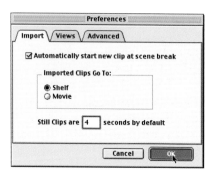

3. Choose Edit ▷ Preferences (iMovie ▷ Preferences in OS X). Set your default still length to 4 seconds and click OK.

4. Select your new title clip. In the Monitor, move the playhead. Locate the position where your text block looks pretty-much centered in the screen. You do not need to select this position precisely. All this project needs is a good estimate.

5. Split your clip at this near-center point (Edit ▷ Split Video Clip At Playhead, ⌘-T) and create a still of this frame (Edit ▷ Create Still Clip, Shift-⌘-S).

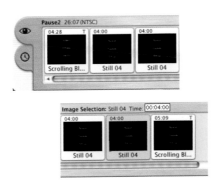

6. Holding the Option key down, drag your new still clip from the clips shelf to the Clip Viewer. Place it between the first and second portions of your title clip. Repeat to add three more copies of your still. After doing so, you should have added a total of four still clips between your titles.

7. In the Transitions palette, select GeeThree's Rotate Out & In (www.geethree.com). Choose the Up direction from the circle on the palette. If you do not own the GeeThree transitions, choose Push and use the Right direction, instead. Set your speed to 3 seconds.

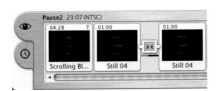

8. Drag your transition between the first and second stills.

9. Return to the Transitions palette. Set your direction to Left, leaving all the other options as they are.

10. Drag this transition into place between the third and fourth stills. Wait for iMovie to finish rendering.

continues on next page

tumblescroll.mov, mollyoverlay.psd, mollyoverlay-PAL.psd, scrollcaps.mov

Drag a CD Track

Did you know that you could simply drag a track from your CD to the iMovie Timeline? You can. Select the Audio palette, insert your CD into the Macintosh, and wait for the tracks to load. To preview a track, select it and click the Play button.

When you find the track you want, drag the purple track icon down to your Timeline. iMovie will import, convert, and add the track to your movie.

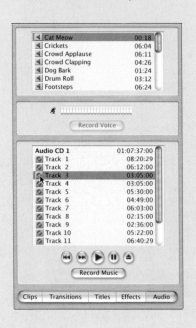

A Tumbling Scroll *continued*

11. Press the clock icon to switch from the Clip Viewer to the Timeline. Drag your third still clip to the left, completely collapsing your second still. Repeat with the second title clip to collapse your fourth still. Next, drag both transitions to fully collapse the remaining two stills.

12. Select File ▷ Export (⌘-E). Choose Export To QuickTime and select Full Quality, Large from the list of Formats. Click Export and save to ScrollTitle.mov.

13. In Photoshop Elements, design a full-sized QuickTime overlay (720x480 NTSC, 720x576 PAL) that matches the old-time computer motif (or use the one I've provided on the companion CD). Leave the center of your image blank. Save your image to disk.

14. In QuickTime Pro, open your overlay. Select all (⌘-A), copy (⌘-C), and close the overlay window (⌘-W). QuickTime Pro copies your overlay to the Clipboard.

15. Open ScrollTitle.mov in QuickTime Pro. Select the entire movie (⌘-A) and scale your overlay onto every frame of the movie (Edit ▷ Add Scaled, Option-Shift-⌘-V).

16. Open the Movie Properties window (⌘-J). Select Video Track 2 from the left pull-down menu and Graphics Mode from the right. Choose Premul White Alpha and close Movie Properties.

17. Select File ▷ Export (⌘-E) and export your overlaid movie to a DV Stream.

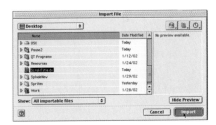

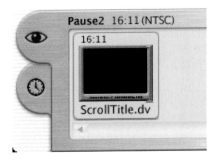

18. Return to iMovie. Select File ▷ Import File (⌘-I). Navigate to your overlaid work, select it, and click Import.

19. Discard the original clips that remains in your Clip Viewer and replace them with the newly imported clip from your clips shelf.

20. Select the Fade In transition. Set the speed to 1 second. Drag it in front of your imported clip. Repeat for the Fade Out transition, dragging it to the right of your imported clip. Wait for your transitions to render. Test your title sequence to ensure that it works as expected, then save your work to disk.

Title Effects

iMovie effects apply a style to a clip, changing the way it appears and plays back. Effects don't just work on video clips; you can apply them to title clips too. A well-chosen effect can turn your iMovie title from blah to wow. With effects, you can change colors or adjust focus, add a mirror effect or a TV "look," and so forth.

Each effect offers a different touch and style. In the next few pages, you'll see how to apply trails and ripples to your iMovie titles. And while these projects are quite specific, you'll learn some techniques that will allow you to expand beyond the specifics into ideas of your own.

Note: iMovie offers a number of built-in effects. You can add more from the Apple Plug-In Pack (**www.apple.com/imovie** for OS X, or **www.apple.com/imovie/macos9** for OS 9.x) and from GeeThree (**www.geethree.com**).

Title Trails

In iMovie's Plug-In Pack, you'll find an effect called Ghost Trails that can add lingering bits to your moving titles. In these steps, you'll apply this effect to your titles to create a snazzy-looking presentation.

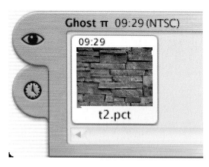

1. In iMovie, move a still image to the Clip Viewer. Select a long still, or expand a still (sidebar). This project won't work over live action footage—the effect in Step 7 affects the footage as well as the titles. Instead, pick a pleasant still as a backdrop or use Over Black to work on a black background.

2. Select the Titles palette. Choose Flying Words. This title style offers a lot of motion and works particularly well with the Ghost Trails effect. Enter your text; select a font, a size, and color. Use a long speed and pause to create more dramatic titles.

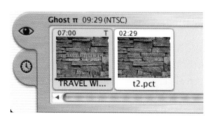

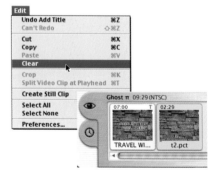

3. Drag your title in front of your still and wait for iMovie to render the frames. Depending on the complexity of your title, this may take a minute or two to complete. The red bar and the red frame count indicator helps you track progress while waiting.

4. After iMovie renders your title, select any remaining portion of your still. Choose Edit ▷ Clear (or press delete) to remove this extra section.

5. Select your title clip, then open the Effects palette. Choose Ghost Trails. This effect adds a trailing visual echo to any motion within your video clip. Because you've added your title over a still, the only portions that will be affected come from the motion of the title animation. Drag the Trail and Opacity sliders all the way to the right to ensure a solid, heavy trail.

6. In the Effects palette, click Preview. Observe the Monitor as iMovie offers a peek of your effect with the current settings. Be aware—this may take a while. Previews tend to run slowly.

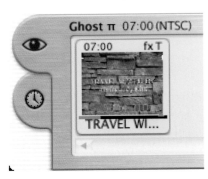

7. Assuming you're satisfied with the preview, click Apply—otherwise, make any needed adjustments. Go get a cup of coffee while iMovie renders your effect.

8. After iMovie finishes your effect, test it. If you're completely satisfied with the result, click Commit and save your work to disk.

Expand a Still

Have you ever imported a still that was a bit too short? Fortunately, iMovie offers a nifty way to expand your still to a more convenient length. With this trick, you can expand your clip to nearly any size needed. Here's how.

1. Drag your still clip to the Clip Viewer (the eye icon).

2. Option-drag the still to the right to create a copy.

3. Press the clock icon to switch to the Timeline view.

4. Drag the copy to the right, lengthening your still.

5. When you're finished resizing, press Delete to remove the copy.

Note: When you select a clip you can set its duration by editing the number at the top of the Clip Viewer or timeline.

traveljudy.mov

Lens Flare

Move beyond ripples and trails. GeeThree's Slick Transitions and Effects Volume 1 (www.geethree.com) offers a Lens Flare effect that looks nifty on a plain black background.

This effect adds a series of colored clouds that waft around your title footage. It doesn't really look like an actual lens flare to me, but it is very pretty. Add the effect to your title clip to create a multicolored band of lights, as you can see in the picture shown here.

To see the effect in action, watch flaremov1.mov. You'll find it on the accompanying CD.

Title Ripples

In these steps, you'll use the Water Ripple effect to make your title undulate as if under water. You'll split and reverse your results to create an effect that introduces your title and then ushers it out.

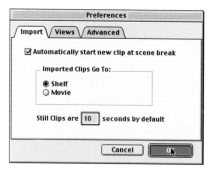

1. In iMovie, select Edit ▷ Preferences (iMovie ▷ Preferences in OS X). Set your default still length to 10 seconds and click OK.

2. Choose the Titles palette. Select Zoom and move the Speed and Pause sliders all the way to the left. Enter your text, select Over Black, and adjust your maximum font size. Drag the title down to the Clip Viewer. Wait for it to render.

3. Select the newly created title. Move the playhead along the slider to find a good, large still of the title at maximum size. Choose Edit ▷ Create Still Clip (Shift-⌘-S). iMovie will create a still of this title and place it in the clips shelf. Discard the remaining Zoom title clip from your Clip Viewer.

4. In the clips shelf, Option-drag your new still clip to create a new copy.

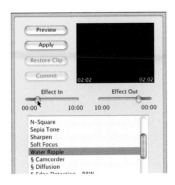

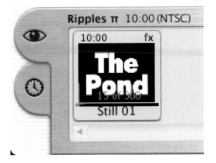

5. Drag the new still clip down to the Clip Viewer. With this clip selected, choose the Effects palette. Select Water Ripple. Set the two sliders to allow the effect to come in and leave approximately 2 seconds from the start and end.

6. Click Apply. iMovie asks if you wish to convert your still clip to a regular clip so it can apply the effect. Click Convert.

7. Wait for iMovie to render your effect. This may take a minute or two.

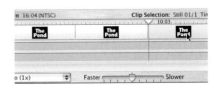

8. After the clip finishes rendering, select your clip. In the Monitor, move the playhead to 5 seconds. Select Edit ▷ Split Video Clip At Playhead (⌘-T). This splits your effect clip in two.

9. Select a clip and choose Advanced ▷ Reverse Clip Direction (⌘-R), then select the other and reverse it. Do not attempt to reverse them both at the same time, as you'll change the order of the clips.

10. Click the clock icon to switch to the Timeline. Drag the clip you created in Step 4 between the two reversed clips. Drag the right clip to squeeze the still clip down to a more manageable size. Play back your movie to test your results, then save your work to disk.

Ripplemov.mov, flaremov1.mov

Artistic Titles

When you build a layered title with Photoshop Elements, you create an image that lends itself to iMovie animation. With layers, you place each visual element in a separate "compartment." This allows you to save different parts of your title to separate files. Extracting pieces in this way offers a convenient opportunity to use iMovie to bring the pieces back together with a dash of transitions and effects.

In this section, you'll use layers to create several title effects, including a title with an exploding glow and a title with a hidden message. You'll learn how to build your source files in Photoshop Elements and then import them into iMovie, where you'll manipulate them to produce your title effect.

Exploding Title

Follow these steps to create a strong visual emphasis behind your title. You'll use a large, blurred version of your title to add a sudden highlight.

1. Design your title in Photoshop Elements. Place your text and background in separate layers. If you include a drop shadow, add a layer for that as well.

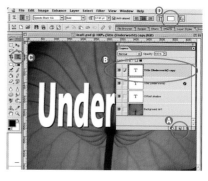

2. Drag your title down to the New Layer icon in the Layers palette (A). Select the copy of the layer (B). Choose the text tool (C), and click the color swatch (D). Choose a bright, contrasting color—here, I use white—from the Color Picker and click OK.

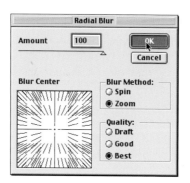

3. Choose Filter ▷ Blur ▷ Radial Blur. Photoshop Elements asks if you want to simplify the layer. Click OK. Choose Zoom, choose Best, and set the Amount slider to 100. Click OK.

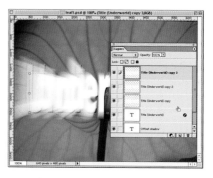

4. After Photoshop Elements renders the blur, copy the blurred layer by dragging it down to the new layer icon in the Layers palette. Repeat to add a second layer. These additional layers reinforce your original blurred layer, making it appear more solid.

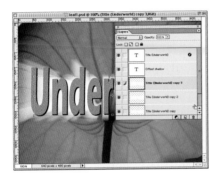

5. Drag the original title and any shadow layer above the blurred images in the Layers palette. You must now save four different images to disk: the background, the title over the background, the blur over the background, and the complete title/blur/background image. Save each to a separate file.

6. In iMovie, set your clip length to 3 seconds each (Edit ▷ Preferences, or iMovie ▷ Preferences in OS X). Import your four images and drag them to the Clip Viewer. Set them in this order: title, title with blur, blur, and background-only.

7. Select Cross Dissolve from the Transitions palette. Set the Speed to between a second and a second and a half. Here, I use 1:10 (one second and ten frames). Drag a copy of this transition between each pair of still clips and wait for iMovie to render.

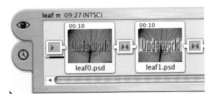

8. Select the Fade In transition and drag it to the left of your first still—use the same timing as in Step 7. Select Fade Out and place it after your last still. Play the movie to make sure it works as expected, then save to disk.

Use More Stills

You can go beyond the simple explode effect shown here by adding more stills to your sequence. In this example, you added all three copies of the radial blur at once. If you wanted to you could have added—and then removed—them one at a time. You can see this extended effect in action on the accompanying CD, fullsplode.mov. Here's some suggestions to keep in mind when varying this effect.

Vary colors Add a number of different colored blurs instead of several copies of a single color.

Vary size Use the Move tool to expand your blurs to create a growing effect of blurs behind your title.

Shorten the transitions and stills The more stills you add to your title sequence, the more compact each transition and still needs to be. Keep your elements short so your animation flows more freely from still to still.

Splode1.mov, SplodeFull.mov, ff.psd

Creating a Glow

To create the glow behind my message that you see in this project, I produced an expanding set of blurred images. This is a simple technique, once you master the trick.

I started by copying my title to a new layer. Then I simplified the layer (Layer ▷ Simplify Layer) and used the magic wand to select it. I filled this selection with white, overwriting the original black color.

Next, I expanded the selection (Selection ▷ Modify ▷ Expand), created a second layer, and filled that copy with yellow. Again, I expanded the selection, created a third layer, and filled it with green.

I applied Filter ▷ Blur ▷ Gaussian Blur to each of these three layers. I used a small blur on the white, a larger blur on the yellow, and a very large blur on the green. To finish, I merged all three layers into a single glowing background.

The Hidden Message

In these steps, you'll create an iMovie sequence that reveals a hidden message within your title.

1. In Photoshop Elements, design your title. Here, I use the words "Gloves & Buttons" to hide the message "Love U". In this design, I placed the letters, the glowing background behind them, and the black background into separate layers. Save a copy of your image to disk as fulltitle.psd, but do not close.

2. Copy the layer, select it, and choose Layer ▷ Simplify Layer. Remove those letters that are part of your message, leaving the rest. Select the original layer and adjust the layer opacity to create an intermediate image. Here, I use 36% opacity. Save a copy of this message image to disk as msg-gray.psd.

3. Hide the semi-opaque original title to fully reveal the background with the glowing message. Again, save a copy to disk, this time as msg-white.psd.

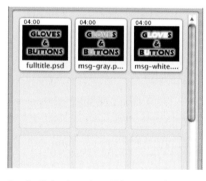

4. In iMovie, select Edit ▷ Preferences (iMovie ▷ Preferences in OS X). Set your default still length to 5 seconds. Select File ▷ Import File and import all three images into iMovie. They will appear on your clips shelf.

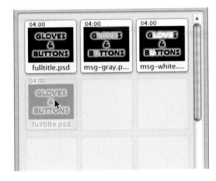

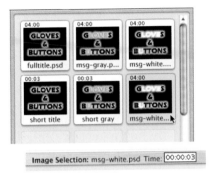

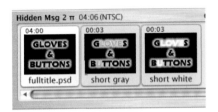

5. Option-drag each of the three stills to create copies of them in the clips shelf.

6. Select the first still copy. In the Clip Viewer or Timeline, edit the still duration, changing it to 3 frames (00:00:03). Repeat to create 3-frame versions of the second and third clips. Rename these three clips to short title, short gray, and short white.

7. Drag your fulltitle still clip to the Clip Viewer, followed by short gray and short white. Select these short second and third clips.

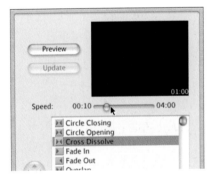

8. Option-drag the selected clips to the right to copy them. Repeat 8 more times to create a total of ten repetitions, or one second's worth.

9. Drag the msg-gray and msg-white into place after the repetitions. The clip sequence will include fulltitle, 10 repetitions of short gray/short white, followed by msg-gray and msg-white.

10. Add a 1-second Cross Dissolve between msg-gray and msg-white, a 1-second Fade In to the start of your movie, and a 1-second Fade Out to the end. Adjust your stills, squeezing them as needed to create the overall flow desired. Save. To accessorize, add electronic hums and buzzes to enhance the illusion as your letters flicker.

HiddenMsg.mov, MsgSrc.sea

Title-over-Title

When iMovie adds a title over part of your movie, it creates a new video clip in your Media folder. This is a perfectly ordinary clip. As you discovered in the last few projects, you can use it just as you would any other—trimming, editing, and even adding further titles. iMovie's ability to add a title over an existing title clip allows you to introduce a variety of interesting text effects.

In the next few demonstrations, you'll use this title-over-title effect to bring a little splash into your movies. You'll see how to layer your titling to create an attention-grabbing presentation. You'll also learn how to use icon-based fonts to build even more creative titles.

Note: Don't forget to turn off Over Black to layer titles over video footage.

Note: In iMovie, the question of "what is a title clip and what is not?" is largely a matter of bookkeeping. Because of this, iMovie does not always reliably add titles onto existing title clips. In this project, you'll import a copy of your title clip, creating a "non-title" clip, before adding your next layer of titling.

Basic Title-on-Title

In these steps, you'll add a series of titles to your movie, each traveling in a different direction.

1. Import your video into iMovie and place your clip on the Clip Viewer.

2. In the Titles palette, select Scroll With Pause. Enter your text and choose a color, a font, and a font size. Set the scroll direction to Left by clicking the small left-arrow. Here, I use a 1-second pause with a 9-second speed to create a slowly travelling title. Enter your text on the top title line.

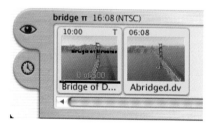 

3. Drag the title down in front of your clip and wait for iMovie to create your new title clip. It marks this clip with a small *T* in the upper-right corner to indicate that a title has been applied. It may take a minute or two for your clip to fully render.

4. Navigate to your project's Media folder and import the clip you created in Step 3 (Scroll With Pause 01) as a new, regular clip, that is not as a title clip.

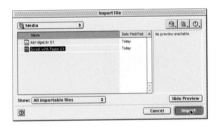

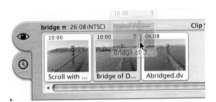

5. To import this clip, select File ▷ Import File. Navigate to the Media folder in your project file. Select Scroll With Pause 01 and click OK. If you've added other titles to your project, the number at the end will vary. As a rule of thumb, the clip with the largest number was added most recently.

6. Drag your new clip down to the Clip Viewer in front of the clip it will replace, and get rid of the original. (As shown here, the cautious will prefer to drag the original title clip away to the clips shelf. The bold will simply delete it.)

7. Select your new clip. In the Monitor, move the playhead to frame 15 (in PAL, select frame 12 or 13 instead). This corresponds to about a half-second. Select Edit ▷ Split Video Clip At Playhead (⌘-T).

8. You're about to add another scrolling title with the same timing used in Step 2. This offset allows both titles to rest for about a half-second together. (This offset is optional—you don't have to offset your overlapping titles.) Return to the Titles palette. Leaving all the other options the same, set the direction of travel to Up. Enter your text on the lower title line.

9. Drag your title into place between the first and second portions of the clip that you split in Step 7. Wait for iMovie to render the new title.

10. Play your movie back to make sure everything works as expected. If you like, add more titles by repeating Steps 5–9. You may want to use the Spaces trick (☞ sidebar on the next page) to position your titles so they may more easily pass each other on the way.

bridge.mov

Off-Center Titles

Sometimes you want to add a title, but there really isn't enough space in the footage. It may overlap or cover important visual elements. Off-center titles can help you overcome this problem. By moving the title to one side or the other, you can better place your text.

There's a trick to off-center titles: the spacebar. When you add spaces before—or after—text, iMovie moves the title, compensating for these extra elements. To move text to the right, add spaces before your text. To move to the left, add them after. iMovie centers the text using the spaces as extra characters.

In the sample shown here, I used the Subtitle title (iMovie Plug-In Pack, **www.apple.com/imovie** or **www.apple.com/imovie/macos9**). Adding twenty spaces before the word *oranges* in the Titles palette proved enough to move the text quite noticeably to the right.

Time Flies

In these steps, you'll use icon fonts to create a title-over-title effect.

1. Select Edit ▷ Preferences (iMovie ▷ Preferences in OS X). Set your default still length to 10 seconds and click OK. Select File ▷ Import (⌘-I). Navigate to your background still and click Import. Drag the new clip to the Clip Viewer.

2. In the Titles palette, select the Zoom title style. Choose the Wingdings font and enter Option-O as your text. This character creates a clock icon (set at nine o'clock). Move the Speed and Pause sliders to their maximum settings. Drag this title into place in front of your background clip and wait for iMovie to render.

3. Select your new title clip. Move the playhead to 2 seconds; this is the approximate time where the clock appears at its full size. Select Edit ▷ Split Video Clip At Playhead (⌘-T).

4. Return to the Titles palette. Select Flying Letters. Add a whole row of Option-O characters (here I use 12 of them) to the second title row. Adjust the Speed and Pause sliders to set your title length to 8 seconds. Choose the Down direction and a color that contrasts with the one used in Step 2.

5. Drag this title to the gap at 2 seconds that you created in Step 3. Wait for iMovie to finish creating your title.

6. In the Titles palette, select Scroll With Pause and a normal font; enter "Time Flies" as your title; place one word in the top space and one in the bottom. Add eight spaces each *after* Time and *before* Flies to offset the words. Experiment with your Speed and Pause until your title lasts exactly 10 seconds.

Beware of Snapz Pro!

Take care when using Snapz Pro with iMovie. Snapz Pro is a terrific package that I used to create all the screenshots in this book. In my opinion, however, it has one major problem. It can actually alter your footage in your iMovies, leaving behind small image flaws like the one shown here.

This embedded icon actually appears in the DV footage in my Media folder. I had to remove three of these, a frame at a time, from the "Time Flies" movie created in these steps. Tech support at Ambrosia Software is currently working on fixing this problem.

7. Set the title direction to Left. Drag your title in front of your first clip on the Clip Viewer. This should combine all your clips back to a single clip of 10 seconds. Wait for iMovie to render your title.

8. In the Transitions palette, select Fade In. Set the Speed to 1 second and drag it in front of your clip. Select Fade Out and drag it to the end of your clip. Again, wait for iMovie to render. Save your work to disk.

timeflies1.mov, scrollcaps.mov

Titles, Transitions, and Art

Transitions can add some real pizzazz to your iMovie titles. They allow you to change a title's look and motion in ways you cannot with simple title styles. In this section, you'll learn how to add a transition or two to fully bring out your title's potential. Some of the snazziest special effects derive from applying one transition over the results of another. In this and following projects, you'll learn how to clean up a messy title, how you can alter a title's direction, and how you can use the transition-over-transition technique to make your titles twist and turn.

Virtix iMovie Plug-ins

Just as this book was finishing up, Virtix (www.virtix.com) introduced two new sets of commercial iMovie plug-ins. The Bravo and Echo plug-in packages are available for $25 each, or $40 for both. Each package includes about twenty transitions and effects, including some exciting motion-based algorithms like the one shown here.

Cleaning Up

GeeThree's (www.geethree.com) Fluid – Drip transition offers a way to clean up an iMovie title. In these steps, you'll create a title "cleaned" by the drip transition.

1. In Photoshop Elements, create a new iMovie-sized image (640x480 NTSC, 768x576 PAL). Fill it with your background color and use the text tool to add a title into a new layer. Save to disk, without closing your work.

2. Select the title layer and open the Layer Styles palette. Choose Complex from the pull-down menu of style families, and click the Pepper style. This style adds a dirty fringe around the edges of your title. Save a copy to disk, so you do not overwrite your clean title image.

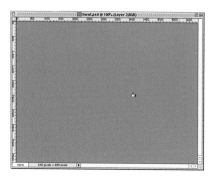

3. Create a new image of the same size and fill it with a light blue color. Save this to disk as well. You will use this still to "wash" your dirty title with "water."

4. In iMovie, import all three stills. (File ▷ Import File, ⌘-I). Drag them down to the timeline in this order: dirty, water, clean.

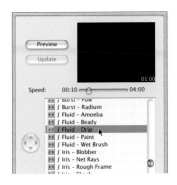

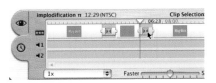

5. Select Fluid – Drip from the Transitions palette. Set your speed to 1 second. Drag two copies to the Timeline, one between the dirty and water stills and one between the water and clean stills. If you do not own the GeeThree transitions package, you can use Cross Fade instead—but you'll lose the drip-clean effect.

6. In the Timeline, drag the second transition to the left until you completely collapse the blue still.

7. Select the clean still. Press the right arrow one time, to move one frame into the clip. Choose Edit ▷ Split Video Clip At Playhead (⌘-T). This step separates the remaining portion of your clip from the transition, leaving one frame to anchor the transition.

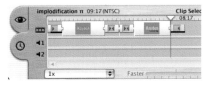

8. In the Titles palette, create a subtitle for your image. Here, I use "Cleaning." I've added a space between each letter to lengthen the title somewhat and added spaces before the first letter to move it to the right. Drag this title into the space you created in Step 7 and wait for iMovie to create your title.

9. Select any remaining still portion after your newly added title and choose Edit ▷ Cut (the Delete key) to remove it.

10. Finish by adding short (1- to 2-second) Fade In and Fade Out transitions to either side of your title.

Hayden2.mov

Zoom Direction

GeeThree's (**www.geethree.com**) Zoom In transition allows you to set a direction for your Zoom. This project skips this functionality so the instructions will work for those using Warp Out as well as those using Zoom In. You can, however, save a step or two by setting your first direction using the circle with the arrows, found to the left of the transitions list.

Scale Down

This project is not unique. Use the Scale Down transition to achieve a similar (but, in my opinion, not quite as good-looking) effect. While this takes fewer steps to achieve the same general look, the transition adds an unattractive black border. You must use black backgrounds to hide this border. You may also have to reverse the transition to create the appearing (rather than the disappearing) effect.

Off-Center Zoom

In these steps, you'll learn how to create a title that zooms in from a corner. You'll use the Push transition to help position the entry point.

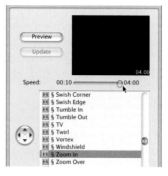

1. Drag 5-second-long versions of your background-only clip and your title clip to the Clip Viewer. Place the background first, followed by the title.

2. In the Transitions palette, select GeeThree's Zoom In transition. If you don't own the GeeThree package, choose Warp Out instead. Set the speed to 4 seconds, the maximum transition length allowed by iMovie. Drag the transition between your two clips on the Clip Viewer and wait for iMovie to render.

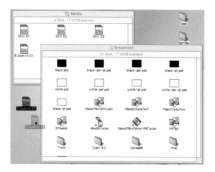

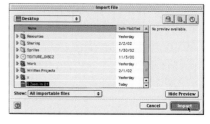

3. Open your Media folder and Option-drag your transition somewhere convenient (usually to the Desktop) to create a copy. Drag this copy onto the DVmaker utility (found on the accompanying CD) to convert the transition to a normal DV file that iMovie can read.

4. In iMovie, select File ▷ Import File (⌘-I) and navigate to your newly transformed transition. Select this file and click Import.

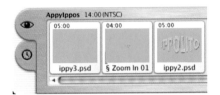

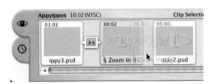

5. In your Clip Viewer, select the in-place transition and choose Edit ▷ Clear (the Delete key) to remove it. Drag your imported clip between your two stills to replace this original transition.

6. In the Transitions palette, select Push. Choose the Left direction. Set the speed to 3:28—that is, 2 frames shy of 4 seconds (iMovie will not allow you to add a 4-second transition using a 4-second clip)—and drag it between the first (blank) still and the imported Zoom transition.

7. Wait for iMovie to finish rendering the Push transition. Option-drag the 2-frame portion that remains of your Zoom to the right, to create a copy just before the title still. Each time you apply a transition to a transition, you need to preserve these two frames so your final footage does not contain jumps in the motion.

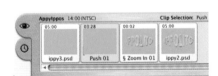

8. Repeat Steps 3 through 5 to import your Push clip, replacing the Push transition in your Clip Viewer. Discard the imported Zoom transition clip, but keep the 2-frame copy.

9. Return to the Transitions palette, and select Push again. Set the Speed to 3:26 and the direction to Down. Drag the transition between the plain background still and the copy of your Push transition. Wait for iMovie to render this transition.

10. Finish by adding a Fade In and Fade Out transition to each end of your title. If desired, switch to the Timeline and adjust your still lengths. Play back your movie. You will have created a title that zooms in from the upper-left corner. Save your work.

appyippos.mov, DVmaker

Organize Your Clips

Have you ever found your clips shelf in chaos? Do you want to restore some order? Here's a cute trick that can put all your clips back in place.

Choose any clip on your Shelf. This lets iMovie know that you're working with your Shelf. Then select Edit ▷ Select All (⌘-A). iMovie will select all the shelf clips. Grab the bottom-most clip you can see and drag it to the top-left-most slot on your Shelf. When you drop it there, iMovie automatically straightens the clips, sequentially filling the available slots.

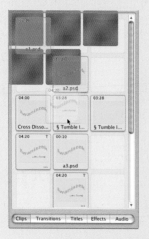

Twist and Turn Title

In these steps, you'll use transitions from GeeThree (www.geethree.com) to create a twisty, spinning, rotating title effect. Unlike most of the other projects, this one doesn't really work if you don't own the GeeThree package.

1. In Photoshop Elements, create your title using iMovie sizes (640x480 NTSC, 768x576 PAL). Here, I used the Warped Text button on the Options bar. Save a copy to disk, but do not close the file. Change the font color to a different hue and save a second copy. Also save a blank image filled with the background color.

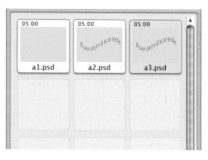

2. In iMovie, use Edit ▷ Preferences (iMovie ▷ Preferences in OS X) to set your default still length to 5 seconds. Select File ▷ Import (⌘-I). Navigate to your three stills and import them.

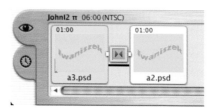

3. Drag your two titles down to the Clip Viewer. Select a 4-second Cross Dissolve transition from the Transitions palette and drag it between the two still clips. Wait for iMovie to finish rendering.

4. Open your Media folder and option-drag your Cross Dissolve transition to the Desktop to create a copy. Drag this copy onto the DVmaker utility (on the accompanying CD) to convert the transition to a file that iMovie can read. In iMovie, select File ▷ Import File (⌘-I) and navigate to your transformed transition. Select it and click Import.

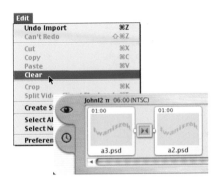

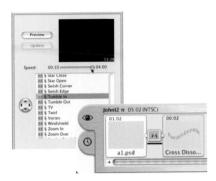

5. Select the *original* Cross Dissolve transition in your Clip Viewer. Choose Edit ▷ Clear (the Delete key) to remove it. Then drag your stills back to the clips shelf.

6. Drag your blank background still and the newly imported Cross Dissolve clip down to your Clip Viewer. In the Transitions palette, select Tumble In. Set the Time to 3:28 and the Direction to down. Drag this transition into place between the background and Cross Dissolve clips.

7. After iMovie finishes rendering your clip, Option-drag the remaining 2-frame Cross Dissolve clip to the right to create a copy. iMovie demands at least one frame on either side of a transition. Whenever you apply a transition to a transition, save those final two frames to ensure that your final movie doesn't jump.

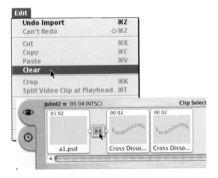

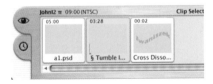

8. Return to your Media folder. Option-drag your new Tumble In transition to the Desktop to create a new copy. Convert the copy to a DV clip with DVmaker and import it back into iMovie.

9. Select the original Tumble In transition in the Clip Viewer. Choose Edit ▷ Clear (the Delete key) to remove it. Deleting it restores the full Cross Dissolve clip. Drag this restored clip back to the clips shelf, leaving the 2-frame version in the Clip Viewer.

10. Drag the newly imported Tumble In clip between the background still and the 2-frame Cross Dissolve.

continues on next page

twisttwirl.mov, mwd.mov, linger-old.mov

A Look Back

Each project in this book went through a three-step development process. For each, I first created an experimental version. My editor and I used these experiments to plan the various chapters in this book. These versions were fairly crude and often involved extraneous steps that were trimmed from the final project. Later, I created new prototypes to help design individual steps. As I snapped the screen shots for each project, I created my final versions. For the curious, I've included several experimental versions of these title movies on the accompanying CD. A couple—most particularly mwd.mov and linger-old.mov—were particularly influential in developing this section.

Twist and Turn Title *continued*

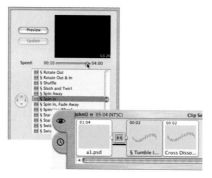

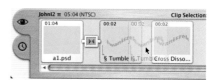

11. In the Transitions palette, select Spin In. Set the time to 3:26—2 frames shorter than the Tumble In clip. Drag this transition between the background still and the Tumble In clip, and wait for iMovie to render the transition.

12. Option-drag the 2-frame Tumble-In clip to the right, creating a second copy before the 2-frame Cross Dissolve clip.

13. Return once again to your Media folder. Option-drag the Spin In transition to the Desktop, creating a new copy. Convert this copy to a DV clip by dragging it to DVmaker and dropping it. Return to iMovie. Select File ▷ Import (⌘-I) to import a copy to your clips shelf.

14. Select the original Spin In transition in the Clip Viewer. Choose Edit ▷ Clear (the Delete key) to remove it. Next, drag the full Tumble In clip back to the clips shelf, leaving the 2-frame version in the Clip Viewer.

15. Drag the newly imported Spin In clip to the Clip Viewer. Place it between the background still and the 2-frame Tumble In clip. Then drag the background still back to the clips shelf.

16. Select all three clips in your Clip Viewer. Option-drag them to the right to copy them. While keeping all three selected, choose Advanced ▷ Reverse Clip Direction (⌘-R). iMovie will reverse all three clips *and* reverse the order of the clips.

17. Drag your original second-color still back to the Clip Viewer. Place it in the middle, between the two Cross Dissolve clips. Make sure the color matches! Select this still and trim it down in the Monitor. Select all but a second or two. Choose Edit ▷ Clear (the Delete key) to remove the extra frames.

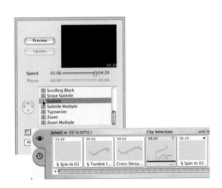

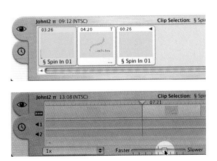

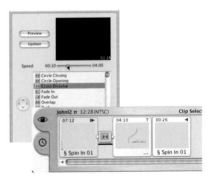

18. In the Titles palette, select the Subtitle style. Enter your secondary title and set the Speed to a nice, long duration. Drag this title down to the Clip Viewer. Place it before the final still clip you just added. Wait for iMovie to finish rendering.

19. Slowing down your clips (as you're about to do) can make the Tumble In and Cross Dissolve clips jerk. To avoid this, select the two 2-frame clips. Choose Edit ▷ Clear to remove them. Next, select the longer Spin In clip. Switch to the Timeline and move the time slider one notch to the right.

20. Click the eye icon to return to the Clip Viewer. In the Transitions palette, select Cross Dissolve. Set the speed somewhere between 1 and 2 seconds and drag the transition between the slowed Spin In clip and your title clip. If desired, add Fade In and Fade Out to the ends of your movie. Save your work.

Retain Your Title Settings

When you want to reuse title settings you created in a different clip, or even a different project, iMovie offers a very convenient shortcut. Let's say you created a title in some project that you really liked. You can recover those settings with just a few steps. First, save your work in your current project. Then load up the old one. Select your clip, and examine the Titles palette.

Whenever you select a title clip, the palette automatically loads the settings related to that clip. These settings include text, speed, direction, font, color, and so forth. After selecting the clip, reload your original project. The settings will remain even after you switch projects. You can now apply these settings to a new clip. Be careful, though. If you select another title clip, the Titles palette will update to that clip's properties, instead.

Lingering Text

You can focus attention on a single word by allowing it to linger after the text it accompanies has faded away. In these steps, you'll create a sequence where your held word changes color.

1. In this project, you'll create a visual version of that old joke about time and bananas. Start by creating a new title, "Time flies like an Arrow", on a black background. Use the Flying Words style and set the Speed to 5 seconds. Drag your title to the Clip Viewer.

2. Select Edit ▷ Preferences (iMovie ▷ Preferences in OS X). Set your default still length to 4 seconds and click OK. Choose File ▷ Import File (⌘-I). Navigate to your background image and click Import. Option-drag your new still in your clips shelf to create a copy, and then drag these two still clips to the Clip Viewer.

3. In the Titles palette, select Subtitle. Set Speed exactly to 4 seconds. Place your message in the first title line and the lingering word in the second—here, "Fruit flies like a" and "Banana". Use the same font and color from Step 1 but don't choose black background. Drag this title in front of the first banana still clip.

4. Return to the Titles palette. Remove the first line of your subtitle. Drag this title in front of your second banana clip.

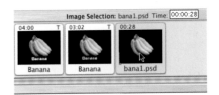

5. In the Clip Viewer, Option-drag your third clip (the second of the two banana stills) to duplicate it.

6. Select this newly copied clip. Return to the Titles palette. Change the Speed to 3:02 (three seconds plus two frames) and select a contrasting color. Here, I select yellow to match the color of my bananas. Click Update and allow iMovie to re-render your title.

7. After following Step 6, iMovie returns a 28-frame still clip to your Clip Viewer. Select this still and choose Edit ▷ Clear (the Delete key) to remove it.

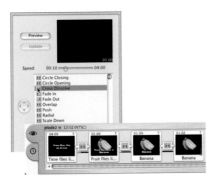

8. In the Transitions palette, select Cross Dissolve. Set the Speed to 1 second. Drag a copy of this transition between the first and second clips, and another between the second and third clips. Increase the speed to 2:00 seconds and drag the transition between the third and fourth clips to create a slower effect.

9. Wait as iMovie renders your clips. Return to the Transitions palette and select Fade In. Set the Speed to 1 second (1:00) and drag the transition to the very front of your title sequence. Then select Fade Out and drag it to the end.

10. (Optional) To turn your completed title sequence into a single clip, use the "Transform Footage with Empty Titles" trick (↷ Chapter 1). Select a title style without text. Set the time to the exact length of your sequence and drag it in front of your clips. After rendering, you will have transformed your sequence into one, unified, reusable clip.

fruitflies.mov

QuickTime Title Effects

QuickTime Pro offers titling tricks that you cannot replicate in iMovie. Chief among these are QuickTime's ability to add subtitles that change over time and its general masking ability. These features allow you to go beyond iMovie titles and add text with a unique flair.

You can direct QuickTime to display a subtitle starting at a particular moment and lasting for a particular duration. With QuickTime Pro's scripting abilities, you can set the font, color, and other properties of your subtitles. Unfortunately, the program doesn't offer a cute, interactive system to add this text. Instead, you must script your subtitles in a text editor, import them into QuickTime Pro, and convert them to a text track. This can prove daunting to the first-timer but is actually a lot easier than it sounds.

QuickTime masks add location-specific shading to your scrolling titles. These masks allow you to fade your titles in and out at different locations on your screen.

This section just touches on the various titling tricks offered by QuickTime Pro.

QuickTime Subtitles

In these steps, you'll design and add subtitles to a QuickTime video.

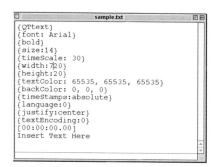

1. Open sample.txt (from the accompanying CD) in your favorite text editor and save a copy to disk. This file provides the basic skeleton you need when designing your subtitles.

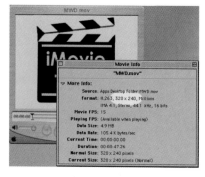

2. Open your movie in QuickTime Pro. Choose Window ▷ Show Movie Info (⌘-I). Make a note of your movie's properties, particularly the width.

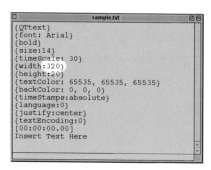

3. Return to your text editor and adjust the width to match this number. I suggest you leave the remaining defaults alone. They create a 20-pixel high subtitle area using the popular Arial font in white over black.

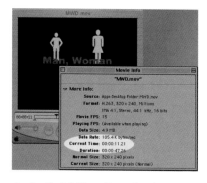

4. In QuickTime Pro, slowly move the playhead along the scrubber bar and decide where you wish each subtitle to appear. Write down the title and the exact time where it begins, in the Info window. Make a careful note of all the numbers in the time. (Also note the time for your final frame.)

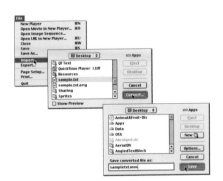

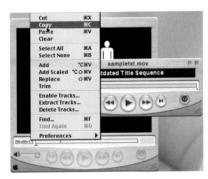

5. Transfer your notes into your text editor. For each title, add the exact time in square brackets, followed by the title itself. Keep your titles brief. Use a period rather than a colon between the third and fourth set of numbers. Also add an ending time so your titles end with your movie. Save your updated text file.

6. In QuickTime Pro, select File ▷ Import. Navigate to your text file, select it, and click Convert. QuickTime Pro asks you how to store your converted movie. Enter a new movie name and click Save. QuickTime Pro converts and saves your movie and then automatically opens it up in a new window.

7. Select your entire new text movie (⌘-A), copy it (⌘-C), and close it (⌘-W). QuickTime Pro copies your new text track to the Clipboard.

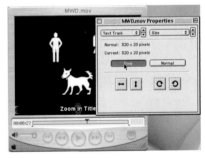

8. Return to your original movie. Move the playhead to the start of your movie, select nothing (⌘-B), and choose Edit ▷ Add (Option-⌘-V). QuickTime Pro adds the text track you copied in the previous step to your movie.

9. After adding, the text track appears at the top of your movie. Fortunately, you can easily move it down into place at the bottom. Open the Movie Properties window (⌘-J). Select Text Track from the left pull-down menu and Size from the right. Click Adjust.

10. Holding the Shift key, drag the text track to the bottom of your screen. The Shift key ensures that you can only move the track in a single direction—vertically, in this case. When you're satisfied with the track placement, click Done. Save your work to a new file or export your movie to disk.

sample.txt, subtitled.mov

A Quick QuickTime Title Effect

I'd feel remiss if I didn't include this oddball QuickTime Pro titling technique. In this project, you'll add a mask to your scrolling block title to make it fade out at the top. I use this technique a fair bit to add all sorts of fades to scrolling material—it doesn't have to be text, although text provides the most common scrolling medium in my repertoire.

Get Creative

Don't limit yourself to fades at the top and/or bottom of your video. In the example shown here, I used a gradient in the middle of the screen to create the illusion that the titles scroll across the pages of a book. In the center of the book, the titles scroll down to the binding and then up again. Get creative and discover what you can do with QuickTime masks and iMovie titles.

Fade Away

In these steps, you'll add a mask to the top of your scrolling block that fades your text away.

1. Create your scrolling block title in iMovie and export it to a full-quality QuickTime movie.

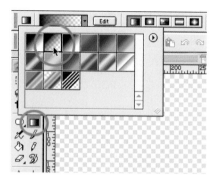

2. Create a new, transparent, RGB image in Photoshop Elements using QuickTime sizes (720x480 NTSC, 720x576 PAL). Select the gradient tool from the Tools palette. Move your attention to the Options bar. Open the Gradient Picker (click the down arrow to the right of the current gradient) and select Foreground To Transparent.

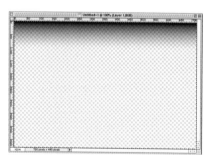

3. Press Shift-D to set your foreground color to black and your background color to white. Select your entire image (⌘-A). Shift-drag the gradient tool to draw a line from the top of your image to about 100 pixels down. This gradient darkens the very top of your image while leaving the rest transparent. Save this image to disk.

4. Open the image you just created, in QuickTime Pro. Select it (⌘-A), copy it (⌘-C), and close the window (⌘-W).

5. Open the movie you created in Step 1. Select all (⌘-A) and scale the gradient image over every frame of your movie (Edit ▷ Add Scaled, Option-Shift-⌘-V).

6. Open the Movie Properties window (⌘-J). Select Video Track 2 from the left pull-down menu and Graphics Mode from the right.

Other Masks

In this project, you learn how to add a fade at the top of your screen to allow your title block to gently fade away as it leaves the display. You need not stop there. You can use this technique to add any number of masks to your scrolling footage.

I've included several other masks in the gradmaterials.sea package on the companion CD. These include a symmetrical mask that fades both at the bottom and top, one that distorts in the middle, and one that extends across your entire display. Experiment with these masks and consider designing your own.

An important thing to consider when working with these masks is the graphics mode you use. Try each one with Straight Alpha, Premul White Alpha, and Premul Black Alpha to see how the graphics mode affects the overlay. You may be surprised and occasionally amused by the elegant or oddball results you create.

7. Choose Premul White Alpha from the list of graphics modes. Your overlay should disappear and provide a gradual shading effect as your movie scrolls.

8. (Optional) If you like, select Video Track 1 from the left pull-down menu and Size from the right. Click Adjust, and resize, move, and skew your text to create an angled effect. (First squeeze before you skew!) Finish by adding a blank, black QuickTime-sized still to the back of your movie for a backdrop.

gradtitle.mov, tiltgrad.mov, gradmaterials.sea

7 iMovie Artistry

Express Yourself with iMovie Tricks

Don't let the utilitarian need to finish an iMovie project blind you to the fun you should be having. iMovie offers one of the most artistically satisfying software packages around. In this chapter, you'll discover a fair number of cool effects. These effects can help set a mood or define a setting. Most importantly, they're fun, artistic, and useful. You'll learn how to play with color. You'll see how to build pro edits. You'll investigate exports and find out how to create a "skin." Working through these projects, you'll see how far a little artistry will take you.

Color Tricks

iMovie Artistry

Finishing Up

Color Tricks

When you manipulate color, you change the way people view your iMovies. People react to color at a very direct and emotional level. Bright, saturated colors make your movies seem real and alive. Black-and-white or sepia images create an old-fashioned feel. Colors can set a mood, a time, or a feeling.

In this section, you'll discover interesting ways to control color. You'll use iMovie and QuickTime Pro to create a variety of effects. These projects will allow you to adjust and control the color in your videos. You'll see how to move from black-and-white to color. You'll learn about color overlays and blends. You'll also find out how to use iMovie plug-ins to add basic color effects to your footage.

Note: In Step 2 in the project on this page, you make a selection that helps lay out the position of your first cut. By Step 4, iMovie has unselected that portion. This is not a problem. That selection already played its role, providing enough space for the split in Step 5.

From Black-and-White to Color

In these steps, you'll create a video that transforms itself from black-and-white into color in an ever-growing cloud of tint.

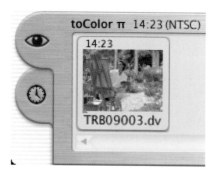

1. Import your video into iMovie. Select a clip that lasts at least 7 seconds and drag it to the Clip Viewer. To apply your special effect, you'll use a portion of 4 seconds or less from the middle of your clip. Choose a clip that's sufficiently large to support this portion. (The 4-second limit comes from iMovie's maximum transition length.)

2. Use the crop markers to select a 4-second-or-less segment in the middle of your clip. (Drag below the scrubber bar in the Monitor to make the crop markers appear.) You'll find the duration of the current selection at the top of the Clip Viewer or Timeline. Use this timing to help set your crop markers.

3. If the playhead is not at the left crop marker, click the triangle-shaped marker. When you click a crop marker, the playhead jumps to it. Select Edit ▷ Split Video Clip At Playhead (⌘-T). iMovie splits your clip in two at the point you selected.

4. Select a piece of the second portion of your clip, approximately the same less-than-4-second section as Step 2. Although I used the Time: indicator here to duplicate the selection from Step 2, you do not need to be exact when doing it yourself.

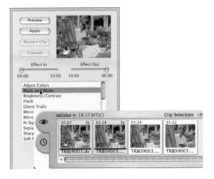

5. Click the right crop marker and select Edit ▷ Split Video Clip At Playhead (⌘-T). iMovie makes a second cut, creating a total of three clips in your Clip Viewer. After following Steps 2–4, the second clip will last 4 seconds or less.

6. Option-drag the second video clip—your less-than-4-second clip in the middle of your movie—to the right to create an exact copy.

7. Select your first two clips in your Clip Viewer. In the Effects palette, choose Black And White. Click Apply and wait for iMovie to remove the color from those two clips.

8. In the Transitions palette, select GeeThree's Fluid–Amoeba transition. If you do not own the GeeThree package, choose Cross Dissolve instead. Set your speed to just less than the length of your middle clips.

9. Drag this transition between the two middle clips and wait for iMovie to render.

10. Play back your movie. A blob of color will appear in the center of your black-and-white movie and grow out to the edges until your entire movie transforms into color. Those who used Cross Dissolve will watch a movie that starts out black-and-white and gradually fades into color.

amoebacolor.mov

Emotion and Color

People react to the *type* of color as much or more than they do to the color itself. Use different color schemes to create different moods. The Adjust Colors option on the Effects palette allows you to manipulate your colors.

Oversaturated color

Oversaturated color lends a 1960s look to your videos. The colors appear a little too rich and too deep. In the Adjust Colors palette, slide the Color handle towards Vivid, or use GeeThree's Film Noise-Saturated Color effect.

Undersaturated color   Washed-out colors create a distance between the movie and your viewer. Many westerns desaturate their color to take advantage of this effect. To desaturate, nudge the Color handle a little bit towards B&W or use GeeThree's Film Noise-Faded Color effect.

Black And White   Black And White offers a starkness and simplicity that creates a less-real setting for your video. Use this to artificially age your images or apply a cold artistic touch. Drag the Color Handle completely to B&W to convert to a black-and-white image.

Color shifts (Adjust Colors)   When you shift the natural colors in a video, you can create dreamy out-of-step images. To create this effect, move the Hue Shift handle in either direction.

See these color types in action. Watch ColorType2.mov on the accompanying CD.

Nostalgia

In these steps, you'll create a movie with an old-time feel using QuickTime's Sepia and Film Noise effects.

1.   Open your original footage in QuickTime Pro. Select File ▷ Export (⌘-E). Select QuickTime movie from the Export pull-down menu. Click the Options button.

2.   You're about to apply a sepia (brownish) tone to your video. To accomplish this, you'll need to use a QuickTime filter. Click the Filters button in the Movie Settings window to open up the Choose Video Filters window.

3.   Select Color Tint from the scrolling list of filters on the left side of the window. Choose Sepia from the pull-down Tint Type menu. Click OK to set your filter and return to the Movie Settings window. Click OK to close that window. Enter a name and click Save to export your file with the sepia filter.

4.   Open your new sepia-toned movie in QuickTime Pro. Select File ▷ Export (⌘-E) and again click the Options button. Click the Filters button.

5. Select Film Noise from the list of filters and then Dust And Film Fading from the pull-down. Crank up the Dust Density and Dust Size; more works better than less here. Select Faded Color Film from the Film Fading pull-down menu. This fades the sepia tone to a more gentle color that I prefer to the orange-looking default.

6. Click OK to set the filter. Click OK to close the Settings window. Enter a name and click Save to export your file to disk.

7. Open this new scratched movie in QuickTime Pro. Select File ▷ Export (⌘-E) and export to a new DV Stream. PAL users may want to click Options and confirm that the correct Country System has been selected. Open iMovie and import the DV file into a new iMovie project.

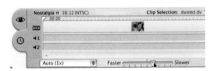

8. Drag your imported clip to the Timeline. Move the Speed slider one notch to the right to slow your clip down just a bit. Please note, this step and the ones that follow assume that your sound track won't be used in your final movie. These steps play total havoc with original audio.

9. Select your slowed clip. In the Monitor, use the crop markers to select just a few frames at a time (between 2 and 5 frames). Choose Edit ▷ Clear (the Delete key) to remove these frames from your movie. Repeat several times, selecting a different portion each time, to add a jerky look to assorted parts of your movie.

10. After repeating Step 9 many times, you will have fragmented your clip to a series of cliplets in your Timeline. Test the movie to make sure it works as you like, adding more cuts as needed. Save your work to disk.

 NostalgiaFeel.mov, ColorType2.mov

Choosing Colors

When you select colors in Steps 4 and 5 of this project, make sure to pick bold, clean tints. You'll obtain the purest colors when you follow these hints.

- Set your colors to 0, 100, or 200. These settings correspond to all-off, half-on, and all-on. By limiting yourself to these numbers, you ensure that your tints correspond to primary or secondary colors. Avoid wishy-washy middling colors.

- Use just one or two colors at a time. Set one or maybe two sliders to 0. When you use three colors at once, you introduce grays, whites, and blacks into your tones rather than the rich colors of this exercise.

In the first of these pictures, the colors are set to Red:0, Green:200, and Blue:0. Notice the pure green effect. In the second, the colors are set to Red:100, Green:200, and Blue:100. This misses a rich color effect, leaving a sickly greenish overtone instead.

Rich Color Tints

In these steps, you'll break your movie down into a series of segments, add rich colors to them, and then rebuild them into a single movie.

1. Open your movie in QuickTime Pro. Use the scrubber bar to select a portion of your movie—say, a quarter or a fifth. Choose Edit ▷ Cut (⌘-X) to remove that section from your movie and copy it to the Clipboard.

2. Keep your original file open; select File ▷ New (⌘-N) and create a new player. Choose Edit ▷ Paste (⌘-V) to add your cut portion to the new movie.

3. Upon pasting, your new movie resizes to fit the copied footage. Select this new movie. Choose File ▷ Export (⌘-E) and choose QuickTime movie from the pull-down menu. Click the Options button to open the Movie Settings window.

4. Click the Filters button and choose RGB Balance from the list. Set the Red and Blue sliders to 0 and the Green slider to 200. Click OK to set your filter. Click OK to close your settings window. Enter a name (include a sequential number for later reference) and click Save to save your rich, tinted image to disk.

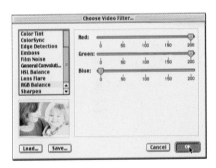

5. Return to your original movie. Select another segment, cut it (⌘-X), and repeat Steps 2–4, this time choosing a new combination of sliders to add a different color tint to these frames.

6. Repeat Steps 1–4 until you've segmented and colored your entire movie. Close your now-empty original movie and open up all your segments in QuickTime Pro.

7. Choose File ▷ New (⌘-N) to create a new player. In order, choose each movie, select it all (⌘-A), copy it (⌘-C), and close it (⌘-W). Then paste (Edit ▷ Paste, ⌘-V) that portion of your movie into the new player. Make sure the playhead stays at the end of the movie after each paste.

8. After you've reassembled your movie in order, select File ▷ Export (⌘-E) and export your completed movie back to disk.

Dissect Your Movie With Care

When you split your movie apart, dissect by numbers—don't try to "eyeball" it. Each time you cut away part of your movie, the proportionality changes. A 3-second clip forms one-third of a 9-second movie. The same clip will occupy fully half of the scrubber bar in the 6-second movie that remains after you remove a 3-second portion. Use math to plan and execute your splits. The Movie Info window (Window ▷ Show Movie Info, ⌘-I) offers precise timing and playhead location information to assist you.

Use Your Rich Colors for Titling

Color overlays work particularly well for title segments and video montages. For titles, make sure to use colors that contrast well with the overlays and produce readable text.

RichColor.mov

Free Yourself!

Although I used a rectangular design for the example, this project allows you to use nearly any layout. Feel free to use circles, zigzags, curves, and more.

The key to this project lies more in the bold color overlay than any particular design. So long as you keep to a bright and vibrant color scheme, the blending operations you perform in Steps 4 and 5 will produce a video with rich, colorful shading. (However, you may need to adjust the degree of blending to bring out different colors when you use darker hues such as blues.)

See AltDesign.mov on the accompanying CD to view an example with the exact same colors used in this particular project but a free-hand design.

Color Grid

Why settle for a single color overlay when you can add several at once? In these steps, you'll design a bright multicolor overlay and add it over your video.

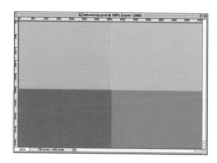

1.   In Photoshop Elements, create a new QuickTime-sized image (720x480 NTSC, 720x576 PAL). Design your multicolor overlay using bright, saturated colors. Save this image to disk.

2.   Open the image you just created in QuickTime Pro. Select the entire image track (⌘-A), copy it (⌘-C), and close the window (⌘-W). QuickTime Pro copies your image to the Clipboard, ready for reuse.

3.   Open the video you intend to overlay. Select all (⌘-A) and scale the copied image over each frame of your movie (Edit ▷ Add Scaled, Option-Shift-⌘-V).

4.   Open the Movie Properties window (⌘-J). Select Video Track 2 from the left pull-down menu and Graphics Mode from the right. Choose Blend from the list of modes offered to you.

5. The default blend is a little too light for my taste. Click the Color button and select the Crayon Picker. OS 9.*x* users, click on the fourth crayon from the left on the top row, Concrete. OS X users, pick a slightly darker gray. This lightens the blend color, making the overlay a bit more prominent.

6. Return to Photoshop Elements. Design a title using a QuickTime-sized RGB image with a transparent background. Add your title over the blank background and save to disk.

7. Open your title in QuickTime Pro. Select all (⌘-A), copy (⌘-C), and close the title (⌘-W). QuickTime Pro copies your title to the Clipboard.

8. In your overlaid video, select the portion of your video that you wish to receive the title. This may include all or just part of your movie. Choose Edit ▷ Add Scaled (Option-Shift-⌘-V) to add the title over the selected frames.

9. If needed, move the playhead back into the gray selected area so you can see your new title. Return to the Movie Properties window (⌘-J). Select Video Track 3 from the left pull-down menu and Graphics Mode from the right. Choose Premul White Alpha to remove the background from your title.

10. Repeat Steps 6–9 to add any more titles to your video. Here, I've added several small words to the individual rectangles, staggering the appearance of each. ✍ See Chapter 3, "Overlays," for more details on adding, moving, and adjusting overlaid titles. When finished, save your work to disk.

 altdesign.mov, mag8.mov, overlaypkg.sea

iMovie Artistry

A lively presentation can go a long way in enhancing your video productions. In this section, you'll discover a variety of artistic ideas that will transform your iMovie source materials from one thing into another thing entirely. You'll learn how to make your clip look like it's playing back on a television set. You'll add that "public television documentary" style to your work. You'll gradually add a filtered effect using QuickTime gradients, and you'll find out how to turn your movie into a reflecting pond. You'll also see how to import PowerPoint presentations and wide-screen footage into iMovie. Finally, you'll learn how to add some pro touches to make your iMovie presentations even more stunning.

"Look! I'm on TV!"

In these steps, you'll use GeeThree's (www.geethree.com) Jittery TV effect and a QuickTime overlay to create the illusion that your subject appears on TV.

1. In iMovie, import your video clip and add it to the Timeline or Clip Viewer. Select this new clip. In the Effects palette, choose Jittery TV, one of the GeeThree effects. Click Apply and wait for iMovie to add the effect to your clip.

2. Choose File ▷ Export (⌘-E). Select a Full-Quality, Large QuickTime movie and click Export. Navigate to where you wish to save this movie, enter a title and click OK.

3. In Photoshop Elements, design a television in a new QuickTime-sized (720x480 NTSC, 720x576 PAL) transparent RGB image. Make sure to leave a blank central area where your video will appear. Save your work to disk.

4. In QuickTime Pro, open the TV image you just created. Select all (⌘-A), copy (⌘-C), and close the window (⌘-W). QuickTime Pro copies your image track to the Clipboard.

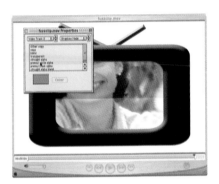

5. Open your jittered clip from Step 2 in a new QuickTime Pro player. Select all (⌘-A) and scale the copied TV image over each frame of your clip (Edit ▷ Add Scaled, Option-Shift-⌘-V).

6. Open the Movie Properties window (⌘-J). Select Video Track 2 from the left pull-down menu and Graphics Mode from the right. Choose Premul White Alpha. Your jittery video should appear behind the hole you created in your TV image.

7. Select Video Track 1 from the left pull-down menu and Size from the right. Click Adjust. Red resizing handles appear around your frame.

8. Use the handles to resize and position your video behind the TV overlay. Make sure that your overlay hides all the edges of your clip—don't break the illusion by allowing one of the clip sides to show. Keep your proportions roughly the same as the original clip. When you're satisfied with the placement and sizing, click Done.

9. Select File ▷ Export (⌘-E) and export your work back to a DV stream. After QuickTime finishes saving to disk, return to iMovie and select File ▷ Import. Load the processed video back into iMovie.

10. In iMovie, remove the original clip from your Clip Viewer and replace it with the newly imported one. Add further effects and transitions as desired. Here, I've created stills from the start and end of my TV clip and added Push transitions to bring the TV into view and then push it away after the clip finishes.

 tvlook.mov, tvthing.psd, tvthing-PAL.psd

Extra Sections

When working with an especially wide image, you can adapt this project to create additional image subsections. Keep the following in mind:

- To create three subsections, use a 12:3 ratio in Step 2. For four, use 16:3, and so forth.

- In Step 5, the width will update to reflect this added size.

- In Step 8, after performing Undo, choose Select ▷ Invert Selection and crop your image down to the remaining portion with Image ▷ Crop. This allows you to remove one portion of your image at a time, using Photoshop Elements' snap-to feature to perfectly select each sub-image.

- In Step 9, double your still length. If you used 4 seconds for two stills, use 8 seconds for three or more. This extra length allows you to add your Pushes (Step 10) between each pair of stills for a longer pan through your entire image.

Note: The extra black area in Step 1 allows you to better match your rectangular selection in Step 2 to your subjects. When you can't quite fit in all the faces and important features, the black area offers convenient padding and better geometry.

The KB Effect

You've probably seen an effect in TV documentaries where a camera slowly pans along an old black-and-white image to some awful Civil War tune. In these steps, you'll learn how to duplicate this effect.

1. Open your elongated image in Photoshop Elements. Copy it and paste it onto a larger, much-wider image filled with black. You'll need this extra black area to help plan your panning.

2. Choose the rectangle marquee selection tool. In the Options bar, select the constrained aspect ratio option and enter 8 and 3 into the width and height fields. This ratio allows you to create two 4x3 selections in Steps 6 and 8, corresponding to iMovie's default proportions.

3. Drag out your selection, carefully covering as many subjects as possible within the selection bounds. Choose Image ▷ Crop to trim your image down to this selection.

4. Next, you'll down-sample your image to use iMovie's 480-pixel height (576-pixel height for PAL). To begin, select Image ▷ Resize ▷ Image Size.

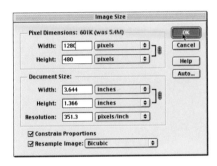

5. The Image Size adjustment window appears. Check the box labeled Constrain Proportions. Enter 480 (or 576 for PAL) in the Height field; the Width automatically updates to 1280 (or 1536 for PAL). Click OK and allow Photoshop Elements to resample your image.

6. Again select the rectangle marquee selection tool. This time choose the Fixed Size option in the options bar. Set your width to 640 pixels and your height to 480 pixels. (Use 768x576 pixels for PAL.)

7. Move the selection to the left half of your image until it snaps into place. Select Image ▷ Crop. Save a copy of this cropped image to disk as part1.psd. Do not close the image.

8. Choose Edit ▷ Undo (⌘-Z). Photoshop Elements will restore your original image. (Users of Photoshop 5.5 and earlier may need to re-open the original image.) Move the selection to the right half of your image until it snaps into place. Again, select Image ▷ Crop. Save a copy of this cropped image to disk as part2.psd. Do not overwrite part1.psd.

9. In iMovie, import your two source images and drag them, in order, to the Clip Viewer.

10. In the Transitions palette, select Push. Set your direction to left and your timer to at least 2 frames less than the length of your still clips. Drag your transition into place between your source images and wait for iMovie to create the transition clip. After, test your movie and save to disk.

ottolenghi.mov, leftpic.psd, rtpic.psd

Effect Tracks

QuickTime offers a number of effect track varieties. These special effects include Fire, Cloud, and Ripple. You can see each one in action by launching MakeEffectMovie. Select ⌘-1, but when the Open File dialog appears, click Cancel. The Effect Track dialog will appear, allowing you to play with each of these three effect types.

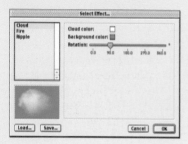

Note: I created the rippled effect movie you open in Step 7 in Totally Hip's LiveStage Pro (**www.totallyhip.com**, $999). LiveStage Pro allows advanced QuickTime programmers to interactively design and customize all sorts of QuickTime effects.

The Great Flood

In these steps, you'll create the illusion of a river or pond, complete with reflections.

1. In Photoshop Elements, create a full-sized QuickTime image (720x480 NTSC, 720x576 PAL). Create two rectangles, black on top, white on bottom, each occupying one half of the image. Save this image to disk.

2. In QuickTime Pro, open the movie you intend to work on. Bring up Movie Properties (⌘-J). Select Video Track 1 from the left pull-down menu and Mask from the right.

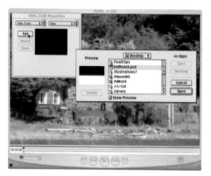

3. Click Set. Navigate to the mask you created in Step 1 and click Open. QuickTime resizes your image, cropping it down to half-height.

4. Select all (⌘-A) and copy the masked video (⌘-C). Then add this copy right back into your video using Edit ▷ Add Scaled (Option-Shift-⌘-V). After this, you'll have two copies in the same movie.

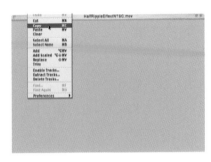

5. Return to the Movie Properties window (⌘-J). Select Video Track 2 from the left pull-down menu. Select Size from the right.

6. In the Size palette, click the up-down vertical mirroring button. QuickTime inverts your second track and place it at the bottom of your screen. This placement trick works because you're mirroring a masked image. QuickTime uses the full size of your movie when mirroring and rotating.

7. Open HalfRippleEffectNTSC.mov (or the PAL version) on the accompanying CD-ROM. This movie will appear entirely gray and look somewhat odd—there may not be a control panel at the bottom of the movie. Select all (⌘-A), copy (⌘-C), and close the movie (⌘-W).

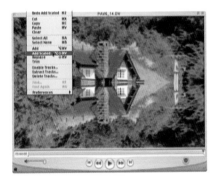

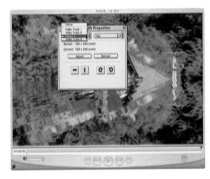

8. Return to your mirrored movie. If needed, select all (⌘-A). Then use Edit ▷ Add Scaled (Option-Shift-⌘-V) to scale the ripple effect over your entire movie. The bottom of the movie will begin to ripple (I designed the ripple to affect only the bottom half).

9. Your effect exists as a separate QuickTime track, not as a real part of your movie. (To see this, stop your movie. The effect continues.) Open Movie Properties (⌘-J) and you'll discover the Effect track. (The extra video track arrived with the effect. It's a full-sized blank image that positions the ripple at the bottom.)

10. Select File ▷ Export (⌘-E) to export your video to a new DV Stream file. This combines your overlaid ripple into your footage so you can use this altered footage in iMovie.

reflected.mov, ripplepkg.sea

Design Your Own

The Gradient Wipe effect proceeds by changing one portion of your image at a time. It starts from white and works its way to black, wiping each shade of darker gray in turn. This predictable behavior offers a novel way to design your own wipe patterns. In the sample shown here (NumberGrad.mov on the companion CD), I created a series of numbers using ever-darker shades of gray. The Crayon Color Picker helped me choose each color in turn. I added a white 1, a slightly darker 2, and so forth. To finish, I added a circle gradient behind the numbers, using the remaining shades of gray. When you watch this effect in action, each digit changes in order as the wipe reaches that particular shade. The pauses between each number reflect the intermediate shades not used in my gradient.

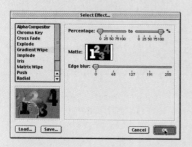

An Arriving Effect

In these steps, you'll use MakeEffectMovie's gradient wipe to transform one version of a movie into another.

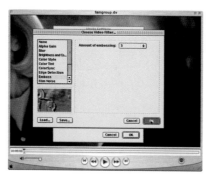

1. To start this project, use a QuickTime filter to export your movie to disk as a QuickTime movie with a new look. Here, I chose File ▷ Export (⌘-E), clicked Options, clicked Filter, and chose Emboss. (↶ See "Rich Color Tints" earlier in this chapter for more details on using filters in QuickTime Pro.)

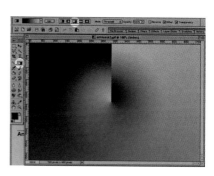

2. In Photoshop Elements, create a new RGB full-sized QuickTime image (720x480 NTSC, 720x576 PAL). Press Shift-D to set your foreground color to black and your background color to white. Choose the gradient tool and select any of the gradient styles offered. Add a gradient to your image.

3. Select File ▷ Save As (Shift-⌘-S). Choose to save to a CompuServe GIF file. When the Indexed Color window appears, choose an Exact Palette and forced Black & White. Click OK. Select Normal (rather than Interlaced) and click OK.

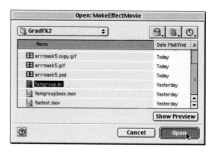

4. Launch MakeEffectMovie. Press ⌘-2, ⌘-1 to begin to build your effect movie. Navigate to the movie you created in Step 1 and click Open. Navigate to your original movie and click Open.

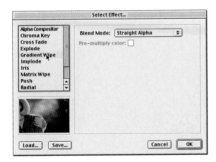

5. Select Gradient Wipe from the list of effects on the left side of the window.

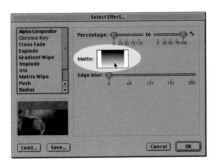

6. Click the Matte image that appears in the center of the Gradient Wipe window. Clicking this image launches an open file dialog, which allows you to select a new matte for MakeEffectMovie to use.

7. Navigate to the image you saved in Step 3. Select it and click Open.

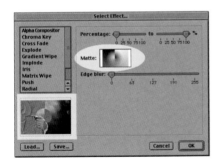

8. The Gradient Wipe window should update. Your new mask replaces the simple gradient in the center of the window. The animation changes to reflect the wipe pattern you just loaded.

9. Click OK. Navigate to where you wish to save your new effect movie. Enter a name and click Save.

10. Open your new movie in QuickTime Pro and play it back to make sure it works as expected. If you're ready to return to iMovie, select File ▷ Export (⌘-E) and save your file to a new DV Stream.

GradFX.mov, NumberGrad.mov, GradFXpkg.sea

Fonts Matter

Thin, delicate fonts will not survive the transformations from PowerPoint to QuickTime to a DV stream. Avoid fonts with serifs (small accent elements) and fonts with thin lines. Large, bold fonts work much better for this project—the stronger your font, the more it will hold up throughout. In this project, I used Admisi Display and Arial Black. These fonts share a few features that make them good candidates for this project. Here are some overall pointers to help you choose a font.

- Use wide, thick fonts with few (or preferably no) thin features.

- When selecting a font, pay attention to the holes. Thin holes will disappear during compression, smudging your text. Use round, large holes in your letters.

- Where possible, apply a bold weight to your text to thicken the letters.

- Big works better than small. Crank up the font size.

- Be concise. Fewer words work better than more.

- Assume poor quality results and be delighted when things work out better than expected.

PowerPoint Movies

Did you know you could convert your PowerPoint presentations to a movie? In these steps you will import your PowerPoint work into iMovie.

1. In PowerPoint (the Office 2001 release or later), design your presentation. Use large, bold fonts and avoid the default Times font. (☞ See sidebar at left for tips on how to choose effective fonts.)

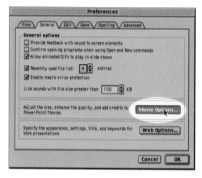

2. Select Edit ▷ Preferences. When the preferences window appears, click Movie Options.

3. Select Quality from the Optimization pull-down menu.

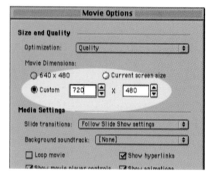

4. In Movie Dimensions, click Custom. Set your new size to 720x480. (PAL users, enter 720x576 pixels instead.)

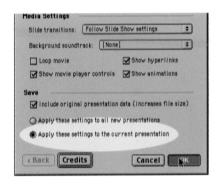

5. Select Apply These Settings To The Current Presentation and click OK. Click OK to finish setting preferences.

6. Choose File ▷ Save As and select PowerPoint Movie from the Format pull-down menu.

7. Enter a name for your new movie, navigate to where you wish to save this movie and click Save.

8. Launch QuickTime Pro. Select File ▷ Open Movie in New Player (⌘-O). Navigate to your movie and click Open. (You cannot double-click your new movie in the Finder. That would launch PowerPoint rather than QuickTime Pro.)

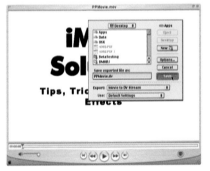

9. Select File ▷ Export (⌘-E). Select Movie to DV Stream from the Export To pull-down menu. Navigate to where you wish to save this movie, enter a name and click Save. QuickTime Pro exports and compresses your movie, saving it to a new DV file.

10. In iMovie, select File ▷ Import (⌘-I). Navigate to your movie, select it, and click Import. When iMovie finishes opening your video, play it back to make sure that your text remains somewhat readable. Because of DV compression, your final movie may never look wonderful, but it should remain legible.

PowerPoint.mov

Download MakeEffectSlideShow

Point your web browser at the following address and download your own copy of MakeEffectSlideShow: **http://developer.apple.com/samplecode/Sample_Code/QuickTime/Effects/MakeEffectSlideShow.htm**

Your slides will work best when you pre-convert them to QuickTime Sizes (720x480 for NTSC, 720x576 for PAL). GraphicConverter (**www.lemkesoft.com**, $30 shareware) offers the best batch resizing utility available for the Macintosh. GraphicConverter works under both OS 9 and OS X.

Understand the "Jerk"

After slowing your movie down, your slide show may appear to jerk slightly. This is due to repeated frames. iMovie can only do so much in the way of calculations when it slows down footage—particularly computed footage in these slide shows rather than real footage from a video camera. You can make better slide shows with Totally Hip's LiveSlideShow (**www.totallyhip.com**, $50). LiveSlideShow offers much finer user control, including speed adjustments, voice-overs, custom themes, and background sounds.

Quick and Easy Slide Movies

Although you can import stills into iMovie and add transitions to create a slide show, it's fun to let another program do the work. In these steps, you'll use MakeEffectSlideShow to create a slide-show video.

1. Follow the directions in the sidebar to download a copy of MakeEffectSlideShow from Apple. Open the downloaded folder and double-click the program icon to begin.

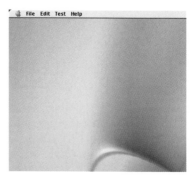

2. When MakeEffectSlideShow launches, it changes the menu bar but does not open any windows.

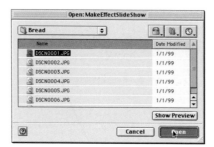

3. Type ⌘-1. The open file dialog appears. Navigate to your first image, select it, and click Open.

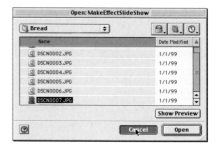

4. Navigate to your second image, select it, and click Open. Repeat until you've added all the slide images in your show. Then click Cancel.

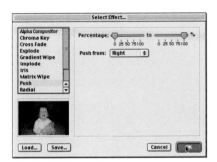

5. Select the effect for your movie. Here, I chose Push and selected Right from the pull-down menu. (You can choose many other wipe effects from the list offered.)

6. Click OK. Navigate to where you wish to save your slide movie, name it, and click Save.

7. Open your new movie in QuickTime Pro. Select File ▷ Export (⌘-E) and save to a new QuickTime movie, merging effects and slides into a single track. (If you skip this extra save, your effects may disappear from the DV video.) Open your merged movie, select File ▷ Export (⌘-E), and now save to a new DV stream.

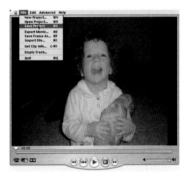

8. In iMovie, open an existing project or create a new one. Select File ▷ Import (⌘-I), navigate to this new DV file, and click Import. iMovie opens your video and adds it to the clips shelf.

9. Drag your new clip to the Timeline. I find the default slide show timing to run way too fast. Select your clip and drag the speed slider a notch or two to the right to slow your video down.

10. After adjusting the speed, play the video back to test it. If needed, further adjust the timing. Save your work to disk.

 slideshow.mov

Shrink the Height... or Stretch the Width

Take either of two approaches to restore image proportion when using wide-screen footage. In Step 9 of this project, you shrink the relative height of your video to 360 pixels (432 pixels for PAL). The width remains unchanged. You can use a second approach: expand the width and leave the height unchanged. Stretch your video width to 960 pixels (both NTSC and PAL users) and pad above and below with 80-pixel high black bars (96 for PAL). Here's a convenient reference table.

SMALL LETTERBOX

NTSC 720x480, 60-pixel padding
(720x360 video)

PAL 720x576, 72-pixel padding
(720x432 video)

LARGE LETTERBOX

NTSC 960x640, 80-pixel padding
(960x480 video)

PAL 960x768, 96-pixel padding
(960x576 video)

Note: As this book went to press, Virtix (www.virtix.com) introduced a brand new letterbox plug-in. This plug-in offers control and manipulation features specific to wide-screen footage. Download a free version (it's part of their sample pack) from the Virtix site.

Wide-Screen Fun

Many cameras offer 16:9 aspect ratio wide-screen shooting options. Here's how you can use this footage in iMovie.

1. Import your wide-screen footage into iMovie. Your video will look compressed, squashed from side to side. Many features will look elongated, particularly faces. This occurs because iMovie uses a 4:3 aspect ratio while your footage uses a 16:9 aspect ratio.

2. Select File ▷ Export (⌘-E). Export your work to a Large, Full Quality, QuickTime movie.

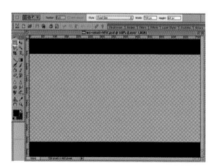

3. In Photoshop Elements, create a letterbox mask. Start by opening a new, QuickTime-sized (720x480 NTSC, 720x576 PAL) transparent RGB image. Use the fixed-size rectangular marquee tool to add 720x60-pixel black rectangles (720x72 for PAL) to the top and bottom of your image. Save your image to disk.

4. In QuickTime Pro, open the image you just created in Step 3. Select the entire image track (⌘-A), copy it (⌘-C), and close the image (⌘-W).

5. Now open the movie you created in Step 2. Select your entire movie track (⌘-A) and scale the letterbox mask over each frame of your movie (Edit ▷ Add Scaled, Option-Shift-⌘-V).

6. Open the Movie Properties window (⌘-J). Select Video Track 2 from the left pull-down menu and Graphics Mode from the right.

7. Select Straight Alpha to restore the transparent center area you designed in Step 3. You'll now be able to see your video underneath the letterbox overlay.

8. Select Video Track 1 from the left pull-down menu and Size from the right. Click Adjust. The red resizing handles will appear around your underlying video track.

9. Carefully resize your video to match the cutout. As you resize, your subjects' faces should return to their proper proportions. Make sure to check the Normal Size data in the Movie Info window (⌘-I) to make sure you do not stray from your original pixel dimensions. Click Done to finish resizing.

10. Select File ▷ Export (⌘-E). Choose Movie to DV Stream, navigate to where you wish to save the movie, enter a name, and click Save. You can now reimport your properly proportioned footage back into iMovie to use in your project.

 widescreen.mov

Add a Pro Feel

Give your videos an overall pro feel by mastering these basic techniques.

Use fades Throughout this book, I've promoted fade-ins, fade-outs, and cross-fades (called Cross Dissolves in iMovie) to gently bring the viewer into your sequence and to ease back out. Fades produce smoother edits. This all goes back to what my graduate advisor called the Principle of Least Astonishment. Don't shock your audience unnecessarily with sudden changes. Use fades instead.

Use a variety of cut techniques In this project, you learned to use L-cuts and J-cuts. In Chapter 1, you discovered how to create cutaways. Start using these techniques in your videos. They allow you to add visual interest and continuity in a subtle and nonsurprising fashion. You'll be startled at how these three simple procedures can make a huge difference in your final productions.

Keep it simple A video should tell a story without calling attention to the techniques it uses. Don't fill up your movies with special effects and cool tricks unless these serve a specific reason. Have fun. Just don't go overboard.

Learn more Many fine books can teach you about video planning and technique, such as my *Digital Video! I Didn't Know You Could Do That...* (Sybex, 2001). Pick up one of these books and start reading. You'll discover a wide variety of shooting and editing methods that will make your videos more interesting and professional.

Advanced Cuts: A Pro Touch

In these steps, you'll learn how to add J-cuts and L-cuts to your iMovies. These cuts refer to ways you can extend audio into a separate clip to smooth the transition between clips.

1. In iMovie, select a primary video clip and a background shot. Place these clips in your Clip Viewer, the primary clip to the right. Background clips work well for your second video segment in the J-cut you're about to build. Their audio doesn't matter as much. You know you won't overwrite some important timeless statement with your extended audio track. In J-cuts, the sound from the second clip begins before the cut.

2. Select your background clip. You're about to start the audio from your main clip as this clip finishes. Determine the length of overlap time you want; for this exercise, we'll use 3 seconds. Use the crop markers in the scrubber bar to select the final 3 seconds of your background clip. Look for the selection duration at the top of your Clip Viewer.

3. Choose Edit ▷ Cut (⌘-X) to remove the selection from your clip and copy it to the Clipboard.

4. Select your primary clip. Choose Advanced ▷ Paste Over At Playhead (Shift-⌘-V). iMovie pastes the video over at the playhead, discarding any audio from the background clip and preserving the audio from the primary clip.

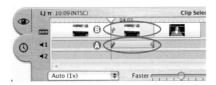

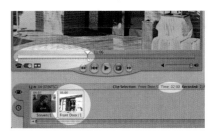

5. By pasting over, you've instructed iMovie to create a J-cut. Here, the audio from the primary clip (A) extends into the last three seconds of the background clip (B). Play back the sequence you just created. You'll start hearing the second clip before its video begins. You're now ready to try an L-cut.

6. L-cuts work in the opposite way from J-cuts. In these, a clip's audio extends into the next visual sequence, adding continuity from the other direction. In iMovie, move your primary video clip and a second shot to the Clip Viewer—again, we'll use a background video clip. For an L-cut, place your primary clip to the left.

7. As in Step 2, select your background clip. This time, however, use the crop markers to select the *first* few seconds—here, I use 2 seconds. Again, you'll find the current selection duration at the top of your Clip Viewer.

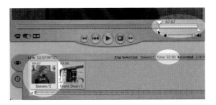

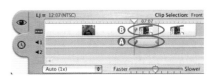

8. Choose Edit ▷ Cut (⌘-X) to remove the selection from your clip and copy it to the Clipboard.

9. Select your primary clip. Use the crop markers to select the final seconds of the clip. Be exact: Use the duration at the top of your Clip Viewer to make sure you've selected exactly the same number of frames that you cropped in Step 8. Then click the left triangular crop marker to move the playhead to that location.

10. Choose Edit ▷ Select None (⌘-D) and then Advanced ▷ Paste Over At Playhead (Shift-⌘-V). iMovie will create a perfect L-cut. The audio from your main clip (A) continues into the video from your second clip (B).

LJCuts.mov

Finishing Up

Even after you finish your iMovie, you can still play with it further. In this section, you'll see how to push the limits to create a custom QuickTime skin for your movie.

Skins offer just one sharing solution for your completed iMovies. There are many other ways to do so. You can distribute your work on tape, on disc, or over the Internet. Each method uses a different technology, but the bottom line remains the same: Allow others to watch and enjoy your work. The fun shouldn't end just because your movie has.

Investigate the new and cool tools out there, such as iDVD (**www.apple.com**) and Roxio Toast (**www.roxio.com**). They allow you to burn your videos to disc for playback in DVD players and on computers. Other solutions include Terran's MediaCleaner EZ (**www.terran.com**) and RealSystem Producer (**www.realnetworks.com**). These packages allow you to create streaming movies to share over the Internet so you and others can enjoy them in a new way.

The Fish Movie

In these steps, you'll create a whimsical QuickTime presentation in which you offer the illusion of being underwater and then play back your movie in a fish.

1. In iMovie, select File ▷ Export (⌘-E) and export your work to a large full-quality QuickTime movie.

2. In Photoshop Elements, create a new QuickTime-sized (720x480 NTSC, 720x576 PAL) RGB image with a transparent background. Using the shape tool, add a random series of white circles around your image.

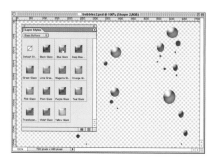

3. Using the Layers Style palette, select the Glass Buttons subpalette, and choose Blue Glass to create a landscape of bubbles. Save this image to disk. Then design a new image full of circles and apply the Blue Glass style to it to create a second, different bubble image. I named my images bubbles1.psd and bubbles2.psd.

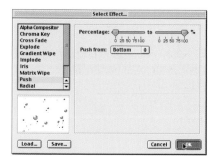

4. Launch Make Effect Movie. Press ⌘-2, ⌘-1. Navigate to your first bubble image and click Open. Navigate to your second bubble image and click Open. Select Push, set your direction as Push From: Bottom, and click OK. Save your work to bubbles.mov.

5. Open bubbles.mov in QuickTime Pro. Select all (⌘-A), copy (⌘-C), and close the movie (⌘-W). QuickTime Pro copies your entire effect movie to the Clipboard.

6. In QuickTime Pro, open the video you exported in Step 1. Select all (⌘-A) and scale the effect movie over your video. (Edit ▷ Add Scaled, Option-Shift-⌘-V).

7. Open the Movie Properties window (⌘-J). Select Video Track 4 from the left pull-down menu and Graphics Mode from the Right. Choose Premul White Alpha. Your original video appears behind your bubbles, adding an undersea look to your movie.

8. Choose File ▷ Export (⌘-E). Choose QuickTime Movie from the Export pull-down menu. Click the Options button, then click the Size button.

9. Select Use Custom Size. Set your width to 240 and your height to 160. (PAL users, use 192 as your height.) Click OK, name your new movie, and click Save. Wait a few minutes as QuickTime Pro resizes and saves your movie to disk.

10. Open your new movie in a new player. Press Play and watch your movie. Is the audio missing? If not, skip to Step 15.

continues on next page

FishMovie.mov

Stream Your Movies

Want to share your movies over the Internet? Stream them! Streaming works by establishing an Internet connection between a video data server and a viewing program, called a player. It provides controlled, on-demand delivery of both real-time (live event) and previously recorded data.

To stream, save your iMovie to a special streaming file. Then upload your file to a video server. Apple offers limited free streaming from their iTools accounts (**iTools.mac.com**). RadicalZoo (**www.radicalzoo.com/ video_index.php**) offers unlimited free streaming for now.

You can save direct from iMovie to a streaming file (Export To Streaming Web File, Small). For finer control, use one of the many programs with more professional features. Consider these:

Totally Hip's HipFlics
www.totallyhip.com, $100

Sorenson Squeeze
www.sorenson.com/products/ squeeze.asp, $149 intro price, $300 normal price

Discreet's CleanerEZ
www.discreet.com/products/ cleaner_ez/, $500

The Fish Movie *continued*

11. Return to your original movie. Choose Edit ▷ Extract Tracks.

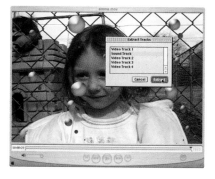

12. Select your Sound Track and click Extract. QuickTime Pro opens a new window with a copy of your audio. Your original movie remains unchanged. This step does not alter it in any way.

13. Select the entire sound track (⌘-A), choose Edit ▷ Copy (⌘-C), and close the window (⌘-W). QuickTime Pro copies the audio to your Clipboard.

14. Return to your silent new movie. Select all (⌘-A) and choose Edit ▷ Add Scaled (Option-Shift-⌘-V). QuickTime Pro restores your audio track.

15. Select File ▷ Save As. Save your movie to a new, self-contained file. I called mine UnderSea.mov.

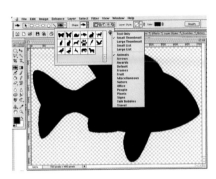

16. In Photoshop Elements, create a new RGB transparent image. I used my normal QuickTime sizes, but you can really use any size you want. Set your foreground color to Black (Shift-D). Choose the shape tool. Select the custom shape and choose the fish shape from Photoshop Element's shape library. Add a large fish to your image.

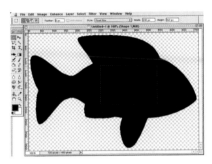

17. Select Layer ▷ Simplify Layer. Choose the fixed-size rectangular marquee tool. Set your selection size to 240x160 (PAL users use 240x192). Center this selection in your fish and press Delete to remove a movie-sized section from your fish's interior.

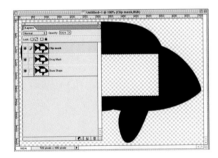

18. In the Layers palette, drag your fish layer down to the New Layer icon to create a copy. Repeat to create a second copy. You'll end up using each of these layers in a slightly different fashion. Double-click each layer to give it a new name: Base Shape, Clip Mask, and Drag Mask.

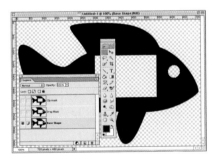

19. Make the Drag Mask layer visible and select it. Choose the fixed-size circle marquee (48x48 pixels). Move this "fish eye" into place and press Delete to remove the black beneath. Make the Base Shape layer visible and select it. Again, press Delete to remove the black beneath the selection.

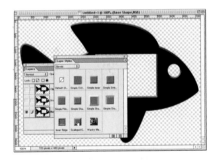

20. Open the Layers Styles palette. (You'll find it in the Shortcuts bar.) Select Scalloped Edges and give your Base Shape a nice 3-D feel.

continues on next page

Design Your Own Sprites

In Step 28, you open a special movie called PlayButton.mov. I built this movie, called a sprite, using Totally Hip's LiveStage Pro (**www.totallyhip.com**, about $900). Sprites are fully programmable QuickTime elements that allow you to add all sorts of interactive behaviors to your movies. Here, I added a Play/Pause button, but you can design sprites as diverse as movie controllers, picture adjustment tools, and even tic-tac-toe games.

LiveStage Pro offers a power toolbox for QuickTime. In it, you can do just about anything with QuickTime that the QuickTime specifications allow. It's not easy to learn and it's certainly not cheap, but it's amazingly powerful and convenient. When you know what you're doing, you can create and program new sprites in a matter of minutes.

Read more about sprites here: **http://developer.apple.com/ techpubs/quicktime/qtdevdocs/ RM/rmWiredIntro.htm**

The Fish Movie *continued*

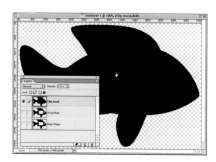

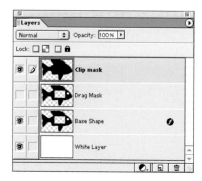

21. Press ⌘-D to remove the current selection. Option-double-click the Clip Mask layer visibility icon and select the layer. Use the paint bucket tool to fill the rectangle in the middle of this layer.

22. Click the New Layer icon at the bottom of the Layers palette. Drag this layer below your fish layers and fill it with white.

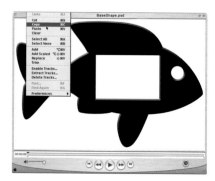

23. Save three new files as follows: Make the Base Shape layer and the white layer visible, hide the others, and save to BaseShape.psd. Save the Clip Mask layer and the white layer as ClipMask.gif (note the format), and save Drag Mask plus the white layer as DragMask.gif.

24. Return to QuickTime Pro. Open BaseShape.psd from within QuickTime Pro. Select all (⌘-A), copy (⌘-C), and close the window (⌘-W). QuickTime Pro copies your image track to the Clipboard.

25. Open UnderSea.mov in QuickTime Pro if it isn't already open. Select all (⌘-A) and scale the copied image over your movie (Edit ▷ Add Scaled, Option-Shift-⌘-V).

26. Open the Movie Properties window. Select Video Track 2 from the left pull-down menu and Layer from the right. Click the up arrow until your original video appears in front of your fish image.

27. Now select Video Track 1 from the left pull-down menu and Size from the right. Click Adjust and move your movie into place in the rectangle provided in your fish's belly. Click Done when you're satisfied with the placement.

28. Open PlayButton.mov (on the accompanying CD). When this movie opens, you probably won't see a normal QuickTime display—the scrubber bar and playback keys should be missing. That's because this is a sprite—an interactive QuickTime component—not a normal movie. Nevertheless, Select All (⌘-A), copy (⌘-C), and close (⌘-W).

29. In UnderSea.mov, Select All (⌘-A) and Edit ▷ Add Scaled (Option-Shift-⌘-V). The play button will appear in the upper-left corner of your screen. This is, by the way, a fully functioning Play button (👉 sidebar). Go ahead and try it out yourself.

30. Open the Movie Properties window. Select Sprite 1 from the left pull-down menu and Size from the right. Click Adjust. Move your play button into place as your fish's eye. (Hint: Select your movie window and then use the arrow keys to move the eye around.) When you're satisfied with placement, click Done.

continues on next page

Burn Your Movies

Recordable DVDs offer a new and exciting medium for distributing your movies. Create your own with an Apple SuperDrive (actually a Pioneer A03 unit) and a copy of iDVD or iDVD 2 (the latter runs under OS X). These programs provide simple and interactive solutions for authoring your own DVDs. Be aware, it often takes several hours to burn a single DVD because of the time it takes to convert your movies to the MPEG-2 format. If you want to go the super-deluxe route, check out the MPEG SuperCharger (Discreet, **www.discreet.com**, $999). SuperCharger works with Discreet's Cleaner product to speed up your MPEG-2 compression, greatly reducing the time involved to produce iDVD2-compliant files.

The Video on CD format (VCD) offers an inexpensive alternative to DVDs. VCDs can play in many low-cost DVD set-top units, particularly those built in East Asia. Easily create VCDs with Roxio's Toast Platinum (**www.roxio.com**, about $90) and a blank CD-R or CD-RW.

The Fish Movie *continued*

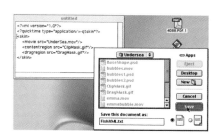

31. Select File ▷ Save (⌘-S) and save your work to date. Be aware, this saved file uses references. You'll need to keep your original fish artwork and play button file around to open this movie file. Close this movie (⌘-W).

32. In a plain-text editor, open FishXML.txt (provided on the companion CD and shown here). This file instructs QuickTime how to create your custom skin using the masks you created in Step 23. Save a copy of this file into the same folder as the rest of this project.

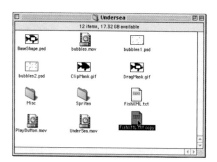

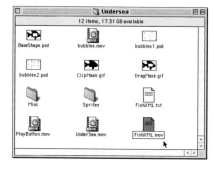

33. Option-drag FishXML.txt to create a copy. Select FishXML.txt Copy.

34. Rename this file to FishXML.mov. As you do so, its icon changes from a SimpleText file to a QuickTime movie.

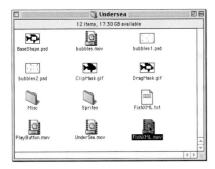

35. Double-click FishXML.mov to open it up in QuickTime Pro.

36. When your movie opens in QuickTime Pro, it will appear differently than a normal movie. It should look like a fish with a movie in its tummy. You can drag the fish around the screen and play it by pressing the Play button.

37. Select File ▷ Save As from the QuickTime Pro menu bar at the top of the screen.

38. Navigate to where you wish to save your movie and name it. Make sure to choose Make Movie Self Contained. Click Save and wait as QuickTime Pro saves your new, self-contained movie to disk. You can now you're your movie to disk, send it to a friend by e-mail, etc. It's a fully self-contained QuickTime movie.

Export to VHS

In a world of digital video cameras and high-tech DVD players, don't overlook the humble VCR. The VHS format provides the most universal video playback medium available today. Most digital cameras allow you to connect your unit to a VCR for playback (check your owner's manual for specific details). Export your movie back to the camera using the FireWire link. Then connect to your VCR, add a fresh tape, press Record, and play back the movie on your camera.

Some cameras even offer what's called *video pass-through*. This feature allows you to send video directly from your Macintosh through the camera to the VCR without needing the export step. Other video devices, including the Sony DVMC-DA2 (**www.sony.com**) and the Miglia Director's Cut (**www.miglia.com**), allow you to connect your VCR to your FireWire port and export directly to your video player.

Index

Note to the Reader: Throughout this index **boldfaced** page numbers indicate primary discussions of a topic. *Italicized* page numbers indicate illustrations.

A

B

N

O

T

W

X

Z

Dear Reader

Thank you for choosing *iMovie 2 Solutions*. At Sybex, our goal is to bring you the best graphics and digital video books on the market. We're working hard to find the best authors and to bring our love of these topics to the look and feel of each book.

I hope you've seen all of that reflected in this title. We're very excited about the way author Erica Sadun has opened up Apple's surprisingly powerful software, making potentially complex tips and tricks accessible.

Our goal is to make each title better than the last. You're our partners in this effort, and I'd be very interested in hearing your feedback. To let us know what you think about this book, please visit us at www.sybex.com. Once there, go to the product page, click on Submit a Review, and fill out the questionnaire. Your input is greatly appreciated.

Now comes the best part. This book and iMovie are both tools. The real fun begins when you pick them up and see where they lead you.

Best regards,

DAN BRODNITZ
Associate Publisher
Sybex Inc.

About Sybex

Sybex has been part of the personal computer revolution from the very beginning. We were founded in 1976 by Dr. Rodnay Zaks, an early innovator of the microprocessor era, and the company's president to this day. Dr. Zaks was involved in the ARPAnet and developed the first published industrial application of a microcomputer system: an urban traffic control system.

While lecturing on a variety of technical topics in the mid-1970s, Dr. Zaks realized there wasn't much available in the way of accessible documentation for engineers, programmers, and businesses. Starting with books based on his own lectures, he launched Sybex simultaneously in his adopted home of Berkeley, California and in his original home of Paris, France.

Over the years, Sybex has been an innovator in many fields of computer publishing, documenting the first word processors in the early 1980s and the rise of the Internet in the early 1990s. In the late 1980s, Sybex began publishing our first desktop publishing and graphics books. As early adopters ourselves, we began desktop publishing our own books in-house at the same time.

Now, as we move toward the start of our fourth decade, we publish dozens of books each year on topics related to graphics, web design, digital photography, and digital video. We continue to explore new technologies and over the last few years have been among the first to publish on topics like Maya and Photoshop Elements.

With each book, our goal remains the same: to provide clear, readable, skill-building information, written by the best authors in the field—experts who know their topics as well as they know their audience.

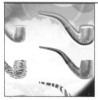

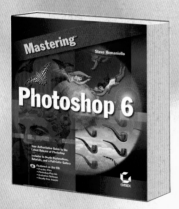

What's on the CD

The *iMovie 2 Solutions* CD provides many of the tools you need to work through the projects in this book—including project videos, source images, and software.

You can access videos and source files from the CD interface by clicking Movie Files or Chapter Files. The Software button takes you to demos, tools, and other software goodies:

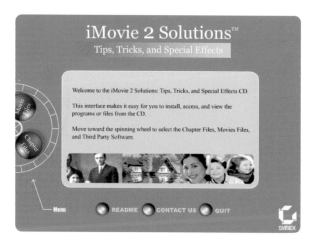

Adobe Photoshop Elements— 30-Day Fully Functional Version

Adobe Photoshop Elements presents the best image processing bang-for-the-buck available on the market today. Offering many of the features of the pro-level Adobe Photoshop, Photoshop Elements provides hobbyists and home users with high-end algorithms in an affordable software package.

GeeThree Slick Transitions and Effects, Volumes 1 and 2 Sample Packs

These fully working plug-ins allow you to sample GeeThree Slick effects before you buy the full package. GeeThree offers dynamic plug-in packages that expand the range and vocabulary of iMovie transitions and effects. Demos are included for both OS 9 and OS X users.

Ulead Royalty-Free Media

Ulead offers some of the most cost-effective royalty-free media on the market today. On the CD, you'll discover some sample videos that you can use in your videos for free—and never have to pay another penny. Ulead sells several collections of royalty-free stock video footage as well as images and sound effects in a variety of themes.

FileTyper

A terrific shareware utility, FileTyper allows you to associate file type and creator information with any Macintosh files. FileTyper helped create several special-purpose utilities used in this book. (You'll also find these special-purpose utilities, including DVmaker, MakeSimpleText, and others on the CD.)

Totally Hip LiveStage Professional and HipFlics trial versions

These powerful and innovative packages allow you to take QuickTime Pro to the edge. With LiveStage Professional, you can build effect tracks, sprites, and many other special-purpose QuickTime components. With HipFlics, you can prepare your QuickTime movies for sharing over the Internet. Compress, optimize, and even add watermarks with this easy-to-use program.

iMovie Solutions readers will also find a special discount coupon for purchasing these products.

Other Software

There isn't enough space here to detail all the goodies you'll find on the CD, but you'll also find such gems as the Apple QuickTime Player; a terrific freeware app called SoundRecorder; SoundEffects, a wonderful shareware sound editor; and more.

Sybex strives to keep you supplied with the latest tools and information you need for your work. Please check **www.sybex.com** for additional content and updates that supplement this book and CD.